# Kurdish Nationalism on Stage

# Kurdish Nationalism on Stage

*Performance, Politics and Resistance in Iraq*

Mari R. Rostami

**I.B. TAURIS**
LONDON • NEW YORK • OXFORD • NEW DELHI • SYDNEY

I.B. TAURIS
Bloomsbury Publishing Plc
50 Bedford Square, London, WC1B 3DP, UK
1385 Broadway, New York, NY 10018, USA

BLOOMSBURY, I.B. TAURIS and the I.B. Tauris logo are trademarks of Bloomsbury Publishing Plc

First published in Great Britain 2019
Paperback edition first published 2021

Copyright © Mari R. Rostami, 2019

Mari R. Rostami has asserted her right under the Copyright, Designs and Patents Act, 1988, to be identified as Author of this work.

For legal purposes the Acknowledgements on p. xi constitute an extension of this copyright page.

Cover design: Adriana Brioso
Cover image: 'Kurdish Dance' by Shirin Baran

All rights reserved. No part of this publication may be reproduced or transmitted in any form or by any means, electronic or mechanical, including photocopying, recording, or any information storage or retrieval system, without prior permission in writing from the publishers.

Bloomsbury Publishing Plc does not have any control over, or responsibility for, any third-party websites referred to or in this book. All internet addresses given in this book were correct at the time of going to press. The author and publisher regret any inconvenience caused if addresses have changed or sites have ceased to exist, but can accept no responsibility for any such changes.

A catalogue record for this book is available from the British Library.

A catalog record for this book is available from the Library of Congress.

ISBN: HB: 978-1-7883-1400-8
PB: 978-0-7556-3855-0
ePDF: 978-1-7883-1870-9
eBook: 978-1-7883-1869-3

Typeset by Newgen KnowledgeWorks Pvt. Ltd., Chennai, India

To find out more about our authors and books visit www.bloomsbury.com and sign up for our newsletters.

# Contents

| | |
|---|---|
| List of Illustrations | vii |
| Acknowledgements | xi |
| Translation and Transliteration | xiii |
| | |
| Introduction | 1 |
| 1. Kurdistan's performance traditions | 19 |
| 2. The origin and development of Kurdish theatre in Iraq, 1920–75 | 49 |
| 3. Kurdish theatre and resistance, 1975–91 | 111 |
| 4. The construction of leftist-nationalist identity in Talat Saman's theatre | 155 |
| 5. Ahmad Salar's theatre: The mythical 'Golden Age' | 181 |
| Conclusion | 217 |
| | |
| Timeline: Iraqi Kurds | 225 |
| Bibliography | 229 |
| Index | 245 |

# Illustrations

## Figures

| | | |
|---|---|---|
| 1 | Mîrmîren carnival in Mahabad, Iran, in 1944 | 29 |
| 2 | A Çemer ritual in Ilam | 42 |
| 3 | *Nîron* (Rawanduz, 1931) | 70 |
| 4 | Rafiq Chalak in *Gilkoy Tazey Leyl* (Leyl's New Grave, 1956) | 72 |
| 5 | *Bûkî Jêr Dewarî Reş* (The Bride under the Black Tent, Sulaymaniyah, 1961) | 72 |
| 6 | *Serbazî Aza* (1935) | 81 |
| 7 | *Le Rêy Nîştimanda* (1946) | 84 |
| 8 | Actors Taha Khalil, Salah Muhamad Jamil and Fuad Omar with artists Khalid Saeid and Azad Shawqi in dressing room for *Pîskey Terprîr* (1956) | 93 |
| 9 | *Mem û Zîn* (1958) | 94 |
| 10 | Narmin Nakam in *Tawanî Çî Bû* (1958) | 95 |
| 11 | Narmin Nakam in *Emrekey Begim* (1958) | 96 |
| 12 | Kurdish delegations showing support for the 1958 Revolution | 98 |
| 13 | Gaziza's Friends Theatre Group | 104 |
| 14 | The Iraqi Ministry of Culture's approval for the staging of *Pîlan* in 1977 after the implementation of the ministry's alterations to the text | 116 |
| 15 | A page from the play *Pîlan* shows the extent to which the Ministry of Culture controlled and censored dramatic texts. The circled parts with the Arabic word 'yahdhif', meaning delete, next to them are to be completely removed from the play | 117 |
| 16 | Badea Dartash in *Ey Gelî Felestînî Rapere* (1988) | 118 |
| 17 | *Receb û Piyawxoran* (1975) | 121 |
| 18 | Badea Dartash in *Nexşey Xwênawî* (1976) | 124 |
| 19 | First drama professors at Sulaymaniyah Institute of Fine Arts: (sitting from left) Azad Jalal, Badea Dartash and Ahmad Salar | 136 |

| | | |
|---|---|---|
| 20 | Midiya Rauf (right) and Nigar Hasib Qaradaqi in *Le Çawerwanî Siyamend* | 139 |
| 21 | *Ragwêz* (Transfer), a play performed by PUK peshmerga fighters in the village of Bilekê in Saqez, Iran, 1989 | 143 |
| 22 | *Tewbey Gurg Merge* (A Wolf's Penitence Is Death), a play performed by PUK peshmerga fighters in 1980 | 144 |
| 23 | Letter by the Ministry of Intelligence demanding the arrest of the listed Kurdish intellectuals including Hussein Barzanji, Fuad Qaradaqi, Fuad Majid Misri, Rauf Hasan, Ahmad Salar, Karim Kaban, Sherzad Hasan and Taha Khalil | 186 |
| 24 | Actors playing Daf in *Nalî w Xewnêkî Erxewanî* | 198 |
| 25 | A musical ensemble in *Nalî w Xewnêkî Erxewanî* | 198 |
| 26 | *Katê Helo Berz Defrê* | 214 |

# Maps

| | | |
|---|---|---|
| 1 | Distribution of Kurds across Turkey, Iran and Iraq | ix |
| 2 | De facto autonomous Kurdish region | x |
| 3 | Major Kurdish principalities | 51 |

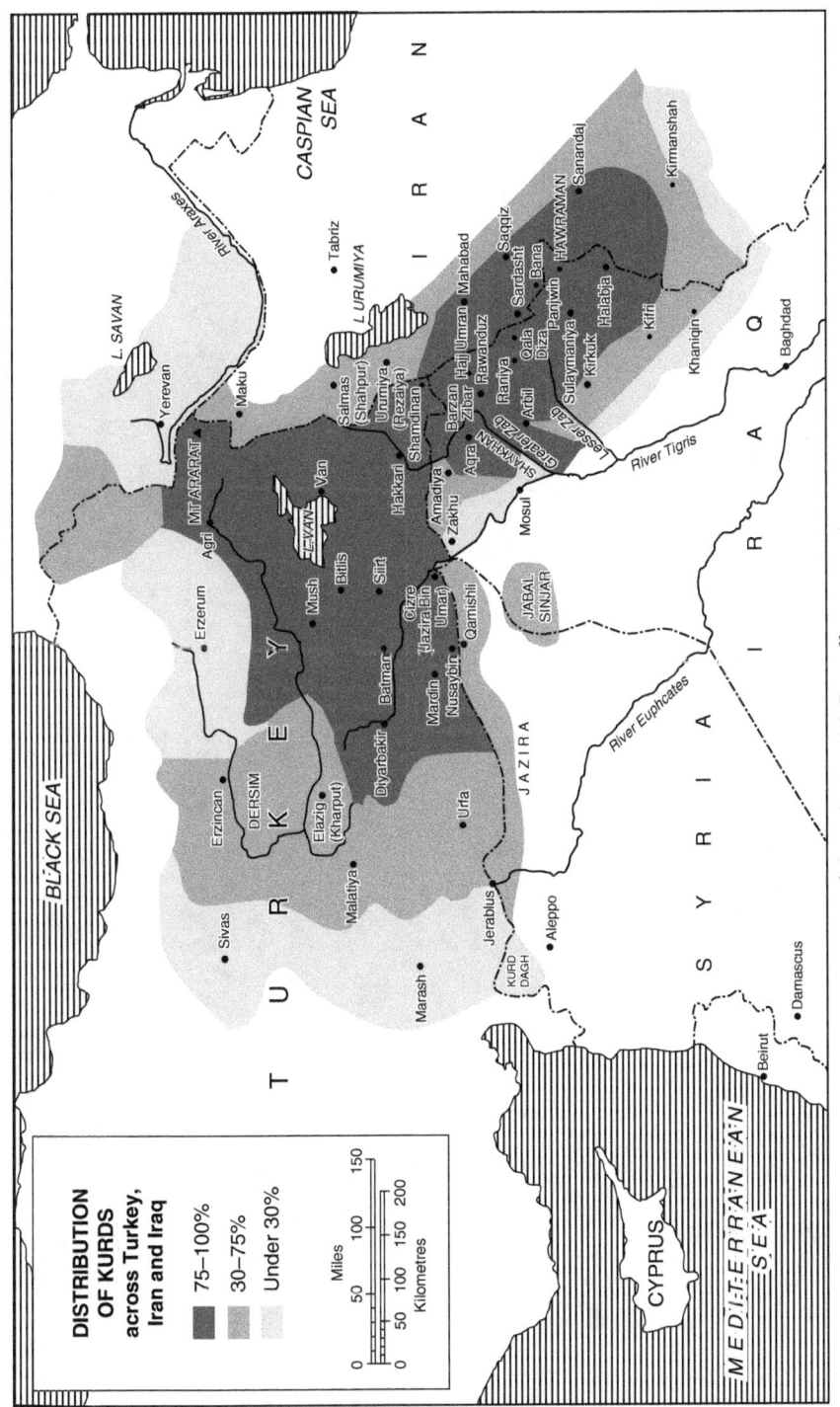

Map 1 Distribution of Kurds across Turkey, Iran and Iraq. *Source:* McDowall 2004, p. xiv.

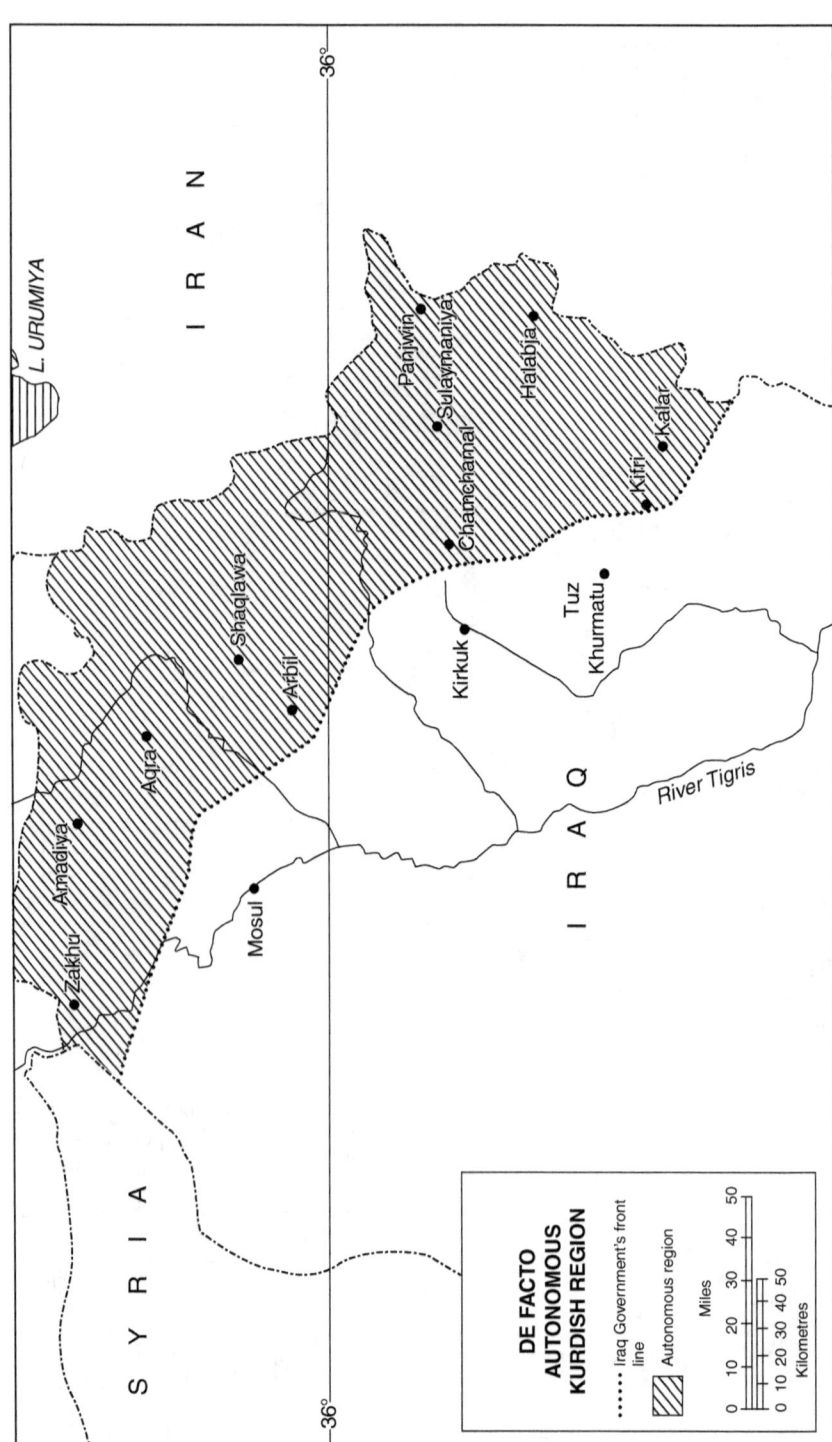

**Map 2** De facto autonomous Kurdish region. *Source*: McDowall 2004, p. 374.

# Acknowledgements

The most significant acknowledgement for this volume must go to my family for their emotional and intellectual support over the years. I am particularly indebted to my mother, Fereshteh Naleini, who enriched this book with her knowledge of Kurdish folk tradition.

The University of Exeter awarded me the doctoral scholarship which made this research possible. I am grateful for that and also for the hospitality, advice and cooperation from various government organizations and individuals within the Kurdistan Region, where I conducted my fieldwork.

I would like to thank the University of Salahaddin for accommodating me during my field research in Kurdistan and both the University of Salahaddin and the Erbil Central Library for giving me access to their invaluable resources. I am also grateful to the General Directorate of Erbil Theatre and the organizers of Erbil's Third International Theatre Festival for their generosity and hospitality. My attendance of the week-long festival was made possible by the Directorate's invitation and this afforded me a precious opportunity to meet and interview several theatre artists whom I had not met during my fieldwork, as well as witness several performances by Kurdish artists.

I would like to extend my most sincere gratitude to all the theatre artists, academics, family and friends in Kurdistan without whose unfailing support this book would not have come to fruition. My dear friend Siham Mamand not only helped me with my research but, more importantly, made me feel at home during my time in Erbil. I am forever grateful for her and her family's kindness and hospitality. Among the theatre artists, I should particularly thank *mamosta* Ahmad Salar and Muhsin Muhammad who made time to sit with me and answer my many questions about theatre under the Baath rule. I also interviewed veteran director and playwright Talat Saman who, to my utmost regret, passed away recently. I am deeply sorry that I cannot share this book with him and so I would like to dedicate it to his memory instead.

I should also thank Dr Ben Boulton for his careful reading of the manuscript and his extensive comments and corrections. Any errors that remain despite his assistance are, of course, my own.

Last but not least, I would like to pay tribute to my partner, Dr Jeremy Wildeman, whose unwavering encouragement and support made this journey possible. His belief in me and my work has got me through tough times and I count myself fortunate to have benefitted from his critical guidance so freely during the process of writing this book.

# Translation and Transliteration

The playtexts, theatre histories and most other sources used by this research are written in Kurdish Sorani and in Arabic script. The transcription system which has been used for the texts in this work follows the scheme developed by Celadet Bedirxan for writing Kurmanji in Roman script. In this system letters are pronounced as in English with the following exceptions: Long vowels *ê* as in the French mère, *î* as in keen, *û* as in pool and short vowel *e* as in pat. Other exceptions include *ç* as in chip, *ş* as in ship, *c* as in jail, *q* as pronounced in the Arabic Quran and *x* as in loch. The vowel *i*, as in tip, corresponds to the [ɪ] symbol in English and *u*, as in hook, corresponds to the [ʊ] symbol in English.

To make the reading experience easier and the book more accessible to a wider public, I have refrained from using this transcription system and Kurdish pronunciation for Kurdish proper names. As for place names, such as Erbil and Sulaymaniyah, I have again chosen to keep to common English norms. However, for lesser-known places, such as Pîremegrûn Mountain, I have chosen to use the Kurdish transcription system.

Also, translations of all Kurdish texts, including plays and most poems, are, unless otherwise stated, my own.

# Introduction

With an estimated population of over 30 million, the Kurds are the fourth largest nation in the Middle East, inhabiting lands that comprise parts of today's Iran, Iraq, Syria and Turkey.[1] Divided between the Ottoman and Safavid Empires in the early sixteenth century, these lands were ruled by Kurdish dynasties and principalities up to the mid-nineteenth century when those principalities were overthrown by their ruling empires. Kurdish regions were divided again between Turkey, Iraq and Syria after the First World War and the partition of the Ottoman Empire. Despite these territorial divisions, which have caused many cultural, linguistic and political fragmentations, a sense of belonging to a Kurdish nation, albeit locally and within one's native area, has existed among the Kurds for a long time (Nezan 1996, pp. 10–12). The existence of Kurds as a distinct ethnic group is confirmed by the Ottoman and Persian administrators of the sixteenth century and the travellers who spent time in various parts of Kurdistan (see Rich 1836; Fraser 1840; Southgate 1840; Bruinessen and Boeschoten 1988). However, it was in the twentieth century that the modern Kurdish nationalism emerged as a movement and gained momentum.

While the idea that the Kurds constituted a distinct nation in the modern sense of the word began to gain ground during the second half of the nineteenth century, it was only in the aftermath of the 1908 Young Turk Revolution that an organized Kurdish movement emerged into being. In their attempt to foster a sense of common nationality and pride, the early Kurdish nationalists formed societies and published periodicals in which they drew on collective memories and values, ethnic myths and popular culture. They hoped to create a national

---

[1] The Kurdish Institute of Paris estimated the total Kurdish population in 2016 to be between 36 and 45 million (see: https://www.institutkurde.org/en/info/the-kurdish-population-1232551004).

identity based not on tribal or religious affiliation but on a shared culture and language. Influenced by the European orientalists' glorification of oral culture, these pioneers of Kurdish cultural nationalism began to focus on the existing Kurdish oral culture as a rich and valuable source of cultural distinctiveness which could help their claims of political independence. Therefore, although of elite backgrounds, these early nationalists began idealizing the Kurdish peasantry and incorporating their culture into the dominant ethnie (Bruinessen 1994, pp. 12–14).[2] In their attempts to create a shared sense of national identity, they established cultural societies and journals that emphasized national themes, propagated the Kurds' common heritage of splendour, and stressed the value of education as a necessary requirement to survive as a nation in the modern world.

Cultural nationalism, which has been defined as the cultivation of a unique national history and culture (see Hutchinson 1994a; Smith 2009), continues to be an important and resonant aspect of Kurdish national identity-construction. Efforts have been made to standardize the Kurdish language, and these efforts have served as a major thrust in the Kurdish struggle for nationhood (see Hassanpour 1992). Folklorists continue to collect Kurdish folktales, anecdotes and songs (e.g. Akyol 2008; Fidanî 2014); and printing houses in Iraqi Kurdistan and Turkey continue to publish national classics while, at the same time, these classics continue to inspire the modern genres of novels and plays (e.g. Ronî War 2011; Boynukara 2008).

This book attempts to contribute to the scholarship on Kurdish culture and nationalism by examining the development of Iraqi-Kurdish theatre and situating it within historical context. It is focused upon the question of how Kurdish theatre in Iraq has engaged issues of national identity, nationalism and the struggle for independence during moments of profound change during the period 1975–91. While the development of Kurdish theatre since its emergence

---

[2] For example, Kamuran Bedirxan (1895–1978), a descendant of the ancient Bohtan principality, incorporated elements of Kurdish 'low' culture by drawing from the traditional Kurdish tales in his nationalist novel *Der Adler von Kurdistan* (The Eagle of Kurdistan) (Strohmeier 2003, p. 153). This novel which was written to promote the image of Kurds in their brave and just struggle for freedom, presented the image of 'Kurdishness' through the Kurds' 'heroism, patriotism, reverence for their land, identification with their mountains; their pride in their language and heritage, the beauty of their folk tales and songs, the rich variety of their material culture; their strong and patriotic women; the solidarity among Kurds from all backgrounds' (p. 203).

to the defeat of the Kurdish nationalist movement in 1975 is also explored, the 1975–91 period is particularly instructive because it encompasses events such as the loss of Kurdish autonomy, the resurgence of the Kurdish guerrilla struggle, and the genocidal *Anfal* campaign. Taking into account the extensive literature that affirms the role of theatrical performance in constructing and contesting national identity, it is therefore appropriate to ask whether theatre performed this role in Kurdistan during the period 1975–91.

In answering this question, this book seeks to demonstrate that theatre is a genre that is capable of providing evidence that is relevant to the understanding of Kurdish history. It demonstrates that an exploration of the history and voices of those involved in creating theatre can highlight hidden, marginalized or suppressed narratives; furthermore, it can also highlight moments that indicate the critical importance of the theatre as a charged political space that cultivated Kurdish nationalism. This will hopefully contribute to a revisionist historiography of the Kurdish national struggle that takes into account performative and oral genres, by locating and retrieving experiences and voices of those engaged in powerful acts of theatrical resistance.

In his study of Irish drama and cultural nationalism, Ben Levitas points out that in attempting to follow the relationship between literature and politics, there is perhaps no form more appropriate for investigation than drama and its performance (Levitas 2002, p. 5). Drama, as Levitas highlights, is a public art which shares the immediate benefits and also the risks of speaking directly with its audience (p. 5). Because of the ability of a play's performance to generate a shared public response, tracing the interaction between literature and politics can be more reliably done through theatre than the printing of essays, poems or novels which have so often been used by scholars to judge the mindset of the Kurdish society and the relationships between politics and literature in Kurdistan.

With a background in English and having previously researched the politics of English Romantic drama, I was drawn to explore Kurdish theatre's engagement with politics for my doctoral thesis in Kurdish Studies at the University of Exeter. Due to the lack of any such study in the Kurdish context, particularly Iraqi Kurdistan where the environment has been more favourable for the development of a theatre in Kurdish, I became interested in an integrated study of Kurdish theatre and politics in Iraq during the 1970s and 1980s, the height of the Kurdish nationalist struggle against the Baath regime. A review of Iraqi-Kurdish theatre history in the preliminary stages of my research immediately validated my interest by revealing a serious committed theatre that not only promoted national Kurdish identity, solidarity and consciousness but also encouraged resistance against the tyranny of the Iraqi regime. The Iraqi-Kurdish theatre of that era, as I discovered, consistently participated in providing possibilities for resistance through the use of Kurdish mythology and folklore, re-enactment of oppressed histories and revival of Kurdish historical stories. This not only promoted national consciousness and identity but also brought the public together and aroused a spirit of resistance by portraying legendary and heroic national characters from their past.

The Baath regime's response to such theatrical productions demonstrates the impact of theatre in Iraqi Kurdistan during perhaps one of its most difficult times. In the presence of theatre as a powerful cultural force, Iraqi authorities resorted to keeping theatre under control not only by censoring the texts of the plays but also by observing the rehearsals and performances of those playtexts which had been previously approved, banning those which were deemed subversive and punishing those involved in them. The state response to theatre in the form of banning orders, censorship and imprisonment reflects the regime's anxiety and fear of the power of theatre to influence and mobilize the masses. Therefore, while the distinctive features of drama as a nationalist tool informs this study, the Iraqi government's attention to theatre and its regulation and censorship of it, invite further emphasis on the genre.

In his introduction to *Literature and Nation in the Middle East*, Yasir Suleiman emphasizes the role of novel and poetry in constructing, articulating or challenging notions of national identities in the Middle East. He mentions that drama is not dealt with in his edition because of its 'marginal' position in the national cultures of the region (Suleiman and Muhawi 2006, p. 1). This position may be because it is easier for the literary historian and critic to access, document and study written and published literature rather than the fleeting world of theatrical performance which so often lacks archived scripts, especially in the case of stateless Kurds who lack national institutions to safeguard and promote their cultural heritage, or even the freedom to keep and develop a written language. Precisely due to the lack of such institutions, theatre assumes greater importance not only as a means for cultural survival but also as a vehicle for commenting on the political scene and even disseminating resistance within the community.³

Despite its important role in the Kurdish cultural and political nationalism, Kurdish theatre has received no attention from Western scholars whose primary focus has been on the dominant languages and literatures in the region, at the expense of the Kurds who have been left in the shadows produced by four powerful nation-states that each rule over a distinctive corner of their lands. Even the studies of Kurdish literature and culture have almost all ignored the existence of theatre in Kurdistan.⁴ Within this small scholarship, theatre is doubly ignored as a repository of culture and also as a social space utilized by Kurdish artists to reflect and comment on the turbulent political history of their nation.⁵ The lack of attention to Kurdish theatre in academic texts is understandable given the historical marginalization of the Kurds in the Middle East, theatre scholars' unfamiliarity with Kurdish language and literary texts, and Kurdologists' general lack of interest in exploring the Western-style theatre tradition in Kurdistan. Theatre in the Arab world has itself only recently received attention from Western scholars with Egypt dominating most studies (see Badawi 1987, 1988, 1992; Sadgrove 1996).⁶

An examination of the scholarship on Kurdish culture and nationalism shows that the emergence and development of Kurdish identity is usually analysed mainly within the genre of poetry, from Ahmadi Khani (in Kurdish, Ehmedî Xanî) to Haji Qadiri Koyi who inspired early Kurdish nationalists in their struggle, to the nationalist twentieth-century poets, Pîremêrd, Cegerxwîn and

---

³ On theatre's positive political and social interventions in a range of cultures around the world, see Boon and Plastow (1998).
⁴ For instance, Kreyenbroek and Allison's edition of *Kurdish Culture and Identity* (1996) deals with Kurds' written and oral literature, publishing, media, religious beliefs, material culture but not theatre. Also, in its chapter on Kurdish written literature, the growing interest in and publication of plays in Iraqi Kurdistan, especially since the 1970s, have been ignored (Blau 2010).
⁵ The only book written on this subject in a European language is the German *Theater als Form des Widerstands in Kurdistan* (2002) by Hawre Zangana. I have made several references to this book in my discussion of guerrilla theatre.
⁶ Within the growing field of Middle Eastern theatre, there have been a few studies on the relationship between theatre and politics in the Middle East. Some examples of these studies are Stone's *Popular Culture and Nationalism in Lebanon* (2007), Shiva Balaghi's chapter on 'Theatre and Nationalism in the Nineteenth-Century' (Balaghi 2002), Hammond's *Popular Culture in the Arab World* (2007) and Khalid Amine and Marvin Carlson's *The Theatres of Morocco, Algeria and Tunisia* (2011). All these studies place the development of theatre into a wider sociopolitical context of the region by showing the use of theatre by artists to propagate nationalism (Balaghi 2002), states' sponsorship of theatre as a propaganda tool (Hammond 2007, p. 365) and the relation of theatre to the production of national identity (see Stone 2007; Amine and Carlson 2011, pp. 131–216).

others. Studies of Kurdish identity and nationalism in literature have referred to the works of poets, essayists and, more recently, novelists (see Hassanpour 1992; Strohmeier 2003; Vali 2003; Galip 2015). Oral and popular culture, which has played an important role in the preservation of Kurdish cultural identity, had until recently remained largely understudied.[7] In recent years, the field of Kurdish studies has witnessed a growing interest in Kurdish oral and popular culture, this vital component of Kurdish identity. The tradition of *dengbêj* (Kurdish storyteller), in particular, has been the subject of a few academic studies which all contribute to a better understanding of how power relations and everyday politics are articulated through and played out in cultural productions (see Yüksel 2010; Aras 2013; Hamelink 2014). *Dengbêj* tradition has also been studied in relation to Kurdish theatre in Turkey in Duygu Çelik's doctoral thesis *Dengbêjî Tradition and its Effects on Kurdish Theatre in Turkey* (2017).[8]

This book affirms that Kurdish theatre, like storytelling, its traditional predecessor, participated in the preservation of Kurdish culture and history and their promotion in the public sphere. Not only that, theatre promoted resistance and called for revolution against the oppressive Iraqi regimes. By its engagement with Kurdish history through the history of its theatre, this study challenges the predominant focus on the Kurds from within the framework of politics and from the viewpoint of the political elite. Instead it places particular emphasis on Kurdish culture as an important terrain for retrieving marginalized voices of dissent.

Theatre is usually defined as a live performance for live audiences which may or may not take place in purpose-built buildings. In the *Cambridge Introduction to Theatre Historiography*, Thomas Postlewait explains that by theatre he means 'the comprehensive field of the performing arts, including theatre, dance, opera, folk theatre, puppetry, parades, processions, spectacles, festivals, circuses,

---

[7] In his famous notion that nations can be considered 'imagined communities' (Anderson 1991), Anderson proposes that the invention of printing press and the rise of print media provided the technological means for the dissemination of nationalist ideas. Anderson remarks that the regular shared reading of novels and newspapers created awareness of a wider community and produced the idea that readers shared a set of interests as members of the same nation ( pp. 39–40). Anderson's *Imagined Communities* has been criticized for excessive focus on literacy and printed media and offering a reductive view of culture which, among other things, ignores the role of the embodied performances in imagining the nation (see Edensor 2002). For a critique of Anderson's print-capitalism model in the context of Kurdish studies, see Allison (2013).

[8] For an overview of Kurdish theatre in Turkey between 1991 and 2013, see Mîrza Metîn's encyclopedic *Jêrzemîn* (Underground, 2014).

public conventions, and related performance events' (Postlewait 2009, p. 2). It is therefore clear that theatrical productions in purpose-built buildings are only one of several different types of cultural performance.

This form of theatre emerged in the Middle East only in the nineteenth century. It was introduced to the region mainly by non-Muslim minorities, some of whom had travelled to Europe where they had developed a liking for theatre. In the Ottoman Turkey, Armenian theatre companies were among the first groups to stage plays which were mainly adaptations of European classics. During the latter half of the nineteenth century, as part of the modernization projects by Middle Eastern rulers, first Opera Houses and theatres were built throughout the region and the first local productions were introduced to stage.

Pirbal notes that, within Kurdish literary discourse, the word 'theatre' first appeared in a late nineteenth-century poem by Mahwi:

*Dinya tiyatroye, meweste tiya biro*
The world is a theatre (stage), do not pause in it, keep going
*Kê mayewe ke nebûbê tiya tiro*
No one has stayed on this stage forever. (Pirbal 2001, p. 11)

In the early twentieth century, a number of European words, such as *pièce* (play) and drama, began to appear in Kurdish journals and papers. In 1919, when *Memê Alan*, the first play in the Kurdish language, was published in Istanbul, its author, Abdurrahim Rahmi Hakkari (1890–1958), described it as both a Kurdish *pièce* and *teatro*. The influence of French and Italian can be attributed to the fact that French and Italian theatre troupes were frequent visitors to Istanbul during the course of the nineteenth century (Faroqhi 2005, p. 260).

In Iraqi Kurdistan, *namāyesh* (a Persian word) and *tamsīl* (an Arabic word) were used, in addition to European terms, to describe theatrical performances in the late 1920s. It seems that these borrowed words continued to be used until the mid-twentieth century, when the word *şano* appeared in Kurdish. Pirbal suggests that the word *şano*, which has come to replace non-Kurdish words to denote theatre, had first been introduced to the Kurdish language by the poet Goran in 1950 (Pirbal 2001, p. 13); Pirbal suggests that Goran's use of the word in *Cîlwey Şano* (The Splendor of Stage) appealed to Kurdish writers, who then continued to use it in their publications (Pirbal 2001, p. 14). He suggests that the term itself derives from the Italian *scena* (p. 14). While *şano* has been used to denote both drama and theatre (see Subhan 2012), the addition of the suffixes *name* and *gerî* produces *şanoname*, which refers to the text of the play, and *şanogerî*, which refers to the play and the act of performing it.

Tanya (1985), who wrote the first book on Kurdish theatre history in Iraq, presents Greek drama as the beginning of world drama and proceeds to trace the history of Kurdish drama mainly in Sulaymaniyah, but also in Baghdad, Qaladiza, Koya, Erbil, Kirkuk, Khanaqin, Duhok and Halabja. He argues that Middle Eastern nations have not had an indigenous dramatic tradition and that the Kurds were first introduced to drama through their Arab and Turkish neighbours, who had themselves adopted it from the Europeans. Although he extends a cursory acknowledgement to old games and rituals such as *bûkebarane* (rain bride) and seasonal festivals of *semenî* (a pudding-like dish made from wheat), *sawerkutan* (making burghul), *diroyne* (harvest) and *seyrekanî behar* (spring excursions), he rejects the proposition that they provide clear evidence for the existence of a native theatre tradition in Iraq, citing the fact that they fail to conform to Aristotle's definition of drama as justification. He also refers to Claudius James Rich (1787–1821) and the narrative of his residence in Kurdistan in 1820 in which he makes no reference to theatre in the region (Tanya 1985, p. 44). Tanya maintains that the lack of theatre in Kurdistan was attributable to several factors including: the feudal governing system – which, in his view, opposed any intellectual endeavour – wars and occupation by foreign powers.

In other Kurdish theatre histories, which have drawn heavily upon Tanya's accounts of the early years of Kurdish theatre and the archives of old Kurdish periodicals, the names of certain actors, directors and performances are repeated. This has constructed the canon of an early Kurdish theatre that could trace its origins to the 1920s when Western-style, text-based theatre emerged in Iraqi Kurdistan. These works, like Tanya's, are conservative histories of theatre that consider Greek drama to be the starting point of Western theatre and contend that Kurdish drama began in 1919 with the publication of Hakkari's *Memê Alan* in Istanbul (Pirbal 2001, pp. 47–56).[9] This book will engage with

---

[9] Hawrami traces the birth of Kurdish drama in Iraq back to 1952. This was the first time that a Kurdish play was printed and published in Iraqi Kurdistan (Hawrami 2001, p. 305). Prior to that, in 1932, Pîremêrd had printed his *Mem û Zin* in sequential parts in his *Jiyan* newspaper. Having his own printing house, he later printed *Mem û Zin* as a play in 1934 and *Mehmûd Aqay Şêwekel* in 1942 (Pirbal 2001, p. 109).

the history of *şano* (or theatre in the Western use of the term) which first appeared in Iraqi Kurdistan in the 1920s.

Due to a lack of sources on Kurdish theatre in other languages, I have relied almost exclusively on Kurdish sources in order to explore how theatre emerged and developed within the sociopolitical context in which it was produced and performed. Kurdish researchers have made a vital contribution to this project, most notably Yasin Barzanji, Hasan Tanya, Kawa Ahmadmirza, Farhad Pirbal, Hawre Zangana, Hama Karim Hawrami, Ibrahim Ahmad Simo and Salam Faraj Karim. Their theatre histories and studies of Kurdish dramatic texts and performances paved the way for and significantly contributed to my own research.

The works mentioned above are all in Sorani Kurdish which, along with Kurmanji, constitutes one of the two major speech varieties spoken by the Kurds in Iraq. Kurmanji is mainly spoken in the Duhok governorate and its speakers account for about 20–25 per cent of Iraqi Kurds, with Sorani accounting for almost all of the remainder. In large part due to sociopolitical circumstances, these two speech varieties have not developed equally in Iraqi Kurdıstan. When the Babans established the city of Sulaymaniyah in 1784, the speech of the city gained prestige, becoming the language of poetry and the basis of standard Sorani in the twentieth century. At the time of the British occupation (1918–20) and mandate (1920–32), Sorani was used in local administration, education and print media. Despite increasing demands by Kurmanji speakers that education and administrative services be offered in Kurmanji, Sorani has retained its dominant position in the cultural milieu. It should be noted that the choice of Sorani as the dialect of administration and education was based on political considerations. In Iraq, speakers of Sorani were more urbanized and more active in the emerging Kurdish nationalist politics. By contrast, the Kurmanji speech area was more tribal-rural, and numerically smaller than the rest of the Kurdish-speech community (Hassanpour 2012, p. 56). It cannot be denied that the two important Kurdish cities of Erbil and Sulaymaniyah are located in the Sorani-speaking zone, and that most intellectual discourse amongst Iraqi Kurds has been conducted in Sorani.

In writing this book, I have chosen to focus upon Sorani for three main reasons. First, the centrality of the cities of Erbil and Sulaymaniyah within any discussion of theatre; second, the widespread availability of materials on theatre in these cities; finally, my own familiarity with the Sorani speech variety. These three considerations were foremost when I took the decision to focus upon the history of Kurdish theatre in Sorani and to only analyse plays that have been written and performed in Sorani. It should be clarified from the outset that this decision was not intended to denigrate the existence of Kurmanji-language theatre in Kurdistan. By virtue of the fact that it does not engage with this output, this book should not be understood as an authoritative account of theatre that encompasses the entirety of Iraqi Kurdistan.

While surveys of Kurdish theatre, such as Barzanji's, Tanya's, Ahmadmirza's and Pirbal's, provide invaluable insight into the history of theatre in Iraqi Kurdistan, most remain silent on the conditions of the production of the plays at the time of their performance. Also, apart from occasional plot summaries, they do not provide detailed analysis of performances or dramatic texts or provide an extensive in-depth exploration of the relationship between Kurdish theatre and resistance.[10] Tanya claimed that the lack of resources curtailed his ability to write about all theatrical performances from early years of Kurdish theatre history. This explains why he relied heavily upon interviews with past participants in theatre activities and, to a lesser extent, upon the *Birayetî* (Brotherhood) and *Jiyan* (Life) newspapers. Hawrami and Simo instead offer a general discussion of drama and playwriting, and only discuss particular Kurdish texts with reference to their dramatic characteristics. Of all these sources, Dr. Salam Faraj Karim's study provided this research with a general understanding of the relationship between the different phases of theatre in Iraqi Kurdistan and the wider political developments in the region between 1975 and 1995. His five phases of development engage with political events which include the defeat of the Kurdish struggle in 1975, its revival in 1977, the eruption of the Iran-Iraq war in 1980, the genocidal *Anfal* campaign and the Kurdish uprising of 1991. However, the bulk of his analysis is focused upon

---

[10] Hawre Zangana is one important exception in this respect – his German book on theatre and resistance in Iraqi Kurdistan in the 1980s significantly contributes to the understanding of Kurdish resistance theatre under Saddam Hussein. However, he strongly relies upon the personal archives of a small number of Iraqi Kurdish artists who include Kamal Hanjira, Nigar Hasib and Shamal Omar. This is why he commits a relatively large part of his book to their Experimental Theatre and the analysis of *Xec û Siyamend* (Khaj and Siyamand), one of their productions. While my study of Kurdish theatre under the Baath is more extensive, my discussion of guerrilla theatre in Chapter 3 draws heavily upon Zangana's work.

the stylistic analysis of individual dramatic texts and not theatre's engagement with the nationalist struggle.

The theoretical component of my work follows a different path from (the scant) past research by drawing heavily upon cultural nationalism, which is strongly rooted within folklore, history, legends, myths and symbols. Each one is an attribute of cultural uniqueness and an essential means through which national consciousness is stimulated. This book confirms the cultural nationalist approach to the study of nationalism by highlighting the role of intellectuals and the intelligentsia in introducing and promoting Kurdish theatre since its inception. They utilized theatre as a modernizing tool which helped promote education, literacy and women's rights and also retrieve national cultural heritage. I will suggest that, over the course of its history, Kurdish theatre often acted as a site for staging national history, folklore and myths and for formulating nationalist ideology, and thus played an important role in constructing and promoting Kurdish nationalist identity, particularly during the rule of the Baath regime.

However, a culturally imagined unification in Kurdish drama worked alongside mass mobilization as myths of Kurdish nationalism were used to encourage resistance to the central authority by representing historical legends of Kurdish heroes and their self-sacrifice in the face of foreign invasion. It is therefore noticeable that Kurdish theatre under the dictatorial rule of the Baath Party was not merely concerned with preserving and promoting culture; to the same extent, it also sought to promote political liberation and incite rebellion. While this study draws heavily upon theories of cultural nationalism in order to emphasize the role of theatre and theatre artists in promoting nationalist myths and symbols, it also acknowledges that the ultimate goal of Kurdish dramatists, especially during the 1970s and the 1980s, has been a political one; namely, independence for Kurdistan.

In engaging with the relationship between nationalism and theatre, I have been guided by contextual studies of theatre and nationalism which include *Theatre Matters: Performance and Culture on the World Stage* (Boon and Plastow 1998), *Writing and Rewriting National Theatre Histories* (Wilmer 2004), *Staging Nationalism: Essays on Theatre and National Identity* (Gounaridou 2005), *National Theatres in a Changing Europe* (Wilmer 2008), *Theatre and Performance in Small Nations* (Blandford 2013) and *Theatre and*

*National Identity: Re-Imagining Conceptions of Nation* (Holdsworth 2014). The contributors to each of these volumes confirm the close relationship between performance and national identity and explore how theatrical performance can, in the context of specific countries, construct or contest notions of national identity.[11]

When it comes to Kurdish theatre, the lack of national institutions to safeguard Kurdish culture and heritage makes a reliable reconstruction of Kurdish theatre history a challenging task. Many theatre events in Iraqi Kurdistan have gone unrecorded and therefore much of the history of Kurdish theatre has been lost and is unrecoverable or remains hidden. Although since 1991, with the establishment of the Kurdistan Regional Government, attempts have been made to rectify this problem by publishing books and journals on Kurdish theatre and its history, these publications are not widely circulated and easily accessible. I was personally not able to find any books on Kurdish theatre in Erbil bookstores and the materials that I was able to obtain were either provided to me by individuals or were printed and distributed on the occasion of the third annual Erbil Theatre Festival.[12]

In order to redress the inadequate documentation of past theatrical events, I have drawn upon several sources. My research relied mainly on Salahaddin University library, the Central Library of Erbil and the personal libraries of theatre artists Ahmad Salar, Talat Saman and Muhsin Muhammad. These sources enabled me to obtain histories and studies of Kurdish theatre, along with the texts of plays. Historical documents and journalistic accounts also helped me reconstruct the links between Kurdish theatre and history. I have consulted all issues of *Beyan* and *Karwan* periodicals that were published during the 1980s and which are preserved in the Erbil Central Library. These periodicals not only contain the texts of several plays and occasional photographs of certain performances but also provide accounts of past performances and offer valuable insights into the history of Kurdish theatre. Other materials that have been used include biographies of persons associated with theatre, critical

---

[11] In addition to Kurdish studies, theatre studies and studies of cultural nationalism, this research also draws upon feminist studies of female representation in nationalist discourse by Afsaneh Najmabadi (1997) and Diana Taylor (1997).

[12] On the low circulation and consumption of print materials in Iraqi Kurdistan, see Sheyholislami (2011, p. 81).

accounts (of the work of actors, directors and playwrights), general histories of theatre, interviews with theatre artists published in journals, Kurdish histories, legal documents, official records, personal commentaries in papers and on the internet and visual records of performances such as photographs. The bulk of this material provided a sufficient basis for the study of the development of Kurdish theatre in Iraq and its relationship with political developments in the region.

This research uses interviews to contextualize the plays and to provide insight into the viewpoints of dramatists. Upon arriving in Kurdistan, I conducted informal interviews with staff and students at the University of Salahadin, with the intention of identifying the leading dramatists and stage directors in the period 1975–91. I was pointed in the direction of Ahmad Salar and Talat Saman, the two pioneering stage directors in Erbil and Sulaymaniyah (this selection was later justified by a review of the literature that was conducted during the course of my fieldwork). Both Salar and Saman were later interviewed in order to elucidate the sociopolitical context in which they were working and to uncover forgotten stories of theatrical resistance, as told by two of the most prominent figures involved in Kurdish theatre.

In addition to Salar and Saman, I also conducted interviews with Muhsin Muhammad, the actor, historian, and playwright, and Fattah Khattab, the theatre director. Muhammad was familiar with the history of Kurdish theatre and had witnessed the performances of Saman's and Salar's plays at the time. He was also building an archive of Kurdish theatre history which I used to obtain the texts of Saman's plays and records of government censorship of his plays. The section of the book that discusses guerrilla theatre draws upon interviews with Salar and Fattah Khattab, both having worked as theatre directors while being actively involved with guerrilla struggle during the 1980s. These oral accounts bring light to marginalized narratives of theatrical resistance and help answer questions such as why theatre mattered to them at the time of strict cultural censorship and political repression and how audiences responded to their works.

This study, therefore, relies both on theatrical texts and oral history (in the form of interviews with the main figures in the Kurdish theatre history) in order to gain a fuller comprehension of the contexts and meanings of plays; in addition, the interviewees' contributions enable a better understanding of the history and voices of the people whose role in the Kurdish national struggle has rarely been acknowledged. The study of the theatre history of an oppressed group helps uncover 'forgotten stories of powerful theatrical resistance' (Bhatia 2004, p. 3) which are undermined by the dominant focus on the written genres of novel, poetry, essays or political journals and pamphlets. The need to examine the oral history of theatre is particularly apparent in the case of the stateless Kurds who have historically lacked national institutions to safeguard their culture and national heritage. Theatre's impact is not in the literary text but in the live performance. This is especially true for the scarcely published Kurdish drama of the 1970s–1980s. While I have tried to take into account the reception of the selected plays, more oral history research needs to be undertaken if the interaction between Kurdish theatre and society is to be understood and grasped in its full significance.

In order to analyse nationalist discourse in the Kurdish theatre during the rule of the Baath regime in the 1970s and 1980s, this study focuses upon representative plays by Talat Saman and Ahmad Salar who, respectively, were pioneering figures in the cities of Erbil and Sulaymaniyah during these two decades. Saman, who began working in Erbil in the early 1970s, was the first theatre artist in the city to write plays for theatre. His work in both television and theatre established him as the most prolific director in Erbil. Saman, who was at the time one of very few drama graduates, co-founded several theatre groups in Erbil between 1970 and 1974. Salar, meanwhile, was the dominant director and playwright in Sulaymaniyah during the 1980s. In his work as a professor at Sulaymaniyah Fine Arts Institute, he trained a new generation of successful Kurdish theatre actors who included Arsalan Darwesh, Kharman Hirani and Kamaran Rauf. With over a hundred plays, Salar was the most prolific dramatist in Iraqi Kurdistan and the pioneer of a new mode of writing for theatre which drew extensively upon Kurdish music, along with Kurdish folklore, history and literature. Salar's theatre has been presented as the first instance of a quintessentially Kurdish theatre, a point that will be drawn out in more detail at a later stage.

The plays that were written and directed by both dramatists engaged with Kurdish nationalism and national identity during the ongoing war between Kurdish guerrillas and the central government. In utilizing theatre as a site for the representation of Kurdish nationalist myths and reviving historical narratives, at a time when Kurdish nationalist sentiment was in the ascendancy, both dramatists attracted large crowds to theatres. For a better understanding of theatre's engagement with the nationalist struggle, I will examine Salar's *Nalî w Xewnêkî Erxewanî* (Nali and a Violet Dream, 1987) and *Katê Helo Berz Defrê* (When the Eagle Flies High, 1988) and Saman's *Mem û Zîn* (Mam and Zin, 1976) and *Qelay Dimdim* (Dimdim Fortress, 1982). These plays were selected upon the basis of their unparalleled popularity during the period 1975–91 and the fact that they provide considerable insight into the methods deployed by both dramatists. They also demonstrate how Kurdish theatre engaged with nationalism and resistance at critical historical junctures.

Talat Saman's *Mem û Zîn* is an overtly nationalistic work that was first staged in 1976, only one year after Kurds had lost their autonomy. *Qelay Dimdim* was staged during a period when the Iraqi Kurds, demanding autonomy and a halt to deportations, rose up in a massive uprising that resulted in the release of a large number of political prisoners. The play, which was written based on historical accounts, oral narratives and modern adaptations of the story, was another overtly nationalistic production whose appeal to the Kurdish public is clearly demonstrated by the fact that it ran for a total of twenty-five days in Erbil in 1982.

Ahmad Salar's plays provide considerable insight into the Kurdish theatre's response to the atrocities committed against the Kurds during the *Anfal* Campaign (1986–9). *Nalî w Xewnêkî Erxewanî*, which was inspired by the regime's genocidal actions, was Salar's first serious attempt to craft a quintessentially Kurdish drama. The play, which is frequently cited as the cornerstone of an original Kurdish theatre, was staged at both Baghdad University and Sulaymaniyah in 1987, where it was very well-received. *Katê Helo Berz Defrê*, Salar's next work, enjoyed even greater success – in 1988, it was staged for three consecutive days (with two performances on each day) in Baghdad and ran for over two weeks in Sulaymaniyah.

The thematic analyses of these plays bring out the invocation of historical narratives, folklore and nationalist myths – these include the 'Golden Age' of the Kurdish self-rule and the Kurds' heroism in protecting their homeland against foreign powers. The recurrence of these ethnic myths and symbols will be interpreted through Anthony Smith's ethno-symbolist model, which elaborates the different myths propagated by nationalists: myth of common ancestry which links all members of the present generation of the community and between this generation and all its forebears; myth of the heroic age which provides models of virtuous conduct and inspires faith and courage in the face of oppression and decadence; myth of decline which tells how the community lost its grandeur and fell into a state of decay; myth of regeneration which explains how to restore the 'Golden Age' and renew the community as in old days (Smith 1999, pp. 62–8). Future chapters reveal the centrality of these myths to the Kurdish theatre of the 1970s and 1980s and the role that theatre played in propagating nationalist myths and symbols.

This book unravels in chronological order in order to demonstrate how the transformation of theatre has coincided with cultural and political change over the years. The first chapter provides an insight into the traditional performance practices that preceded the emergence of Western-style theatre in the region. In Kurdistan, as elsewhere in the Middle East, a wide variety of performance activity existed well before the introduction of European-style theatre in the twentieth century. These performance traditions were not based on written texts and as such were disparaged or disregarded by conventional Kurdish theatre histories, which tend to trace the beginnings of Kurdish theatre to the early twentieth century. While these performances may not be described as theatre practices by traditional Western standards, their impact on contemporary Kurdish theatre has been very strong. Modern text-based theatre in Kurdistan, as will be discussed later, has been greatly influenced by a long tradition of folk performances and oral literature.

Chapter 2 engages the history of Kurdish theatre in modern-day Iraq from its emergence in the mid-1920s to the fall of the autonomous Kurdistan region in 1975. While the majority of plays from this period have not survived, this chapter not only offers a historical survey of performances but also seeks out the sociopolitical conditions that define and explain aspects of their productions. The chapter explores the sociopolitical developments that contributed to the emergence of theatre in Iraqi Kurdistan and closely examines the early debate over the need for a Kurdish theatre around questions of national identity, class and gender. It demonstrates how the growth of Kurdish nationalism and leftist sentiments strongly impacted upon Kurdish theatre productions during the period which extended from the 1930s to the late 1950s. While theatre activities declined and disappeared in the 1960s as a result of political instabilities, this changed in 1970 when the Kurdish armed struggle finally bore fruit and resulted in the creation of autonomy for Kurdistan. Performances from 1970 to 1974 clearly demonstrate that the establishment of autonomy provided Kurdish theatre with the freedom to express and explore nationalistic sentiments. This fleeting glimpse of freedom from censorship was abruptly curtailed in 1975, when Iraq re-established its rule over Kurdistan.

Chapter 3 examines the link between the Kurdish struggle against Iraqi rule and the growth of radical performance culture in Kurdistan in the period 1975–91. It demonstrates that even after the loss of autonomy in the mid-1970s, a failed uprising, and continued rebellion against the regime, Kurdish nationalist and leftist themes continued to appear in Kurdish theatre productions. This chapter explores political developments of the 1970s and 1980s within Iraq and their influence on Kurdish theatre as can be witnessed in the emergence of guerrilla theatre groups and theatrical performances in refugee camps.

Chapters 4 and 5 examine representative plays from the period 1975–91, with a view to better understand the role of Kurdish theatre in resisting Baathist rule and furthering nationalist agendas. Chapter 4 examines two important plays directed by Talat Saman, one of the first graduates of drama in Baghdad University who was arguably the most successful Kurdish director of the 1970s. Saman was viewed as the pre-eminent figure within Erbil's theatre scene of the time, and his productions were frequently well-received. Of his plays, *Mem û Zîn* and *Qelay Dimdim* will be subject to closer examination in this chapter as they clearly exemplify the politicization of Kurdish theatre in the 1970s. They also attest to the considerable courage that Kurdish theatre artists displayed when producing nationalist works in the immediate aftermath of the loss of autonomy in 1975. The leftist-nationalist themes that are expounded in these plays will be related to the influence of an increasingly politicized Arab theatre, the growing interest in socialist ideologies in the Middle East, the loss of Kurdish autonomy and the failure of the 1975 Kurdish uprising.

Ahmad Salar was the most successful Kurdish dramatist and director of the 1980s. His theatre became increasingly politicized in response to growing state repression and the genocidal crimes of the Baathist regime in the late 1980s. Chapter 5 engages with Salar's construction of a distinctively Kurdish nationalist theatre in *Nalî w Xewnêkî Erxewanî* and *Katê Helo Berz*

*Defrê*. It observes that Salar's theatre not only acted as a site for staging national history, folklore and literature, and therefore strengthened a sense of Kurdish national identity, but also served as a cultural medium which implicitly called for revolution by glorifying the Kurdish national heroes and their struggles against foreign invaders. These plays exemplify Salar's extensive use of Kurdish myths, historical figures, poetry, folkloric songs, musical instruments and dance. They clearly demonstrate how Salar utilized theatre as a public medium for collective expression and experience of a distinct Kurdish identity and fostered a sense of pride in Kurdish cultural traditions which were shown to be appropriate components of a distinct Kurdish theatre. Further, by staging myths of a Kurdish heroic age, its loss, and the need for its restoration, Salar's plays contributed to the nationalist struggle and incited resistance.

The concluding chapter confirms that theatre is an appropriate site to look for and access evidence of Kurdish national identity construction and dissemination. The history of Iraqi-Kurdish theatre is a history of a people's desire to build a modern nation, to improve it and to protect it against external and internal threats to its very existence. By reviving and celebrating their culture and history, theatre validated and strengthened people's belief in themselves as a nation and therefore empowered them against the constant assault against their identity and existence. Even under the oppressive Baath regime, Kurdish theatre artists continued to find ways to not only celebrate their culture but take on the state and call for unity and resistance against the regime. By examining theatre's role within the Kurdish nationalist movement in Iraqi Kurdistan, this study will hopefully contribute to the current scholarship on Kurdish culture and nationalism and open up the field to examinations of previously neglected Kurdish dramatic texts and theatre history.

# 1

# Kurdistan's performance traditions

Oral performance has historically been the dominant form of performance in Kurdistan. This orality, however, has coexisted alongside a culture of literacy and, in fact, there is no great divide separating the oral and written cultures which have always interacted with each other and also with the cultures of the Kurds' neighbours (Allison 2010, p. 35). The centuries-old exchange between Kurds and their neighbours has resulted in a rich folklore of both unique and shared elements which has served as a major source of modern Kurdish literature and culture and much of the imagery of Kurdish nationalism (p. 33). To take some prominent examples, Kurdish oral ballads such as *Dimdim*, *Mem û Zîn* and *Xec û Siyamend* (Khaj and Siyamand) have inspired several literary creations in classical and modern literature; meanwhile many other popular ballads have drawn on narratives common in Arabic and Persian literatures including *Lêylî w Mecnûn* (Layla and Majnun), *Şêxî Senan* (Sheikh Sanan), *Yûsif û Zilêxa* (Yusuf and Zulaikha) and *Ferhad û Şîrîn* (Farhad and Shirin).

While this book is focused upon theatrical texts or drama, this does not mean there is a lack of a rich performance culture in Kurdistan or that the Kurdish people were unfamiliar with theatrical spectacles prior to the emergence of Western-style theatre in the region. In fact, traditional and folk performances have served as a major source of modern Kurdish theatre. This is clearly demonstrated by the Kurdish theatre of the 1970s and the 1980s, particularly, in Talat Saman's and Ahmad Salar's plays which are extensively analysed in future chapters. Saman's plays are mainly inspired by folktales while Salar's plays draw heavily on folk dance, storytelling, music and other performance traditions. It is therefore essential to examine these traditions in closer detail. Also, the lack of an English-language review of Kurdish traditional performances makes this chapter a necessary introduction to the field by covering a wide variety of Kurdish performance practices, from dance to spring festivals and rain rituals.

Western theatre studies had long considered theatrical production to be text-centred and playwright-driven. Historians of theatre and performance usually focused on European theatre tradition where evidence existed in the form of written texts or in archaeological ruins of purpose-built performance structures. This, however, shifted radically in the 1980s with the advent of the field of Performance Studies and its recognition that European theatre is only one manifestation of a very broad spectrum of performed cultural activity. The key assumption of Performance Studies is that 'anything and everything can be described "as" performance' (Schechner 2002, pp. 1–2). This definition suggests that a broad spectrum of human actions ranging from ritual, to games, sports, popular entertainment, theatre, dance and music, and even everyday life performances can be a subject of Performance Studies.

The growing interest in the late twentieth century in performance within non-European cultures resulted in research into the performance and theatre traditions of Latin America, Africa, Asia and lastly the Arab World. Theatre in the Middle East had long been ignored by Western theatre scholars, who mistakenly assumed that the representation of the body and, therefore, theatre, was equated with idolatry and therefore prohibited in Islamic thought. This simplistic assumption is gradually ebbing away as the rich theatre and performance traditions of the region receive increasing attention from scholars. Writing in 1981, William O. Beeman, a pioneering scholar of Iranian performance arts, sought to counter the misconceptions that preclude the esixtence of theatrical tradition in the Middle East or denigrate its importance in Middle Eastern cultures. In his contribution to the *Cambridge Guide to World Theatre* (1988), Beeman lists the performing arts which came into being in the Middle East after the advent of Islam as (1) puppet drama, (2) dramatic storytelling, (3) religious epic drama and (4) comic improvisatory drama (Beeman 1988, p. 664). This is a recurring list common to most principal works describing the Middle East's performance tradition. For instance, in his classic *Namāyesh dar Īrān* (Theatre in Iran, 1965), the acclaimed Iranian film-maker, playwright and scholar, Bahram Beyzai, divides performances in post-Islamic Iran to (1) *naqqālī*, (2) puppet drama, (3) *taʿziyeh* and (4) comic drama. Metin And's *A History of Theatre and Popular Entertainment in Turkey* (1963) closely resembles Beyzai's book in that it provides in-depth descriptions of the traditions of the *meddah* (storyteller), the puppet-show, the *karagoz* (shadow-play) and the *orta oyunu* (improvized open-air theatre).

While the Kurds have performance traditions that closely resemble those of their Arab, Persian and Turkish neighbours, there are nonetheless clear variations of both kind and degree. To take one example, while the puppet show is considered a main category of traditional performance art in the Middle East, Iraqi-Kurdish theatre histories only make one brief reference to a puppet show, which purportedly took place in 1944 in Halabja (Tanya 1985, p. 27). In Iran, *ta'ziyeh*, as a Shi'i performance art, is limited to only a minority of Kurds in (the predominantly Sunni) Iranian Kurdistan. In the case of comic drama, there were satirical performance practices in Kurdistan that involved a great deal of improvisation and stock characters that were played by a very small number of local entertainers. There are references to a Nasreddin[1]-like comedian called Ahmadi Korno (whom Tawfiq Wahbi celebrates as 'a great comedian' – see Rasul 2004, p. 78) who performed in the city of Sulaymaniyah during the second half of the nineteenth century. He narrated comic stories and played out the plots along with others who included Faraj Kurdi and Jafar Laqlaqzada (Karim 2009, p. 61). The written material on Korno suggests he was a very well-known figure at his time, a conclusion which is further reinforced by the fact that he was invited by the notables of Sulaymaniyah, such as Osman Pasha Jaff and Sheikh Mustafa Naqib, to perform at their houses (p. 61).

While puppet drama, *ta'ziyeh*, and improvisatory comic theatre have not had a strong presence within the history of Kurdish performance, a number of ancient traditions have persevered among the Kurds and deserve, within the wider context of Middle Eastern performance traditions, a more sustained engagement. While these traditional performances have been ignored by more conventional theatre histories, they have been acted out with great rigour by the Kurds. The following discussion will summarize some of these performance traditions, which range from carnivals to everyday life performances. Some of these performances veer heavily towards drama by including not only a dramatic format but also spoken dramatic interludes; others such as dance

---

[1] A thirteenth-century satirical sufi in today's Turkey remembered for his funny stories and anecdotes.

and lamentation are also worth mentioning as they feature in theatrical productions examined later in the book.

## Dance-drama

Kurdish dance is undoubtedly the most well-known form of Kurdish performance art. While 'dance' is known locally as *helperkê* or *govend*, there are a variety of dances among the Kurds and each one possesses its own characteristics, function, meaning and name. Kurdish dance is mainly a hand-holding circle dance that resembles those in the Balkans and Eastern European countries. It is noticeable that many of these folkloric dances are mixed-gender and are known in Kurdistan as *reşbelek* or *genim-û-co* (wheat and barley). Karakeçili maintains that *simsimi, delilo, gowendi, siviki, duzo, giraniye, xwarkusta* and *cepki* are the most common mixed-gender celebratory dances as 'they tend to have basic steps thus allowing everyone to become involved' (Karakeçili 2008, p. 29). There are also dances which are specific to each gender. For example, women's dances such as *lorke, gowendejina, delilo, mim, sirwaniyejina* – which are accompanied by handclapping and ululations – are performed in order to lend cheer to bride on her last night with her family; men, meanwhile, perform their own dances for the groom – which include *keşeo, çaçani, çepik* and *xwarzani* (p. 31).

The theatrical quality of Kurdish dances is clearly depicted within Karakeçili's descriptions of several of these dances. In *şur-u-mertal* (sword and shield), a tribal war dance from Diyarbakır region performed by men, 'theatrically angry and menacing expressions, are used to emphasize the fighting in the dance. These expressions are accompanied by cries of pain and shouts of attack. At the end of the dance the facial expressions of the "winner" of the dance change to expressions of exhilaration and pride' (p. 51). *Çepik* is another example of a tribal war dance by men. As in *şur-u-mertal*, facial expressions demonstrate anger and the body movements evidence strength (p. 53). Synchronized steps are taken and the hands of partners are struck in an aggressive manner; dancers pair up to battle one-on-one while backing music guides their rhythmic, synchronized movements. Dancers can be eliminated by the one-on-one battles but the dance generally ends with peace between tribes (p. 53). Qotbeddin Sadeqi also describes several war dances which are performed by the Kurds in Iran including *zengî, swarane, fetah-paşa* and *simkolane* (Sadeqi 2013, p. 82). While *zengî* and *fetah-paşa* represent warriors in battle, *swarane* and *simkolane* are inspired by the movements of the warrior's horse that has been an integral part of Kurdish warfare (p. 82).

In contrast to the more aggressive male dances, typical women's dances depict themes such as love, beauty of nature and the daily chores of Kurdish women. To take one example, the dance *zeyniko* from the Ağrı region tells the story of a young, beautiful girl, Zeynep, who retrieves water from a village well and of the many admirers who encounter her. *Xwezale* (Gazelle) is another common female dance, which is frequently evidenced throughout all of Kurdistan in Turkey – it is imitative of 'the natural movements of a gazelle with undulating upper body and hip movements and elongated neck positioning' (Karakeçili 2008, p. 55). In the *beri* dance, the daily tasks of Kurdish women, which include baking bread, milking cows and working in the fields are performed. Karakeçili describes one variation of this dance as follows:

> [E]ach woman carries a milk jug. The first sequence represents the milking of a farm animal, generally a sheep. Slowly the dancers descend to their knees and with an alternating hand movement mimic the milking of an animal. The next sequence shows the strain of the work, by the women wiping their brows and holding their lower backs. Following this they mimic the motions of spinning wool with a handheld spindle. The kneading of dough and the baking of bread follow. They brush themselves down and apply make-up and fix their hair. Babies are fed and tended to, and then rocked to sleep in rhythmic unison. All of this is done in rhythm to the music, generally using only their upper bodies. (p. 56)

*Gur-u-pez* (Wolf and Lamb), which derives from the Diyarbakır and Bingöl regions, is another Kurdish dance rooted in village life that is performed by both men and women. In this dance, young female dancers play the lambs while men or boys play other characters, which include the wolf, the shepherd and the dog. The dance conveys how the lambs, who crouch down on their haunches and hold their ankles in their hands, are taken to the pasture by the shepherd before they are then attacked by the wolf as they huddle together (Karakeçili, p. 59).

As expressions of Kurdish identity are increasingly attacked in Turkey, Kurdish dance, which ostensibly takes non-verbal, harmless and apolitical form, has been deployed as a relatively safe form of protest (Nyberg 2012, p. 85). Kurdish folk dances are used to express a distinct heritage that can be clearly distinguished from Turkish culture (p. 53). As a communal dance which requires the participants to hold hands, Kurdish dance can easily assume political significance and appear as an (albeit implicit) expression of Kurdish unity. Karakeçili who describes Kurdish dance of *delilo* as a 'symbol of Kurdish nationalism' (Karakeçili 2008, p. 17), maintains that this (frequently performed) dance 'serves to unify the people' and becomes 'a symbol of passive protest against the government's policy of assimilation and the assaults upon the Kurdish people' (p. 90). Political events sometimes bring more than a thousand participants, who dance together in peaceful protest and who even engage in political discussions while dancing (Nyberg 2008, p. 85). However, this form of peaceful protest is not without risks – in recent years, several individuals have been prosecuted and imprisoned for taking part in 'ideological' dancing as propaganda for the outlawed Kurdistan Workers' Party (PKK) (pp. 86–7).

In Kurdistan there is also a type of dance particular to rituals performed by the members of mystical brotherhoods (dervish or sufi orders) which are led by sheikhs, popular saintly persons. There are two dervish orders present in Kurdistan: the Qadiri and the Naqshbandi. The Qadiri dervishes hold their ritual meeting at a meeting place (*khanaqa* or *tekiye*) which can be a purpose-built building or a private room. There, they engage in a type of dance called *sema* which involves the participants moving their bodies backward and forward. This dance is performed in a state of trance accompanied by the rhythmic sound of *def*, songs and saying of *zikr* (recitation of the divine name). The leader of the dervishes leads the singing and devotional dancing which leads to a trance-like state for the devoted. The head begins to roll side to side in rhythm, at the same time their headscarves are taken off releasing their long hair, which flails about all over their faces. The dance becomes more frenzied as the rhythm of the *daf* accelerates. Martin van Bruinessen has thoroughly captured the spirit of this sufi ritual in his account of a performance by the Qadiri dervishes of Mahabad in 1973:

[After saying the short standard Islamic prayers] the dervishes recited *shahada* (confession of faith), *la illaha illa 'llah* ('there is no god but God'), several hundreds of times, standing up now, and swaying the upper part of the body in cadence with the incantation, bowing to the left on the *la illaha*, and on the *illa 'llah* to the right. The incantation alone had a hypnotic effect even on me; for the participants this effect must have been much stronger, combined as it was with rapid, rhythmical breathing and movements of the head and upper body. The '*la illaha illa 'llah*' gave way to the shorter '*Allah, Allah, Allah,*... Drums joined in, the bodily movements became ever wilder. By now the dervishes had one by one pulled off their turbans and untied their long hair ... Some now experienced (or feigned) a form of ecstasy, and uttered wild shrieks during this zikr. (Bruinessen 1992, pp. 235–6)

The followers of the Qadiri order are not the only religious group in Kurdistan that engage in dance-like rituals. Karakeçili describes a dance called *simsimi* which represents fire and its power and is performed by the Yezidis in Adıyaman region. In this dance, male dancers challenge each other by jumping over fire. The dance concludes with a single female dancer sprinkling salt on the fire signifying the burning of the evil eye (Karakeçili 2008, p. 62). Music and dance are also of central significance in the Alevis' *cem* rituals. The Alevis engage in a religious dance called *semah* which enacts stories related to Prophet Muhammed, Imam Ali, Imam Hussein and others. Its most widespread variants are *Kırklar Semahı* (Dance of the Forty Saints) and *Turnalar Semahı* (Dance of the Cranes) which, respectively, symbolize Prophet Muhammed's and Imam Ali's ascent to heaven (Erol 2010, p. 379). In the rural tradition, *semahs* have no basic choreographic patterns and are performed differently in different regions; however, they ususally include three parts, commonly called Agırlama, Yürütme and Yeldirme: beginning slowly after a prayer (agırlama), then forming a circle and moving around it with various arm gestures and steps (yürütme) and finally moving up to the climax (yeldirme) (p. 380).[2]

---

[2] In a chapter that discusses approved forms of performance in the Persianate world, Beeman only makes a passing remark about the function of music in Kurdish religious ceremonies (Beemam 2010, p. 151). This is unfortunate given the fact that, as Beeman himself notes, music is central to the numerous mystical sects that exist among the Kurds (p. 151). For example, among the Kurdish Ahl-i Haqq, the music, while not a necessary part of religious ceremonies, is performed to enhance and elevate the spiritual atmosphere (Hooshmandrad 2004, p. 35). This is similar to the Yezidi recitation of religious texts to the accompaniment of music (Kreyenbroek 1998; Allison 2001). As mentioned earlier, music is also an integral part of Kurdish sufi ceremonies.

## Newroz carnival performances

There are folk performance traditions which are specific to Kurdistan. The most notable are those that are performed during Newroz, the Kurdish New Year. *Kawey Asinger* (Kawa the Blacksmith), and *mîrmîran* or *mîrmîrên* (king of kings, or, playing king), which are part of the Kurdish springtime festival, are two important examples of these performances. The former takes place during the celebration of Newroz on the March equinox. While the Iranian festival of Nowruz is celebrated throughout several countries in the Middle East as the beginning of spring, the Kurdish version has an important feature which sets it apart: this is its convergence with the legend of Kawa (Kāveh in Persian), the blacksmith who rebelled against the tyranny of King Zuhak (Zahāk in Persian), a ruthless foreign ruler. In Ferdowsi's *Shāhnāmeh* (Book of Kings), Zuhak is possessed by two snakes who grow from his shoulders and feed on the brains of two young persons each day. Zuhak's cooks manage to rescue one person each day and send them to the mountains, where they continue to live and eventually found the Kurdish nation. It is ultimately Kawa, a humble blacksmith, who rises against Zuhak's tyranny, while brandishing his blacksmith apron as a flag. He subsequently joins forces with Faraydun, a person of royal descent, who leads an army under Kawa's flag and captures Zuhak. In the Kurdish rendering of this myth, however, Faraydun is eliminated and Kawa is celebrated as a Kurdish hero who liberates the Medes, the supposed ancestors of the modern Kurds. Also, whereas *Shāhnāmeh* associates the legend of Kawa with the Mehregān festival of autumn, the Kurdish version instead links Kawa's revolt to the Newroz festival.

By virtue of its association with the story of Kawa and the victory of the oppressed against the oppressor, Newroz has attained a considerable political significance for Kurds. The myth of Newroz and the legend of Kawa have enabled the Kurdish national movement to trace the origins of the Kurds to the ancient Medes, thus constructing both an ethno-genesis and a resistance myth (Aydin 2014). This myth has naturally been celebrated in folk performances throughout the Kurdish towns and villages during Newroz festivities. In the folk performances of this mythical account of Kurdish origin, there were numerous characters who included Zuhak, the king; a few guards and councils; Kawa, the hero; three boys as Kawa's sons and others who played the role of townspeople (Jaffar 1992). As we shall see later, the modern theatre groups have also drawn upon the myth of *Kawey Asinger* for nationalist purposes.

*Mîrmîran* (or Mir-e Nowruzi in Persian) is another important example of performances that form part of the Kurdish springtime festival. It bears striking resemblances to the medieval Feast of Fools, in which a mock king was elected to rule temporarily. Beyzai maintains this performance was a continuation of the pre-Islamic *Barneshastan-e Kuseh* (The Ride of the Beardless Man) festival which, in replacing the ruler with an ugly man who issued ridiculous orders, exemplified the populace's disdain for the powerful (Beyzai 2004, p. 53).[3] In spite of its important place in Kurdish culture, Beyzai downplays the significance of this tradition by devoting only a few pages to its discussion and contending that Mir-e Nowruzi was now only practiced in some 'distant' villages (pp. 40, 53). This somewhat dismissive appraisal is all the more surprising because some Kurdish sources claim that *mîrmîran* (which is also referred to as *paşapaşayetî*) was the single most important theatrical event among the Kurds until at least the 1920s (Pirbal, p. 20). On this point, it is also instructive to note that Giw Mukriyani, the Kurdish historian and journalist, uses the term '*mîrmîrên*' as the Kurdish equivalent to the words theatre (English) and *masrah* (Arabic) (p. 20).

*Mîrmîran* was enacted in Kurdish regions of Iraq and Iran during Newroz, which was held at the beginning of spring. During the nineteenth century, Kurdish regions were governed by local rulers. During *mîrmîran* this ruler was temporarily replaced by an ordinary, and sometimes even ridiculous, individual who was chosen from the populace of the area. The props were provided by the people themselves. The lords and nobility would lend the new king their lavish clothes, accessories, horses, boots, swords and other

---

[3] Beyzai suggests that the festival of *Barneshastan-e Kuseh* was an ancient Iranian tradition that was held on the twenty-first of November which was considered to be the last day of winter in ancient Iran (Beyzai 2004, p. 40). The performance involved a beardless man (*Kuseh*) riding a donkey with a crow in one hand and a fan in the other, who would pretend to be hot. The crowds would throw snowballs at him and, at the same time, would bestow him with gifts. Those who failed to give donations were splashed with mud by the beardless man. Beyzai associates this tradition with the religious festival of '*Omar koshān* (the killing of 'Omar) in which Iranian Shi'as celebrate the killing of 'Umar ibn al-Khattāb, the second caliph of Islam who ordered the invasion of Iran in 642 AC, by burning his effigy. Beyzai writes that the *Kuseh* tradition survived centuries after Islam as the Mir-e *Nowruzi* festival which, like its predecessor, served to display people's hatred towards the king (pp. 4–41, 53). In the Sunni Kurdish regions, however, the festive tradition of *mîrmîran* does not appear to have such meaning or function.

valuables (Ashurpur 2010, p. 32). It was also customary for the substitute ruler to have a supporting cast of witty and jovial individuals. Various roles would henceforth be assumed, including the grand vizier, the right-hand and left-hand viziers, secretary, soldiers, executioners, chorus, clown and so on. Ashurpur maintains that the right-hand vizier was responsible for giving reasonable orders, while the left-hand vizier issued unreasonable and ludicrous orders. For example, the right-hand vizier would declare on behalf of the king that innocent prisoners must be freed, families who were not on good terms had to reconcile, the rich had to pay their due *zakat* to the poor and everyone had to clean the front of their houses. The left-hand vizier would command that every man had to shave half of his moustache, all young boys over the age of thirteen had to get married immediately, all city-dwellers had to move to the countryside and all those resident in the countryside had to move to the city (p. 37).

In his *History of Theatre in Iran*, Floor (2005) suggests that this festival of 'false emir' was a three-day festival that was most recently celebrated in the 1890s in the springtime in the Kurdish town of Mahabad (pp. 92–3). A picture from 1944 (Figure 1), however, shows that this tradition was revived seemingly by Kurdish nationalists in Mahabad which was home to the Society for Kurdish Resurrection (*Komeley Jiyanewey Kurd*, 1942–5), a political organization whose activities eventually led to the creation of the Republic of Mahabad in 1946.

There is disagreement as to the actual length of the *mîrmîran* festival, which according to some sources ran for the entirety of the holiday season, or thirteen days (see Ashurpur 2010, pp. 44–5, 92–3). Pirbal maintains that the false emir festival started five days before Newroz and ended on the thirteenth day of the new year (Pirbal 2001, p. 19).[4] As for the coronation of the mock king, it seems that, at least in Sulaymaniyah, the event would take no more than three

---

[4] In his monumental study of religion and mythology, Sir James Frazer describes the old tradition of temporary kings as a modified form of the old custom of regicide which was practiced in places as diverse as Cambodia, Siam, Samarcand, Egypt, Morocco and Cornwall. This tradition, according to Frazer, is a fertility cult common to almost all mythologies in which the death and resurrection of the king/god appears as the personification of the rebirth of earth in the spring (Frazer 1998, pp. 254–60). Frazer notes that these rites have been most widely and solemnly celebrated in Western Asia and Egypt, where the gods of Osiris, Tammuz, Adonis and Attis represented the vegetable life and its yearly decay and revival (p. 301–2).

Figure 1 Mîrmîren carnival in Mahabad, Iran, in 1944. *Source*: Ali Qazi Archive, Kurdistan Photolibrary.

days. Tanya contends that in 1912 a witty mullah called Mala Bichkol had been chosen as king in Sulaymaniyah and his coronation had been a joyous three-day-long festive occasion (Tanya 1985, p. 45). He proceeds to explain that, during this festival, it was customary for the elders of Sulaymaniyah to take control of the city and for all their orders to be implemented. This was the prelude for three days of festivities, which began in the city centre. The inhabitants of the city would then dance to the sound of *duhol*[5] and *zurna*[6] for two days. Later, they would all walk towards Sarchinar, near Sulaymaniyah, where fifty springs form a stream that runs through the city. Upon reaching this point, the new king would sit on the throne and various games would begin with the royal accord. The festivities would end with the participants' joyful return to the city to the accompaniment of music (pp. 45–6).

In Sulaymaniyah, open-air amusements and celebrations had always been popular (Edmonds 1957, p. 84) and traditional festivals such as *mîrmîran* enjoyed the support of Kurdish rulers. They were only interrupted by important events such as the death of Sheikh Said Barzanji, the highest religious authority

---

[5] A large cylindrical drum with two skin heads.
[6] A double-reed woodwind instrument.

in the region. His death brought a halt to celebrations, storytelling and gramophones at teahouses; however, once the appropriate period of grieving had been observed, the carnivals and celebrations were resumed (Taymur 1988, p. 68). A relatively well-documented instance of the false emir festival in the city of Sulaymaniyah dates back to the 1920s. Thomas Bois (1900–1975), the French Kurdologist, draws upon Tawfiq Wahbi's account to present this 'carnival' in the following terms:

> The preparations are entrusted to a special committee, and on the day fixed the people of Sulaymaniyah leave the town for a place where the ceremony is to take place. A king is enthroned and courtiers and a guard are assigned to him. The 'king', sitting astride an ox and accompanied by his court and a large crowd, goes to the encampment where tents and divans have been set up and cauldrons put on the fire. Individuals, disguised as sheep or goats, play the part of these animals during the whole period of celebration, which lasts three days. The 'king' is obeyed without question; he even imposes taxes on people, whether they are present or not. He retains his title until the following year when a successor is nominated. (Bois 1966, p. 68)

It is important to note that the Kurdish false king, as the preceeding quote confirms, possessed genuine power and was respected by local rulers. Edmonds (1957) writes that in Sulaymaniyah he was 'often regaled with stories of an annual spring carnival of ancient origin, a kind of saturnalia, which had fallen into desuetude either during or only shortly before the War' (p. 84). During Newroz, Edmonds notes, 'the whole population of Sulaymaniyah would flock out to the Sarchinar springs for a festival which involved the appointment of a Lord of Misrule with very real powers, the temporary upsetting of many of the canons of ordinary behaviour, and the almost complete suspension of normal administration' (p. 84). This overturning of hierarchies of power and norms of behaviour was sanctioned by the highest authority of the Sulaymaniyah region: up until the mid-nineteenth century this was the Baban princes; subsequent to this date, it was Sheikh Mahmud Barzanji, who both licensed the festival and took part in it. Every year in Sulaymaniyah, Sheikh Mahmud himself would give the order to start the festivities and respect the new king as everybody else (Taymur 1988, p. 68). The nobility would also lend the new king their valuables – this is evidenced by the case of Faraj Kurdi, a local comic figure and a mock king in the 1920s who donned clothes given to him by Mustafa Pasha Yamulki (1866–1936)[7] (Tanya 1985, p. 46).

The licensing of the festival by local rulers legitimized the whole representation wherein the hierarchy of the official order was overturned. This is similar to the sort of performance Terry Eagleton describes as 'a permissible rupture of hegemony, a contained popular blow-off' (1981, p. 9). The subversive play of the carnival consists of temporarily suspending the hierarchical power-structure inherent in the practice of everyday life. It proves the importance of such representation wherein the ruler sees himself reflected through the mirrors of carnivalesque representation. In reviewing a similar African performance, Plastow notes that this type of performance presumably was not only cathartic for the participants but also created an acceptable conduit for public opinion to be passed on to higher authorities (Plastow 1996, p. 26).

Abdurrahman Khama was the last king of these festivals in Iraqi Kurdistan, which ultimately concluded in 1922, the year the British banned the performance. Hawrami claims Khama asserted that his rule was not an act and it was only called a game to fool the British colonizers (Hawrami 2001, p. 296). In reality, the mock king had almost absolute power and his rule was approved by Anwar Beg Tawfiq Beg, the governor of Sulaymaniyah in the 1920s. This rule was only limited by two restrictions which forbade the freeing of slaves and the killing of people. However, it did not take the British long to sense the seriousness of the false king's rule and thus put an end to it.

It is also possible that the banning of the festival was a retaliatory act following the arrest of two Englishmen. Hawrami notes that when two Englishmen laughed at the spectacle they were arrested and only freed after they paid compensation for the offence that had been given to Khama's rule (p. 296). It has also been claimed that Major E. B. Soane, a British political officer to Kurdistan, was once charged five hundred rupees for drinking (Tanya 1985, p. 47). To mock the king and his authority or to ignore his orders was punishable regardless of the offender's rank. This might have provoked the colonizers of the land, as it was an affront to their power to allow punishment to remain in the hands of the natives.

---

[7] The Ottoman military officer and later minister of education in Sheikh Mahmud Barzanji's self-proclaimed Kingdom of Kurdistan.

Local figures, on the other hand, maintain that the British officers who watched the festival games and performances from a distance on horseback disapproved of the representation of king in those performances – this, they suggest, is the reason they were banned in Sulaymaniyah and other Kurdish towns (Taymur 1988, p. 68). Amine and Carlson suggest that the carnivalesque and satiric nature of local festivals could help explain why they were banned by the European colonizers. The Europeans whose understanding of 'theatre' was very much indebted to the European tradition, were predisposed to view these activities as, at best, quaint local customs unworthy of the name of art; at worst, they saw them as 'perverse and unpatriotic locations for the expression of subversive and anti-colonial expression' (Amine and Carlson 2011, p. 52). This may explain why the official colonial attitude towards such performance traditions was either to ignore or, as in the case of the Kurdish false emir carnival, to outlaw them entirely. The banning of the false emir festival, however, did not mark the end of it. Between 1927 and 1930, in Qaladiza, which is to the north of Sulaymaniyah, the festival was held and a Bakr Qasab ruled for forty days before his rule was forcefully terminated (see Taymur 1988).[8] In Iranian Kurdistan, a photo taken in 1944 in Mahabad, as shown above, records one of the latest instances of this performance tradition.

## Seasonal festivals and work songs

In addition to the Newroz festivals, Bois describes seasonal festivals which were celebrated by the shepherds. These rural festivals include *serepêz* (the first lambing time), *barodan* (the time of departure for the *zozan* or summer pastures), *berxbir* (sheep-rearing) and *beran-berdan* (the greatest festival of all, 'when estivation ends and the rams are loosed among the ewes' – see Bois 1966, p. 66). This native pattern of life and activity occasioned a variety of folksongs: the *serêle* or songs of spring; the *paîzok* or autumn songs sung by young men and women at the time of the nomads' descent from their upland summer retreats (*zozan*) to the plains; the *bendolavî* sung by young women at the spinning wheel as they weave their multicoloured carpets; the

---

[8] Teymur does not explain by whom and for what reasons Qasab's rule was terminated.

*lorî* (cradle songs), the *lawêj* (short poems telling of marital deeds, chivalrous exploits and love affairs), *hevalê* (songs that accompany the young bride as she enters her new home) and *dîlok* (various dance songs, which are sung to the accompaniment of drum and flute) (pp. 60–1). Women, in particular, have a variety of household duties in villages which they perform with songs – these help to accomplish specific tasks, reduce feelings of boredom or express plaintive or melancholic feelings. The *bertewnane*, which is a type of plaintive song sung during carpet weaving, is an example of the latter. These melancholy songs can be sung while doing other chores such as milking cows, carrying things, or spinning. However, women's work songs are by no means only melancholy and woeful. During *meşkejenî*,[9] for example, a woman might sing a song that could refer to the beauties and blessings of nature in spring or praise her *meşk* and narrate her daily chores to it.[10]

Bois provides an account of a popular mid-winter festival that was witnessed by the Soviet-Kurdish writer Erebê Şemo (1897–1978) when he was a child. In this festival, which he refers to as *Kose-geldî*, 'a young man is disguised as a sheik or mullah while another is dressed up as a woman. The two then go from house to house collecting butter, cheese and money ... Everything which has been collected in this manner by the young men is distributed to poor families' (Bois 1966, pp. 68–9). *Kose-geldî*, which is still practiced sporadically in Iranian towns and villages, has been described in Iranian sources as the shepherds' celebration of the end of the first forty days of winter. This date is also known amongst the Kurds in Iran as the 'Kurdish Spring'.

---

[9] Traditional way of processing milk by transferring yogurt to an inverted sheepskin (*meşk*) which acts as a churn. The churn is suspended by a tripod and rocked back and forth until butter granules form. The butter can be scooped out by hand or the buttermilk can be drained off by pouring.

[10] Here are some lines from a song sung during *meşkejenî*:

*Meşke bijinyê jinyayî*
*Meşk* beat the milk
*Be kef û kerê kinyayî*
Separate the butter
*Meşke bijinyê dêrme*
*Meşk* hurry up, I'm late
*Hengley ga w gwêrme*
I'm worried about my cows and calves
*Kerêkey bo werzêrme*
I want the butter for the farmer
*Dokey bo şûe kwêrme*
And the buttermilk for my blind husband

In *Kose-geldî*, a group of shepherds boisterously pass through the alleyways and streets, playing musical instruments, ringing bells and singing songs while performing the roles of Kosa, Kosa's bride and goats. Kosa wears a long inside-out robe covered with small bells. The person playing the role of Kosa paints his face white and wears a mask made of goat skin with eye and breathing holes. He also wears a large leather belt and holds a long stick to represent shepherds. The person playing the role of Kosa's bride is usually chosen from teenage boys aged between twelve and sixteen. The bride wears women's dress (sometimes a colourful *chador*) and heavy make-up and ties bells around his waist and hands. Kosa, his bride and the goats, accompanied by musicians, knock on people's doors to wish them abundance, wealth and God's blessing. They perform different plots at people's homes where they receive money and gifts, especially from the wealthy (Heidari 2013).

Salimi's (2003) book on Kurdish winter rituals describes several instances of *Kose-geldî* in the towns and villages of Iranian Kurdistan. Salimi suggests that Kosa is mainly a comic figure who entertains the village people with his make-up, costume, dance and humour (pp. 99–101). However, on some occasions the village youth, usually through the provision of a fake moustache and beard and large fur coat, have changed the Kosa tradition by transforming Kosa into a fearsome figure. They hide themselves while Kosa knocks on people's doors and frightens those unfamiliar with the tradition (p. 104).

In the villages of Sanandaj in Iranian Kurdistan, the shepherds hold a *Kose-Kose* celebration in which some of the shepherds are made up in the mosque's *çeqexane* (a little room by the side of the main hall). Kosa's make-up and costume is meant to make him look frightening. Accompanied by the boisterous youth and children of the village, he starts walking through the streets and knocking on people's doors. A series of questions and answers are exchanged between Kosa and the landlord, such as the following:

Kosa: *Pez be yekane, bizin be dwane,*
 May your sheep and goats be bountiful,
 *Xûa bereket bida bew derk û bane,*
 May God bless your household,
 *Selam xawen mal, koset mêwane,*
 Hello landlord, Kosa is your guest,

>
> *Nabê bêbeş bê, lew xanedane,*
> He shouldn't be deprived of your blessings.

Landlord: *Kose xoş hatî, fermû danîşe,*
> Welcome Kosa, come on in,
> *Le kwêt hênawe em gişte rîşe?!*
> From where have you found this thick beard?!

At this point, the shepherd who is standing behind Kosa sings comic folkloric songs while Kosa knocks his long clutch a few times on the ground and makes amusing gestures which bring sounds of laughter from the crowd. The performers only leave each house after they have received donations in the form of money or food. Therefore, while *Kose-Kose* brings joy to the village by signalling the approach of the srping, it also serves as a reminder of communal values of charity and good will by obliging the rich farmers to share their wealth with the poor.

## Rain rituals

Kurdish rituals such as those of *garwanekî* (cattle-raid) and *bûke-barane* (rain bride) are highly performative and theatrical in nature. *Garwanekî* is a cattle-raid ritual which was previously performed in many villages of Kermanshah, Ilam and Lorestan (western Iran).[11] This ritual, which went out of practice only fifty years ago, was performed by women during drought to invoke rain. *Garwanekî*, also known as *gorwatenî, gaberan, gareba, gabrwa* and *gayl rifanin*, literally translates as 'stealing cows'. It was mainly performed by women in spring and autumn during instances of drought or late rainfall. When there was a delay in the onset of raining, women and girls of the village would gather together to arrange the ritual. They would elect a leader among themselves and would move on to the pastures where the neighbouring village's cattle were grazing. They would drive the cattle to their own village and if the herdsmen or farmers working around that area intervened they would be beaten by the women. On hearing the news, women and girls from the village that owned the cattle would set off to fight the cow-thieves and reassert their ownership

---

[11] All the information about *garwaneki* here is based on fieldwork done by Mahmoud Zarifian (2009), Professor of Linguistics at the University of Tehran. He conducted his fieldwork in villages of Kermanshah, Ilam and Lorestan provinces in western Iran.

of the cattle. However, as the collector of the ritual notes, these efforts were often in vain: the cow-stealers were more likely to win because they were more prepared for the fight (Zarifian 2009, p. 206).

It would be reasonable to suspect the seriousness of the fight and seek to measure and assess its theatrical nature. Unfortunately, the information pertaining to this ritual was only collected after it became extinct, and this clearly mitigates against any careful assessment of it. In any case, when the victorious group entered their village with the stolen cattle, celebrations would break out. The cows would be milked and the milk would then be boiled on fire, mixed with tea and served for all. A pot of milk would also be poured down the rainspouts to create the illusion of rain. In the meantime, the elders of the neighbouring village would come to plead for the release of the cattle. Once the women were successfully persuaded to return the cattle, they would all stand to pray for rain and the ritual would end with the return of the cows to their owners.

*Bûke-barane* is another Kurdish rain ritual which used to be performed by young girls in Kurdistan at times of drought. In this ritual, young girls would surround a wooden doll dressed in a Kurdish woman's costume and sing songs asking her to make rain. In some versions of the event, children would take the wooden doll door to door and people would respond by pouring water over the doll.[12] Songs were sung during the ritual, including the following:

*Bûke baran awî dewê*
Rain bride wants water
*Awî naw dexlanî dewê*
She wants the water for crops

or

*Helaran Melaran*
*Xwaya dayke baran*
O God make rain
*Bo feqîran û hejaran*
For the poor and the needy

---

[12] It has been claimed that the doll in this ritual is the symbol of Anahita, the goddess of water, and that the ritual dates back to the Zoroastrian era (see Azimpur 2006).

The song may vary from region to region. In his description of the 'Bride of the Rain' ritual, Bois writes that children 'make a sort of doll of two pieces of wood in the shape of a Latin cross' which 'they dress up and put a turban on its head' (Bois 1966, p. 105). Then they go from house to house singing,

> Pomegranate and jam,
> God let the rain fall,
> For the sick and the poor.
> God let the rain fall,
> Bald head of the spring,
> O Bride of the Rain,
> Pray water the crops,
> Give us meals of past days. (Bois 1966, p. 105)

The association of women with water can be seen in another rain ritual which has been held in both Kurdish and non-Kurdish Iranian towns.[13] In this ritual, which Ali Ashraf Darvishian describes in his autobiographical novel, *Sāl-hā-ye Abrī* (Cloudy Years), girls were married to lakes that were drying up. The novel speaks of Nazka, an old woman who was wedded to a lake when it was about to dry. Nazka narrates,

> They sat me on a horse and took me to the lake and performed the wedding sermon. I slept at the lake for forty days and each day I woke up before sunrise, undressed and washed my body in the lake seven times. A small hut was set up for me and Kaw Lake... But it did not help... The lake dried out little by little. People lost their farms to drought. (Darvishian 2000, p. 559)

The tradition of women soaking themselves in water in order to bring rain existed in Kurdistan in various forms. In the event of a drought, Bois writes, women 'go to the well where they give one another douches' (Bois 1966, p. 105) or, clothed in their finest dresses, they assemble in the shade of an old venerable tree where 'they pour water over one another's clothes and go back to their homes completely soaked' (p. 105). In the city of Kirkuk, Bois writes,

---

[13] This tradition which might have its origins in Mithraism has been performed in the Iranian villages of Golpaygan, Arāk, Tafresh, Malāyer, Tūyserkan, Mahalāt, Khomeyn, Delījāan, Isfahān, Dāmghān, Shāhrūd, Yazd, Shahrekord and Chārmahāl (see Afazeli 1998).

'the women collect in the street under a rain-water spout, and after a meal has been distributed to the poor, they are drenched with water from the spout' (p. 105).

## Mourning rituals

Perhaps the most widely known mourning ritual in the Middle East is the one performed by Iranian Shi'as during the Muslim month of Muharram. Part of this ritual involves the performance of *ta'ziyeh*, a traditional text-based poetic passion play. Having originated in Iran, *ta'ziyeh* is a type of religious dramatic musical performance that combines elements such as music (vocal and instrumental), recitation, poetry, narration and drama. *Ta'ziyeh* translates directly as 'mourning rituals'; however, in this instance, it specifically refers to a type of religious performance that commemorates the event of Karbala and the death of Hussein, Prophet Mohammad's grandson. According to tradition, Hussein, along with seventy-two of his male children, brothers, cousins and companions, was brutally murdered as he contested his right to the Caliphate.

It has been suggested that the commemoration of Hussein, at the beginning, comprised only of the narration of the events of Karbala (nohe-sarā'ī) (Sattari 2008, p. 94). It later evolved into a dramatic ritual which described the sufferings of Hussein and his supporters (roze-khānī) and their enactments, as well as the enactments of the cruelty of Hussein's enemies (p. 94). In this religious performance, both male and female protagonists are represented by male actors who are dressed in green and sing their parts, while the antagonists are represented by actors dressed in red who shriek their lines in harsh voices (p. 100). The spectators display their anger and hatred towards the antagonists by cursing and shouting at them. On the other hand, the heart-wrenching singing by the protagonists elicits strong emotions of grief and sorrow amongst the audience, who respond by weeping and beating their chests and heads.

The tradition of *ta'ziyeh* is said to have been greatly influenced by the ancient Iranian tradition of *Sūg-e Siyāvash* (Mourning Siyavash) (see Meskub 1971; Sattari 2008). In Ferdowsi's epic, *Shāhnāmeh*, Siyavash is a splendidly handsome and honourable prince who, after being betrayed by his family, is forced into self-imposed exile in the mythical land of Turān where he meets an unjust death. The news of Siyavash's death in exile prompts outbursts of grief and anger in Iran for many more years to come. According to Narshakhi (c.899–959), the tenth-century historian, Siyavash had been mourned in Central Asia for thousands of years by the people of Bukhara who grieved the death of Siyavash on the day of Nowruz, and sang sad hymns in his commemoration (cited in Daryaee and Malekzadeh 2014, pp. 57–8). These songs which were known across the realm were called 'Gristan-e Moghan' or 'the weeping of Magi' by the minstrels (p. 58). Apart from singing lamentations, there were certain mourning rituals which, as described in *Shāhnāmeh*, took place on the occasion of the death of noble figures. The following excerpts, for instance, describe such mourning practices:

> And
>
> the nobles marched before the bier, and their
> heads were covered with ashes, and their garments
> were torn. And the drums of the war-elephants
> were shattered, and the cymbals broken,
> and the tails of the horses were shorn to the root,
> and all the signs of mourning were abroad. (Zimmern 1883, pp. 169–70)

> And Tahmineh cried after
> her son, and bewailed the evil fate that had
> befallen him, and she heaped black earth upon
> her head, and tore her hair, and wrung her hands,
> and rolled on the ground in her agony. And her
> mouth was never weary of plaining. Then she
> caused the garments of Sohrab to be brought
> unto her, and his throne and his steed…
> Then with her sword she cut off the tail of
> his steed and set fire unto the house of Sohrab,
> and she gave his gold and jewels unto the poor. (pp. 170–1)

> And Bashuntan
> marched at the head of the train, and he led the

horse of Isfendiyar, and its saddle was reversed,
and its mane and its tail were shorn. And from its
sides hung the armour of the young King. And
weeping resounded through the ranks, and with
sorrow did the army return unto Iran. (pp. 330–1)

These mourning rites which involve crying, scratching and injuring the body; mourners throwing earth on their heads; women pulling or chopping off their hair; cutting off the tail of the deceased's horse; wailing; describing the good features and traits of the deceased; singing and playing musical instruments are prominent in the Kurdish tradition of *çemer*. This Kurdish funeral tradition is more elaborate among the tribes, mainly in the Iranian provinces of Ilam, Lorestan and Kermanshah, whose mourning rituals bear striking resemblances to the ancient *Sūg-e Siyāvash* (see Farokhi and Kiyayi 2001, pp. 22–5; Sagvand 1999, pp. 10–13). An account by the Englishman, Claudius James Rich (1787–1821), who was in Iraqi Kurdistan in 1820 attests to the deep roots of *çemer* tradition among the Kurds. He observes,

> As I was going to the palace today, I saw at a distance three military standards moving along. I imagined a large body of troops was on the march; but to my great surprise, I was informed it was a funeral. This custom is peculiar to Koordistan. In Kermanshah they accompany the body to the grave with music and singing. (Rich 1836, p. 301)

The *çemer* ceremony is held outside the village where a large crowd of mourners gather. The ritual begins with the sound of *duhol* and *zurna* which summons the black-clad mourners to stand along a circular line. As the ceremony begins, a group of mourners sing dirges in a manner similar to sobbing known as *rara*, *roro* or *çemerîweş*. Every time a group of guests arrive, they pay their respects to the elders of the deceased person's family by standing in front of them and beating their own heads while uttering the words '*hey dad hey bîdad* (alas, alas)'. The elders stop them by hugging them and inviting them inside. The guests then proceed to rub mud on their heads and shoulders before joining the others in line. Women have a similar ritual with both groups of hosts and guests meeting each other while weeping, pulling their hair, scratching their faces, moving their hands in a circular motion and uttering the words '*wey wey* (an exclamation of sorrow or distress)'. Their performance is completely in sync with the melancholic sound of *duhol* and *zurna* which intensifies the feelings of grief (Khaksar 2018, pp. 8–9).

On the occasion of the death of heads of families or important figures, *çemer* becomes more elaborate by involving *elem* and *kotel*. *Elem* is a 4- to 5-meter-long wooden object, usually made from cedar tree, which is wrapped in black cloths from top to bottom – and adorned with expensive scarves at the top if the ritual is held for a man. In this ritual, *kotel* is a caparisoned horse with the deceased's guns and other important belongings mounted on it. The horse is walked around a circle or towards where the corpse is placed. This is accompanied by the mournful singing of women who move their hands in circular motions around each other. These dirges, which are known as *mor*, are designed to convey the vacuum that is created as a result of the death of an elder, or mourn the loss of young men and women and their beauty and bravery. Some examples of *mor* for a deceased young man, young woman and an elder are:

> *Wextî dû e şîrebirakem bikem feramûş,*
> *Mer sifîdî kefen bikem we ten pûş.*
> I will only forget the loss of my brave brother,
> when I wear white graveclothes (when I die).
>
> *Ezîzekem ye xu behare, gulan meyûn nû;*
> *Heyf era wujit, gêl we banit bû.*
> My dear, spring has come, flowers are growing back;
> Alas, a flower like you is buried underneath so much dirt.
>
> *Heyf heyf meclisan bî to menîşin;*
> *Dem dem ahi serd pêy to mekîşin.*
> Alas, the elders will sit at their meetings without you;
> And they will sigh (grieve) over your passing.
>
> (Khaksar 2018, p. 10)

On the last day of the ritual, which may take up to three days, the mourners gather around the *elem* and *kotel* and set off to the deceased person's house

**Figure 2** A Çemer ritual in Ilam. Photo: Sajjad Zolfaghari.

where the elders dismantle the *kotel*. The mourners then walk towards the graveyard while they carry the *elem* and women weep to the sad sound of *duhol* and *zurna*. The ritual ends with the mourners' return to the deceased person's house and the disassembling of the *elem*.

Today at typical Kurdish funerals the rites are not as elaborate as in *çemer*. However, crying, injuring the body, the pulling of hair and lamentation are still considered to be social duties by many. Kurdish lamentation is performed by women who may or may not be closely related to the deceased. They usually sing about the deceased and his good features and traits, coaxing the funeral attendants to cry. Such ritual mourning services serve as a valuable mechanism for remembering the deceased and the purging of grief.

## Mosque performances

Pirbal describes a type of performance which took place in mosques in Kurdistan. According to him, the students of Islamic jurisprudence, or *fiqh*, would entertain themselves on Tuesday and Friday nights, especially during winter, by participating in games and dramatic performances (Pirbal 2001, pp. 17–18). These performances represented the traditions and habits of the different Kurdish towns and cities that these students came from. A number of the people within the neighbourhoods would also participate in the performances, which included: *Mamosta w Feqê* (The Teacher and the Faqih), *Westa w Şagird* (The Master and the Student) and *Bawk û Ewlad* (Father and Children). They also wore costumes and acted out various fables (stories featuring animals) that illustrated different moral lessons (pp. 17–18).

Tanya explains that, in the past, in the mosques and other religious sites, the clergy, who were the educated elite, acted out simple plays in the form of operettas which criticized the ills and the wrong manners of the society. It is suggested by Tanya that these performances, which were customary in many towns in Kurdistan including, Xoşnawetî, Deştî Dizeyî, Hekarî, Rowanduz, Balekayetî and Şukak, were the beginning of drama in Kurdistan (Tanya 1985, p. 49). In Iraqi Kurdistan, Islamic preaching in the form of performance was supported by Sheikh Mahmud Barzanji's family, who were an important religious family in Sulaymaniyah. They had historically supported dramatic performances in mosques, which celebrated the occasion of the graduation of students of Islamic jurisprudence or the *faqih* (Taymur 1988).

Islamic preaching in the form of performance and storytelling is not particular to Kurds. According to Amine and Carlson, in the first centuries of Islam, a form of official storytelling, known as the *qissa*, was sanctioned by the leaders of the faith to provide religious and moral guidance to the illiterate majority. These stories were widely circulated and were presented, often to enormous crowds, in streets, markets and public spaces (Amine and Carlson 2011). Islamic preachers have been divided into separate categories such as *qass*, *mudhakkir*, *waiz* and *meddah*. It seems that the operettas mentioned by Tanya fall in the category of *qissa* whose presenters are described to have drawn upon 'many techniques of the popular storyteller such as song, mimicry, accessories and character interpretation' (p. 24).

## Storytelling

Dramatic storytelling, which is a common tradition across most countries in the Middle East, is the regional native theatrical tradition that most closely resembles the Western-style theatre in form.¹⁴ The storyteller is known by names such as *qawwal, gouwâl, meddah* and, more commonly, *hakawati* in Arabic, *aşik* in Turkish and *naqqāl* in Persian. According to Amine and Carlson, although storytelling is not text-based, it clearly contains many features of drama including role-playing, epic narrativity, body language, the interplay between illusion and reality, high/low rhythms, songs as instruments of blockage and structural fragmentation and a committed audience (Amine and Carlson 2011, p. 20). Friederike Pannewick's description of narrative characteristics of *hakawati*, as quoted by Amine and Carlson, demonstrates its animating quality: the *hakawati* has to take into account that his clientele will desert him if his performance does not meet their expectations. He therefore has to design his narrative performance in such a way that his audience does not lose interest and/or disengage. This is achieved by increasing the dramatic tension whenever necessary (p. 21).

In Kurdistan, the narrator-performers who tell long epic songs without musical accompaniment before a live audience are known as *dengbêj* or *şair* (Chyet 1991, p. 9). In the past, because most of the *dengbêj* were illiterate and a large proportion of Kurdish folk literature was still unwritten, these performers specialized in memorizing and reciting vast repertoires of songs, legends and poems of Kurdistan. Trained in certain schools (Jwaideh 2006, p. 24), the *dengbêj* enjoyed the support and assistance of patrons who were, in return, praised in their *dengbêj*'s songs. In describing the Kurdish *dengbêj* in the first decade of the twentieth century, Oscar Mann, the German Kurdologist, observes,

> It seems that among the Kurds . . . there was and still is a type of singing school, in which they cultivate popular epic poetry. Young people with fine singing voices betake themselves to a master . . . to follow his instruction, and learn the repertoire of these masters exclusively by oral tradition . . . the field where the art of recitation thus learned may be first practiced is in the houses of notables, who gladly pass the evening by listening to the singing of bards and generously repay the latter with Khalat (=gifts). Moreover, in the villages the bard contents himself with a plate of rice as payment for his

---

¹⁴ Izzeddin Rasul, the distinguished Kurdish scholar, believes the traditional storytelling to be an apt introduction to any study of Kurdish theatre (see Rasul 2010, p. 42).

recitation. In the towns, there are also coffee houses in which only tea is served which are packed full with people who have come primarily to hear the performance of whatever singer happens to be there. (cited in Chyet 1991, pp. 10–11)

Storytelling in the Middle East has traditionally been highly interactive. Audiences were encouraged to comment upon or even participate in the presentation of the story, which was interrupted from time to time in order for the performers to collect donations from spectators.

The storytellers would employ a range of dramatic techniques, including gestures and different voices for different characters. For example, in his study of voice and the speed of verbal discourse during the storytelling of *Mem û Zîn*, Chyet writes,

[W]hen Mem awakes to find that Zîn is gone, the narrator-performer loudly interjects Ey-wah! (woe is me): he alters the pitch of his voice . . . moreover, although at the beginning of the story the narrator-performer speaks slowly and deliberately, when he gets to Mem and Zîn's argument over who has come to whom, he is speaking quickly and excitedly: thus he alters the speed of his verbal discourse. (p. 110)

The material in these performances varied from folktales, folk romances, history and legends to popular anecdotes (Amine and Carlson 2011, p. 18). In Kurdistan, there are a number of widely known folk romances that are told in a combination of prose and sung verse. Some of these narratives including *Leylî w Mecnûn* and *Yusuf û Zilêxa* are also shared by neighbouring peoples, who include the Armenian, Nestorian, Chaldean and Jacobite Christians, along with the Kurdish Jews. There are also long Kurdish narratives that include *Mem û Zîn*, *Dimdim* and *Xec û Siyabend* (Allison 2001, p. 13).

Storytelling has historically been the most common and popular form of performance in many parts of Kurdistan. Many of the Kurdish emirs (rulers of semi-independent principalities) and feudal landlords were patrons of the arts, and hosted performances of both literary and oral material. They often had their own court poets to sing their praises, as befitted their status (Allison, pp. 10–11). Shukriya Rasul, for example, states that the court of Abdurrahman Pasha, one of the greatest Baban rulers, was always well attended by singers and poets such as Ali Bardashani, Jamshid and Hama Asmani whose poems, known as *beytî meclîs*, recorded key events, along with epic battles fought by the Kurdish emir (Rasul 2004, p. 10).

The best season for storytelling was long winter evenings and the holy month of Ramadan, when, just after the breaking of fast, local people would gather in coffee houses. In fact, a popular saying among the Kurdish Jews is, 'Two things are necessary in winter, fire and folktale; fire to warm the body and folktale to warm the heart' (Floor 2005, p. 101). The stories told and enacted by the storyteller were mainly folktales and histories of local heroes. In Iranian Kurdistan, the reading of stories from Ferdowsi's *Shāhnāmeh* was so popular that each great family in Kermanshah had their own *Shāhnāmeh-khān*. Many verses of *Shāhnāmeh* stories told by Kurdish storytellers were, according to Floor, translated into Kurdish (p. 103). Izzeddin Mustafa Rasul recounts how, during the nights of Ramadan, the storytellers would narrate stories about the heroes of *Shāhnāmeh*, such as Rostami Zal and Zorab, in the large coffee houses of the Kurdish cities (Rasul 2010, p. 41). He describes how the performers were able to completely engage their audiences, who divided into separate groups that cheered for different characters and grieved for their demise (p. 42).

In Kurdistan, the performers of prose narratives are known as *çîrokbêj*. The *çîrokbêj* were usually itinerant performers who wandered on foot from city to city. Upon arriving, they would select public places to present their tales, which possessed a strong theatrical element including improvized dramatic action, impersonation, singing and dancing, usually accompanied by a tambourine and flute. These performers enjoyed less prestige than the *dengbêj* and, like the *aşik*, they appear to have disappeared (Allison 2010, p. 47).

Perhaps the most prestigious and popular oral genre in Kurdistan is poetry. The long narrative poems are called *beyt* in Sorani and *qewl* or *hozan* in Kurmanji (Allison 2010, p. 47). Some *beyts* relate to the history of a region and significant events in the lives of the noble families who ruled the region. These are told by the *beytbêj*, who are considered to be local historians. They recount the glories of the past and so imbue their people with a sense of local pride and unity. Praise-poem and heroic recitations were particularly used to honour the nobility, who were patrons of local poets and artists. Every great house in Kurdistan had its own poet who would narrate their oral history. The *beytbêj* would sometimes narrate romantic epics or historical narratives in public places such as mosques and teahouses. Between 1901 and 1903, Oskar Mann worked in collaboration with Javad Qazi to collect nineteen *beyts* that had been told by two local *beytbêj* in Mahabad named Rahman Bakr and Mirza Iskandar. These were, along with six Kurdish legends, published in a book entitled *Die Mundart der Mukri*.[15]

Amongst the Kurds, storytelling has historically played an important role in preserving Kurdish culture, history and memories and in ensuring their dissemination throughout the public sphere over the course of generations. The importance of the *dengbêj* tradition as a medium of expression has been confirmed by various scholars who have examined the role of oral narrative genres of lament and *dengbêj* performance as the medium of traumatized people in the Kurdish community to speak about, share and disseminate stories of their experiences of enduring pain and suffering (see Yüksel 2010; Aras 2013). Not only that, in Turkey, it has taken the form of resistance against the state. The Turkish state's denial of Kurdish identity, language and culture further reinforced (an already strong) Kurdish oral culture, which became the only communication channel, instrument and means through which Kurds could express themselves. The *dengbêj* tradition therefore became a politicized narrative genre through which performers criticized and attacked the Turkish state policies by glorifying the Kurdish revolts and praising their leaders, along with Kurdish culture, history and language (Aras 2013, p. 127). In Iraq too, as the following chapters demonstrate, stories of Kurds' resistance to external forces, as idealized in Kurdish *beyts*, have greatly influenced Kurdish dramatists. Ahmad Salar, who resorts to old *beyts* and characters of *beytbêj* and *goranîbêj* (singer) to revive the traditional performance culture and reinforce his message of national unity and resistance, is a particularly significant example in this regard.

## Conclusion

A wealth of traditional folk performance notwithstanding, modern text-based drama was introduced to Iraqi Kurdistan only during the early twentieth

---

[15] In Iran, several researchers including Hemin the poet, Abdullah Ayubian and Qadir Fattahi Qazi have embarked on collecting local *beyts* which are at risk of disappearance.

century. In fact, with all the restrictions on Kurdish cultural expression it is astounding that Kurdish has survived and flourished to the point where it has become established as a literary language. Despite their ability to write in dominant languages, Kurdish writers have continued to write in their native language and sometimes have paid the price with their lives. Divided up between Iran, Iraq, Syria and Turkey, the Kurdish land has been a conflict zone for years and as such Kurdish writers have been preoccupied with issues of national identity and oppression. In a context in which the Kurds are still an oppressed minority, theatre has provided a space for reviving and reclaiming their heritage, and also for commenting on issues of national identity and political oppression. This will be the subject of analysis in future chapters with the following contextualizing the emergence of theatre in Iraqi Kurdistan and exploring its developments up to 1975.

# 2

# The origin and development of Kurdish theatre in Iraq, 1920–75

Hawrami (2001) argues that the emergence of drama in Kurdistan began immediately after the banning of the traditional spring festival that was described in Chapter 1. This, according to Hawrami, suggests that Kurdish drama was born out of the need to perform in a society which had lost its traditional form of theatre to the colonizers' whim. The loss of the traditional Kurdish festival might conceivably have impacted upon the acceptance of theatre in Kurdistan in the 1920s. However, the emergence of theatre in Kurdistan should also be conceptualized with reference to the following developments:

First, theatre emerged in Sulaymaniyah which was historically a socially and culturally vibrant city whose bazars, roads, mosques, schools and caravansaries had been built with the support of its Kurdish rulers (Hawrami, p. 294). Second, due to its long history of self-rule, Sulaymaniyah had become the most nationalist location in Iraqi Kurdistan. Finally, the return of Kurdish intellectuals and notables from Istanbul to their hometown of Sulaymaniyah in the 1920s (following the ban on Kurdish language and culture in Turkey) played an important role in the revival of cultural life in Iraqi Kurdistan. In order to better understand the context in which theatre emerged in Kurdistan, the following offers a glimpse into the history of the city of Sulaymaniyah, along with the sociopolitical developments that contributed to the emergence of theatre.

# Sociopolitical developments leading to the emergence of theatre

## Sulaymaniyah under the Baban rule

Sulaymaniyah was built during the reign of Ibrahim Pasha of the House of Baban (reg. 1783–1803), the last Kurdish principality (emirate) that ruled parts of Iraqi Kurdistan. This powerful dynasty was founded by Baba Sulayman who, in the seventeenth century, rendered important services to the Ottomans in a war against the Safavids and as such was rewarded with all he could conquer (Edmonds 1957, p. 81). In 1783, Ibrahim Pasha moved the Baban capital to Sulaymaniyah, a new town he had built and allegedly named after the then governor of Baghdad. It is the reign of Ibrahim Pasha's successor, Abdurrahman Pasha (reg. 1803–13), that is remembered in local memory as 'a period of sturdy Kurdish independence' (p. 54). After Abdurrahman, Baban rule started to weaken; however, as Edmonds notes, 'to the last the character of the administration remained essentially Kurdish and the rulers maintained their own regular army and other signs of petty royalty' (p. 54). Ultimately, with the defeat of Ahmad Pasha (reg. 1838–47) by the governor of Baghdad Eyalet in 1847, Baban autonomy came to an end and Sulaymaniyah fell under the direct rule of Ottoman Turks.

In his narrative of residence in Kurdistan, C. J. Rich describes his visit to the Baban court in Sulaymaniyah during the rule of Mahmud Pasha (reg. 1813–34), his conversations with various personalities, antagonisms between the Babans and the Ottoman Turks, weddings, funerals, dancing and daily sporting events such as displays of swordsmanship, shooting, dog and partridge fighting, horse racing and wrestling. His accounts of the favourite pastimes in Sulaymaniyah also provide considerable insight into the importance of communal life in Kurdistan. He observed,

> The Koords are the only orientals I ever knew who sit up late at night, and rise late in the morning. Few gentlemen in Sulaimania go to bed till two or three o'clock... When it grows dark they begin going to each other's houses, where they amuse themselves with conversation, smoking and music... About an hour before sunset also, a kind of club or assembly is held before

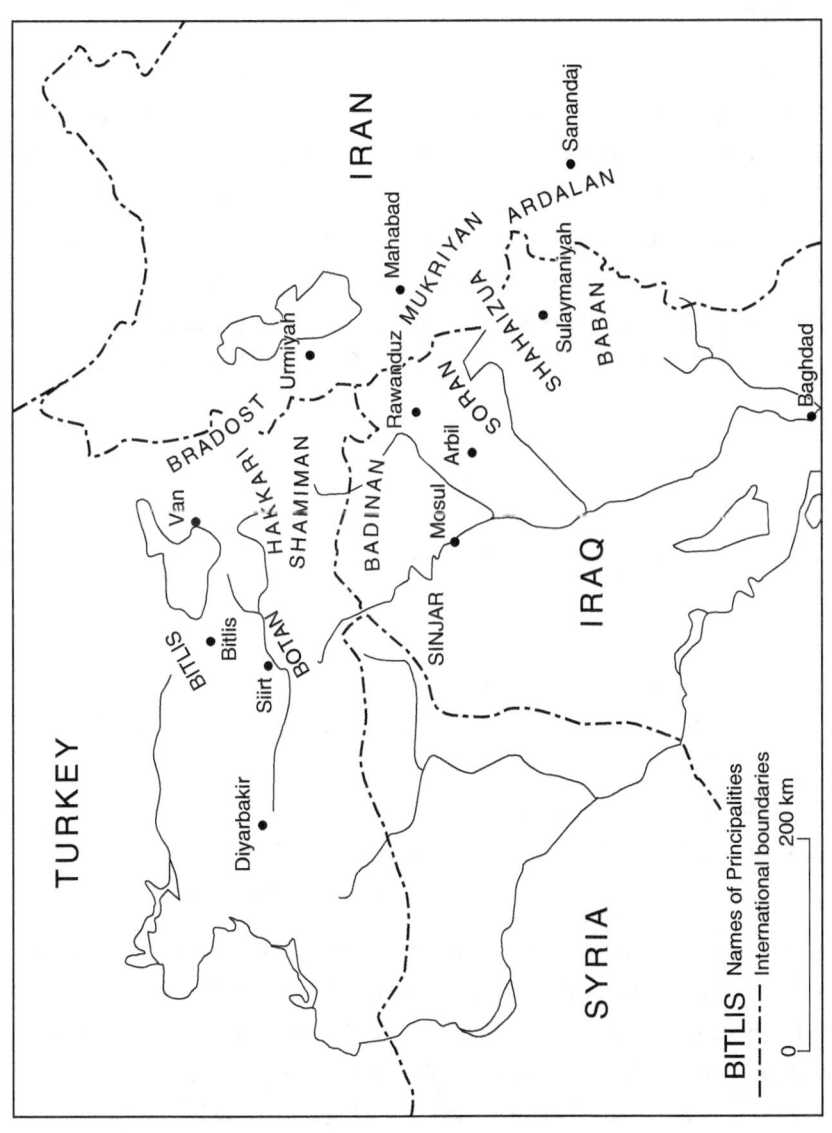

Map 3 Major Kurdish principalities. *Source:* O'Shea 2004, p. 77.

the house of the Masraf,[1] in an open place in the town called the Meidan. Friends meet and chat on various subjects; arms or horses are displayed; and sometimes matches are made of wrestling, partridge or dog-fights ... The Koords are the most determined sportsmen I ever knew...it is the favorite passion of the nation. (Rich 1836, pp. 103–4, 128)

This socially vibrant city was home to singers, poets and other performers who enjoyed the patronage of the Baban princes. The court of Abdurrahman Pasha, one of the greatest Baban rulers, was always well attended by the *beytbêj* who sang his praises in their poems (Rasul 2004, p. 10). Ahmad Pasha's peaceful reign further paved the way for Sulaymaniyah's economic and intellectual revival. In Kurdish literature, the two centuries of Baban rule has been celebrated as glowing days of Kurdish independence. A poem by Sheikh Reza Talabani (1842–1910) is a notable example of this widely shared sentiment a few decades since the extinction of Baban rule:

*Le bîrim dê Silêmanî ke darûlmûlkî Baban bû*

I remember Sulaymaniyah when it was the capital of the Babans

*Ne mehkûmî ecem ne suxrekêşî alî usman bû . . .*

It was neither subject to the Persians nor slave-driven by the House of Usman . . .

*Le ber tabûrî esker rê nebû bo meclisî paşa*

By reason of the batallions of troops there was no access to the Pasha's audience chamber

*Seday mûzîqe w neqare ta eywanî keywan bû*

The sound of bands and kettle-drums rose to the halls of Saturn

(trans. Edmonds 1957, pp. 57–8)

Over the course of many years of self-rule, Sulaymaniyah developed a unique sense of Kurdishness, and this later paved the way for the emergence and development of theatre in Kurdistan. According to the historians, Ahmad Khaja and Shakir Fattah, traditional Kurdish festivals and celebrations which involved dramatic performances were supported by Baban rulers who controlled Sulaymaniyah from the mid-seventeenth century to the mid-nineteenth century – and by Sheikh Mahmud Barzanji in the twentieth century

---

[1] A prominent family in Sulaymaniyah.

(Taymur 1988, p. 68). These included the annual spring carnival which, as described in Chapter 1, was celebrated vigorously in Sulaymaniyah until the First World War (Edmonds 1957, p. 84).

Edmonds notes that within Sulaymaniyah there was an abiding conviction among all classes of the population that the town contained the germs of a revived and extensive Kurdish state of which it was the fore-ordained capital. This belief, according to Edmonds, was always in the air and seemed to give to Sulaymaniyah a 'personality', so strong that few Kurds 'could stay there very long without succumbing to its heady influence' (p. 59).

## The fall of the Ottoman Empire

The events that followed the First World War, most specifically the fall of the Ottoman Empire, had a significant impact upon the development of Kurdish national identity and the revival of cultural life in Iraqi Kurdistan, particularly in Sulaymaniyah. The decentralized policies of the Ottoman state during the late eighteenth century had contributed to the growing independence of Kurdish principalities, the most eminent ones among them being the Bohtan, the Baban and the Hakkari principalities. In the early nineteenth century, the Ottoman and Persian empires adopted a more centralized approach in response to international threats. Sultan Mahmud started the process of eliminating the principalities and subjugating Kurdistan which could provide a bulwark against Russian expansion (Strohmeier 2003, p. 10). By 1850, the last Kurdish principalities were abolished and the Kurdish provinces were governed by centrally appointed administrators. The Kurdish revolts against the Ottoman state proved fruitless and Kurdish leaders were exiled to Istanbul where the state could keep a close eye on them. However, the cultural, political and intellectual atmosphere of Istanbul following the Young Turk Revolution in 1908 provided the exiled Kurdish notables with the opportunity to establish Kurdish cultural and political organizations such as *Kürt Teavün ve Terakki Cemiyeti* (The Society for Mutual Aid and Progress of Kurdistan) and *Kürdistan Teali Cemiyeti* (The Society for the Advancement of Kurdistan). In 1918, the nationalist aspirations of non-Turkish peoples of the Ottoman Empire, in particular the notable families who had lost their power and privileges, were encouraged by the Ottoman Empire's military defeat. In the Kurdish provinces, the notables were composed of the sufi sheikhs especially from the Naqshbandi branch, the tribal nobility and families with local administrative positions (Özoğlu 2004, p. 12).

## Sheikh Mahmud Barzanji's rise to power

As Edmonds notes, sheikhs, sayyids and dervish orders played a prominent role in the daily life of Kurdistan (Edmonds 1957, p. 59). It has been argued that the rise of Islamic mystic brotherhoods of Naqshbandi and Qadiri in Kurdistan could be related to the loss of traditional power structures (Strohmeier 2003, pp. 12–13). While the brotherhoods, particularly the Naqshbandis, had enjoyed the support of the Ottoman sultans, the fall of the hereditary semi-independent principalities and the ensuing power vacuum arguably enhanced the importance of sheikhs. Wadie Jwaideh explains that the suppression and eventual elimination of the Kurdish principalities in the Ottoman Empire was followed by lawlessness and disorder throughout Kurdistan as a result of which 'large segments of the territories of the former princes of Baban, Soran, Bohtan, Bahdinan and Hakari were abandoned to the depredations of numerous petty tribal chieftains' (Jwaideh 2006, p. 75). These feudal lords who were 'hitherto held in check by the powerful princes, were now at liberty to engage in all forms of lawlessness' (p. 75). It was in this context that the figure of the sheikh as 'a power greater than that of the petty feuding chieftains' (p. 76) rose to power and became the only authority outside the tribal organization that could resolve tribal conflicts (Bruinessen 1992, p. 234).

Among the population at large, the influence of the sheikhs increased as the public turned to religion partly 'to find the security and assurance that was so lacking in their daily lives' following the collapse of the principalities (Bruinessen 1992, p. 234). Moreover, Bruinessen maintains that 'missionary activity and fears of Christian domination due to European influence' made the Kurds especially susceptible to the sheikhs' anti-Christian propaganda that stressed the Kurds' Muslim identity (p. 234). Therefore, whereas no sheikh had previously played a leading political role in Kurdistan, in the aftermath of the overthrow of the great Kurdish princes the sheikhs and those belonging to sheikhly families flourished to become the only important political leaders for years to come and the 'focal points for nationalist sentiment' (p. 234).

In Iraqi Kurdistan, the power vacuum left by the disappearance of Baban princes was filled by Barzanji sheikhs while the sheikhs of Barzan gained control over the Hakari-Bahdinan principalities. By the early twentieth century, the old Qadiri sheikhly family of Barzanji, led by Sheikh Mahmud (1881–1956), had become the most important family in Sulaymaniyah. Sheikh Mahmud's great-great-grandfather, Sheikh Maruf, rose to prominence in the early nineteenth century in Sulaymaniyah where the Barzanji family established itself as a powerful political force. Sheikh Maruf's son, Kak Ahmad, secured his family's privileged position by gaining the Ottoman Sultan's favour who granted him revenues from the five villages of Bizênyan, Ezeban, Nodê, Wêladar and Xeraciyan (Edmonds 1957, p. 75).

In the aftermath of the First World War, the Ottoman administration in Kurdistan officially ended, leaving Sheikh Mahmud in sole control of Sulaymaniyah and the surrounding countryside (Jwaideh 2006, p. 163). Shortly afterwards, he was appointed governor of the Sulaymaniyah district and head of the new South Kurdish Federation (p. 164). Convinced of his right to be recognized as the leader of an independent Kurdish state, he rose against the British by imprisoning their officers and appointing his own administration in Sulaymaniyah in May 1919. His rebellion sparked similar incidents across the border in Iranian Kurdistan where tribes declared their solidarity with Sheikh Mahmud's plan for a free and united Kurdistan (p. 180). Sheikh Mahmud was, however, swiftly defeated by the British in June 1919 before being banished to India in 1921.

After Sheikh Mahmud's defeat, Major E. B. Soane, who was the political officer in charge of the Sulaymaniyah district, resumed his authority. Though he ruled with an iron fist, Soane was sympathetic towards Kurds and Kurdistan in general. During his office, Sulaymaniyah achieved greater prosperity than it had known before (McDowall 2004, p. 158). He encouraged agriculture and the cultivation of tobacco and protected the poorer classes. He rebuilt the town which had been destroyed by the Turks. He recognized the Kurdish character of Sulaymaniyah and helped maintain and strengthen it. Schools were opened in which Kurdish, not Arabic or Turkish, was the medium of instruction. He encouraged writing in Kurdish by launching Sulaymaniyah's first Kurdish newspaper *Pêşkewtin* (Progress). Soane believed in Kurdish self-determination and as such did his best to give to the local administration a Kurdish character.

Not only were all his officials Kurds but Kurdish dress was made compulsory. These policies helped 'secure a degree of local autonomy which was not enjoyed by any other part of the occupied territories' (McDowall, p. 159), thus boosting Sulaymaniyah's image as the Kurdish political and cultural centre in Iraqi Kurdistan. However, Britain's policies towards Mesopotamia were about to change towards the end of the 1920s, when the British government decided to abandon the Mandate and set up a unified Iraqi government. Soane's services, which were now in conflict with the policy of creating a unified Iraqi state, were henceforth dispensed with.

By 1922, Turkish agitations in Iraqi Kurdistan had challenged the British administration's authority to such an extent that the British were forced to bring back Sheikh Mahmud and reinstate him as the governor of Sulaymaniyah. He formed a cabinet composed of local notables, issued postage stamps and published a newspaper entitled *Rojî Kurdistan* (Kurdistan Daily). It did not take long before Sheikh Mahmud repeated his previous ambitious move to create an independent state. This time he claimed authority over all Kurdish areas within Iraq and declared himself King of Kurdistan. He replaced *Rojî Kurdistan* with *Bangî Heq* (Call of Truth) wherein he called for war against the British occupiers. His rebellion was again crushed by the British Royal Air Forces (RAF) as Kurds became one of the first victims of the RAF's aerial bombardments in history.

By the time of its occupation in 1924, Sulaymaniyah had developed a distinct Kurdish personality. It was the only city in Kurdistan that had clearly rejected the Arab-Iraqi dominance and refused any form of inclusion under an Iraqi government. It refused to participate in the referendum held in 1921 to determine the validity of Faysal's choice as king of Iraq (Jwaideh 2006, p. 187). Under the British mandate, it had enjoyed special status as the only occupied territory with a Kurdish governor in charge (pp. 155–6), and Kurdish was introduced as the language of administration and instruction in schools (Edmonds 1968, p. 513). While Sheikh Mahmud Barzanji's rebellion was crushed, the nationalists in Sulaymaniyah continued to petition for the independence of Kurdistan to be recognized by foreign powers. Sulaymaniyah also became home to a new class of young educated and urban Kurdish nationalists who would subsequently form left-leaning nationalist groups such as *Komeley Birayetî* (Brotherhood Society), *Darkar* (Woodcutters) and *Hîwa* (Hope).

## Events following the Treaty of Lausanne (1923)

The Treaty of Sèvres, signed in August 1920, made provision for the recognition of Kurdish and Armenian states in Eastern Turkey. This independent Kurdish state was to be carved out of south-east Anatolia, and the Kurds of the Mosul vilayet (Iraq) would be given the option of joining the new state at a later date (Section III, Articles 62–64). However, as a result of Mustafa Kemal's rise in Turkey, this treaty did not come into force and was not ratified. Instead, it was replaced by the Treaty of Lausanne (1923), which included provisions for the creation of Iraq and Syria but made no mention of Kurdistan or Armenia. Therefore, Kurdistan was partitioned between Turkey and Iraq with the oil-rich Mosul province falling under the control of the Kingdom of Iraq under the British administration. The decision to pivot from Sèvres to Lausanne was largely attributable to London's desire to ensure the unity of Iraq for the following reasons: first, to control the oil reserves around Kirkuk which were of great value to Royal Navy's new oil-fired vessels, and second, to avoid further financial losses on overseas projects in the aftermath of the preceding World War.

The Turkish-Iraqi border was identified by a League of Nations commission in December 1925. The commission recognized that the Kurds form five-eighths of the population of the Mosul vilayet and that they are neither Arabs nor Turks. It awarded the Mosul vilayet to Iraq, provided that Britain was prepared to extend its mandate over Iraq for twenty-five years; the reason for this provision being the unstable internal conditions of the kingdom (*Question of the Frontier between Turkey and Iraq*, 1925, p. 88). However, Britain devised a new policy of rapidly liquidating the mandatory regime in Iraq which resulted in several petitions addressed to the League of Nations by Kurdish notables of Sulaymaniyah. In nine petitions dating from July 1930 to April 1931, the signatories demanded the formation of a Kurdish government under supervision of the League of Nations in the event of the mandatory regime in Iraq being brought to an end (Toynbee and Boulter 1935, pp. 130–1). The League, however, rejected the petitions and thus removed the possibility of a

Kurdish state in northern Iraq. Clashes erupted again when Iraq secured its independence from Britain in the early 1930s with Sulaymaniyah becoming the site of mass demonstrations and stone-throwing as a result of which fourteen civilians were killed by the Iraqi troops (McDowall 2004, p. 176). The Hashemite monarchy was established, and Iraq became officially recognized as the Kingdom of Iraq in October 1932.

In Turkey, the liberal political environment that had allowed for the establishment of pro-Kurdish organizations after the Young Turk Revolution did not last long. Following the creation of the Republic of Turkey, the ruling Committee for Union and Progress (CUP) party reversed its liberal multi-ethnic policies and adopted a much narrower and rigid nationalist approach. The crushing of subsequent Kurdish rebellions, in addition to the ban on expressions of Kurdish culture and language, forced many Kurdish notables into exile, a development which significantly impacted the emergence of theatre in Iraqi Kurdistan.

## The creation of Iraq and its consequences for Kurdistan

In 1932, the Council of the League of Nations formally approved Iraq's membership of the League, an action which was conditioned upon the Iraqi government providing formal guarantees on a number of points, including the protection of minorities. In acting in accordance with this decision, the Iraqi government issued a declaration which safeguarded the rights of indigenous minorities including the full protection of life and liberty, equality before the law, civil and political rights, freedom to use any language and the right to maintain independent institutions and educational establishments. Even before this declaration, the Iraqi constitution of 1925 had guaranteed the equality of all Iraqis before the law, their freedom of worship, and instruction in their own languages. The Local Languages Law of 1931 provided that the official language should, in a number of districts, be Kurdish or Turkish and that, in all elementary and primary schools within those districts, the language of instruction should be the mother tongue of the majority of the pupils.

However, the Iraqi government failed to enforce its constitutional provisions that provided minorities with an adequate share in government and army appointments and subsidies to schools. This was anticipated by Kurds who had expressed their concerns in advance about how they would be treated by the Arab-Iraqi government; this is why they had, under British auspices, sought autonomy. As mentioned before, revolts broke out in Kurdistan that were suppressed only with the support of RAF. At home, however, experienced British officers and politicians began to question the validity of Britain's stance towards the Kurds in Iraq. In 1933, Captain P. S. Mumford voiced his concern about the situation of minorities, including the Kurds who, according to him, 'disliked being under an Arab Government and claimed that the promise of limited autonomy held out to them by the Mandatory Power . . . had not been honoured,' the continuous operations against them since the Anglo-Iraqi Treaty proving the truth of their contention (Davidson 1933, p. 76).

From 1932 to 1943 the Kurds did not revolt again; however, they continued to reject the government's authority. Hourani (1947, p. 98) claims that his stance was attributable to two developments. The first was the growth of Kurdish national spirit, a development that was partially attributable to the appearance of a class of educated Kurds and which was, in part, a 'natural' reaction against pan-Arabism. The second development which was considerably more important, derived from administrative grievances. Hourani notes,

> The Iraqi Government made little attempt to carry out the provisions of the various laws passed during the mandatory period. Government departments in Bagdad tended to neglect the claims of districts so far away from the capital; and the Kurds had no way of making their voice heard effectively... In general, Arab officials in the northern provinces failed to understand the mentality and needs of the Kurdish people. (Hourani 1947, p. 98)

The government's neglect of Kurdish concerns was evidenced in a number of different spheres. According to a British foreign office document on Iraqi Kurdistan written in May 1944, there were few educational facilities and those that existed were mainly for education in Arabic. It observes,

> Out of a total population of 180,000 souls, there are only some 3500 receiving education. There are 43 primary schools (of which 12 are in Sulaymaniyah town) with 165 teachers between them, and two intermediate schools (respectively for boys and girls) with a total of 23 teachers. Of the 165 primary teachers, 43 speak no Kurdish and in one or two cases a single non-Kurdish speaker is the only teacher in the school. The teaching in

intermediate schools are in Arabic. ('British Foreign Office Documents on the Kurds', 1944)

The problems in Kurdistan were not limited to education. As Hourani states, nothing was done to extend or improve the cultivation of the land and raise the standard of living in Kurdistan. He observes, 'The mountain districts did not produce enough cereals to feed the population and importation on an adequate scale was rendered difficult by the poverty of the Kurdish peasants, the lack of a food-supply organization and the insufficiency of transport' (Hourani 1947, p. 99). Edmonds's assessment confirms Hourani's by pointing out that the guarantees given to the League in 1925 and 1932 were either being ignored or at best grudgingly implemented and that 'the Kurdish districts were not getting their fair share of social services, particularly education at all levels, or of development projects' (Edmonds 1968, p. 514).

## The return of the elite to Sulaymaniyah

With Iraqi Kurdistan enjoying recognition as a Kurdish region, several Kurdish notables from Sulaymaniyah, who had been involved in pro-Kurdish activities in Turkey, returned from Istanbul to their hometown. Some of them went to Baghdad where they were appointed to high-ranking government offices. The educated elite who returned to Sulaymaniyah took great interest and took part in political and cultural developments in the region. Salih Zaki Beg (1886–1944), Rafiq Hilmi (1898–1960) and Pîremêrd (1867–1950) exemplify how the elite became involved in pro-Kurdish affairs. Salih Zaki Beg was from the prominent Sulaymaniyah family of Sahibqiran.[2] He was a colonel in the Ottoman army until 1921 and later joined Sheikh Mahmud's movement and became the commander-in-chief of the National Armed Forces. After the defeat of Sheikh Mahmud's rebellion, Salih Zaki was exiled to Baghdad where he published a literary, cultural and social journal called *Diyarî Kurdistan* (The Gift of Kurdistan) between 1925 and 1926. This was the first Kurdish journal in Iraq to be printed in colour.

---

[2] The family descended from Ahmad Beg Sahib-Qiran, whose son Mahmud was commander-in-chief of the armed forces under one of the later Babans. The poets Kurdi, Salim and Ahmad Beg-i Fattah Beg, as well as Lady Adila of Halabja, were distinguished members of this family.

The Kirkuk-born Rafiq Hilmi was a renowned Kurdish cultural and political figure and the leader of *Hîwa* party. He studied engineering in Istanbul and returned to Sulaymaniyah in the 1920s, where he actively participated in the political and cultural life of the town. His rare intellectual qualities and mastery of languages, which included Kurdish, Persian, Arabic, Turkish, English and French, earned him the affection of Sheikh Mahmud who referred to him as 'Rafiq Hilmi, the Enlightened (*munewer*).'

Perhaps the single most important literary figure in Kurdistan for three decades was Pîremêrd. He is of particular interest to this study because he printed the first plays in Iraqi Kurdistan, wrote plays himself and helped promote education and build schools where the first theatrical works were performed; In addition, he was the first renowned figure to promote theatre and write critically about it.

## Tawfiq Mahmud Hamza, Pîremêrd (1867–1950)

Tawfiq Mahmud Hamza (1867–1950), known as Pîremêrd (old man), was the most prominent literary figure in Iraqi Kurdistan until his death in 1950. Sulaymaniyah owed much of its cultural and literary revival in the early twentieth century to Pîremêrd's ardent advocacy of education and modernization. A lawyer, diplomat, poet, writer and journalist, Pîremêrd was a man of varied interests and tastes, with his works embracing literature, history, economy, philosophy, religion and politics. During his long literary career, Pîremêrd produced a substantial number of essays, poems, proverbs, stories and translations. For many years, he was the editor of *Jîn* (Life), the outstanding literary magazine in Iraqi Kurdistan. He was a talented poet with a whimsical sense of humour that endeared him to all who knew him (Jwaideh 2006, p. 25).

Pîremêrd was born in 1867 in Sulaymaniyah to an influential landowning family. His great grandfather and grandfather had both served as minister of treasury (*wekil xerc*) in the court of Baban princes. After finishing his primary education, Pîremêrd became a *faqih* (cleric) and studied under the well-known *faqihs* of the time in Iranian Kurdistan. After finishing his studies, he returned to Sulaymaniyah where, after several years of government service, he quit his job to become an adviser to the prominent sheikhly family of Barzanji.

Pîremêrd accompanied the Barzanji sheikhs in a visit to the court of the Ottoman Sultan Abdul Hamid II. Once there, he made a positive impression on the royal secretary which propelled his political career forward. Between 1909 and 1918, he was appointed governor of several districts such as Hakkari, Qeremursil, Balawa, Beytüşşebap in Şırnak, Gümüşköy and Adapazarı in Sakarya. In 1918, he was appointed by the Sultan as the *mutasarrıf* of the city of Amasya where he remained until 1923.

During the twenty-five years of his life in Turkey, Pîremêrd was closely involved in various literary activities. Between 1904 and 1912, he and his son wrote for *Ijtihad*, a monthly paper concerned with literature, science, economics and social issues, which was published by Abdullah Cevdet, the Kurdish physician, poet, man of letters and political thinker. He even contributed to Persian newspapers and periodicals in Iran, including *Shams*, *Farhang* and *Shafaq-e Sorkh*. In Istanbul, Pîremêrd lived in close proximity to and befriended some of the greatest Turkish writers and playwrights including Recaizade Ekrem (1847–1914), Halit Ziya Uşakizâde (1866–1945), Hüseyin Rahmi (1864–1944) and Riza Tevfik (1869–1949) (Pirbal 2001, pp. 105–6). Their literary works and the conversations Pîremêrd had with them substantially impacted Pîremêrd, who was fascinated and inspired by both the Ottoman literature and the translations of European literary works.

In addition to these literary activities, Pîremêrd was also actively engaged in politics. In 1907, he became a member of the Istanbul-based pan-Kurdish organization called *Kurd Teavun ve Terakki Cemiyeti* (Kurdish Society for Mutual Aid and Progress) and the license owner and head writer for the organization's gazette that was published between 1908 and 1909. This organization was founded by Kurdish notables who espoused the idea of a distinct Kurdish identity (see Özoğlu 2004). In *Jîn*, which was published between 1918 and 1919, he contributed with his own writings, poems and translations. *Jîn* criticized what it saw as the deplorable situation of Kurds and demanded their national awakening by reminding them of their distinct history, language and culture. Abdullah Cevdet, for example, wrote in the first issue of *Jîn*:

> Kurds, is it possible to sleep in such a tumultuous era? I do not consider it necessary to shout: Hey, Kurd, awaken! Because if the Kurds are still asleep, that means they died long ago. The Kurds are awake and they will awaken

the masters who have kept them asleep for centuries. They (the Kurds, MS) will repay evil with goodness. 'We are living in an era in which to sleep for an hour means the death of a nation. (Strohmeier 2003, p. 58)

This, of course, was written at a time when old empires were disintegrating into new nation-states and a powerful claim to nationhood could result in the establishment of a new nation-state. The Austro-Hungarian Empire had, largely on the grounds of ethnicity, been partitioned into several states and the Ottoman Empire was about to be divided by the Allies in the aftermath of the Great War. Even Sheikh Said of Palu, in his call to the nation to rebel against the Turkish rule, evoked the myth of the decline of the Kurdish 'Golden Age' and the Kurds' duty to restore it by saying 'we have not made the spirits of our ancestors happy. We have not fulfilled the wishes of Ehmedê Xanî. That is why we live in misery and make our enemies glad' (Strohmeier, p. 90).

Pîremêrd's contributions to *Jîn* suggest that he was a member of the committee for Kurdish Independence which was established in Erzurum in late 1922. After the ban on all Kurdish publications and organizations and the crush of Sheikh Said's rebellion against the Turkish government in 1925,[3] many Kurdish nationalists, including Pîremêrd, were sentenced to death by an Independence Tribunal.[4] To escape the death penalty, Pîremêrd was forced to move back to Sulaymaniyah where he resumed his literary activities.

He initially contributed to a literary journal called *Jiyan*, which was published between 1926 and 1938, before later progressing to *Jîn*, which was published between 1938 and 1950. *Jiyan* was a Kurdish-language weekly paper that was initially published by the Sulaymaniyah municipality in 1926. In 1932, Pîremêrd assumed the position of manager and in 1934 he became the license owner of the paper which later assumed a new life under the name of *Jîn*. Although financial difficulties and a lack of support forced him to mortgage his house to buy paper, Pîremêrd continued to publish *Jîn*, the final (1015th) issue of which was published four days before his death in 1950.

---

[3] This was the first Kurdish uprising since the creation of the Republic of Turkey in 1923. This revolt, which broke out after the abolishment of Caliphate by Mustafa Kemal Ataturk, was led by Sheikh Said of Palu who was executed following the defeat of the uprising.

[4] The Independence Tribunal was formed in the aftermath of the First World War to punish those who had collaborated with the Allies or supported the old regime against the Kemalists. Pîremêrd writes, 'in the Erzurum committee along with Xalid Beg (Cibran) and Yusuf Zia (the prince of House of Bitlis), and Dr. Fuad and Kamal, I was in the service of Mulla Said Bediüzzaman (Nursi) and was sentenced to death by the Istanbul tribunal' (Ashna 2009, p. 103).

Up until his death in 1950, Pîremêrd was the most prominent literary figure in Kurdistan who made a significant contribution to the promotion of literacy and education and the revival of Kurdish literature. In his writings, which covered economic, historical, literary, philosophical and social fields, he advocated reforms in his homeland which had made little progress since his departure in 1898. During his lifetime, he collected and translated poems (from Gorani to Sulaymaniyah dialect) by Mawlawi, Wali Dewana, Besarani and several others. He also published literary works that had long been forgotten. He wrote several histories of Kurds, the Baban principality, the Jaff families and important historical events in Kurdistan. Moreover, he revived the Newroz celebration, including the lighting of bonfires in public spaces, and helped re-establish it as an important national festival (Ashna 2009).[5]

In 1926, Pîremêrd joined together with Ismail Haqi Baban (1876–1913), Rafiq Hilmi (1898–1960) and Amin Zaki Beg (1880–1948) to form a society that would work to promote literacy and education in Kurdistan. Founded in Sulaymaniyah, *Komeley Zanistî Kurdan* (Kurds' Literary Society) would subsequently make a significant contribution to public education and the promotion of arts and literature (Pirbal 2001, p. 31).

## *Komeley Zanistî Kurdan* (Kurds' Literary Society)

The foundation of *Komeley Zanistî Kurdan* was an important step that Pîremêrd and other intellectuals, such as Ahmad Beg Tawfiq Beg and Jamal Baban, took to address the educational backwardness of their hometown. Pîremêrd celebrated this occasion in a poem which clearly conveys his aspirations for the society, with emphasis upon the contribution it could make in building a Kurdish nation visible to the outside world, particularly the Europeans who were determining the fate of the Middle Eastern nations at the time. In the poem, he stated,

---

[5] In reviving the Newroz celebrations, Pîremêrd was accused of promoting the pre-Islamic religion of Zoroastrianism and the rite of fire-worshipping. As a result, *Jiyan* and also Pîremêrd's school of *Komeley Zanistî* were closed down by the mutasarrif of Sulaymaniyah, Majid Yaqubi. Pîremêrd was also accused of being an agent for the British government, with his celebration of the Newroz being attributed to Britain. For more detail on these accusations, along with Pîremêrd's responses to them in his newspaper and poems, see Ashna (2009, pp. 82–90).

*Emşew gulî 'umêdî wetenman epişkwê*
Tonight the flower of our nation's hope blooms
*Mîllet umêdware be zanistî pêşkewê*
The nation is hopeful to progress through *Zanistî*
*Zanistiye sewiyey millet bilind eka*
*Zanistî* moves the nation forward
*Zanistiye ke ême binasêt be ewrûpa*
*Zanistî* can make us known to Europe. (Ashna 2009, p. 119)

Strohmeier notes that early Kurdish nationalists, who had to define and present their nation, sought to inspire an inner Kurdish identification and also enhance the external perception of Kurds, particularly in the West. The first step in this direction was to promote education in Kurdish. Early Kurdish nationalists such as the Bedirxans had emphasized the importance of education as a necessary precondition for the creation of a strong national identity grounded within a shared culture and language. If this was to be achieved, education had to be promoted, Kurdish history had to be documented and literary classics had to be revived (Strohmeier 2003, pp. 21, 39–40, 236–7).

*Komeley Zanistiî Kurdan* was founded with the goal of furthering this nationalist agenda. It promoted education and literacy in Kurdistan through publishing newspapers and historical, geographical and ethnographical narratives about Kurds, translating and compiling textbooks, educational support institutions, enabling students to study in foreign countries and running a series of lectures and seminars. *Zanistî's* activities extended to the opening of a boys' school, the arrangement of free evening classes and the formation of music and theatre groups. Local writers, poets and intellectuals served the society by holding weekly seminars. In *Jiyan*, an appeal was published which gave great tidings to all Kurds. It stated,

> It is known to you, our dear readers, that all we want is to disseminate the knowledge of sciences, and today we thank God to have achieved our wish as we proudly show the public the result of the efforts of some of our countrymen, certified by the Ministry of Interior and supported by the governor and the administrative inspector . . . We announce this news hoping that this society becomes a basis for our scientific development by

educating the masses and also a good omen for our people and our nation; we hope that its steady march will be ensured with the help of notables, scholars, businessmen, and intellectuals. (Maziri 2006)

By 1933, *Zanistî* had taught hundreds of housewives how to read and write. Although *Zanistî* maintained that it was an apolitical society, this claim was drawn into question on 6 September 1930 (known as Black September). On this date, *Zanistîi* teachers led their students in the Sulaymaniyah uprising against the central government. The school was closed down in 1937. It was reopened in 1942 by Kurdish intellectuals who ran the school for three years until the government extended its control over it and turned it into a public school.

The early history of drama in Iraqi Kurdistan is closely intertwined with the history of education. Theatre was one of the key elements of *Zanistî*'s intellectual movement. *Zanistî* was supported by the general public and its schools were maintained by public funding. The first group of Kurdish graduates from the Baghdad House of Teachers (or Teacher Training Institute) who worked in *Zanistî* School were the first in Kurdistan to stage plays in Kurdish. In their hands, theatre served an important social purpose by supporting the education of children from low-income households.

## The emergence of Kurdish theatre: National identity-building

When drama first appeared in Kurdistan during the 1920s, there were no drama schools, neither in Kurdistan nor in Baghdad. The Institute of Fine Arts opened in Baghdad in 1940 and introduced a Theatre Arts programme much later in 1967. Even then few Kurdish students attended it due to the high costs of commuting to the capital and also the social stigma associated to acting.[6] Therefore, it should come as no surprise that there was no real playwriting during the early years of theatre in Kurdistan. Most early plays were either duplications of Arabic plays (which were themselves based on European

---

[6] The social stigma associated with acting was still evident several decades later in the 1970s (see Karim 2013).

classics) or experimental attempts by the educated elite who were not trained in the art. The main purpose of these early theatrical productions was to raise funds for schools and students of low-income households.

In order to retain the interest and engagement of the audience, the plays were usually short and were divided into scenes rather than acts.[7] The actors were mainly the teachers and their students and the plays were mainly Kurdified versions of performances that the teachers had witnessed in Baghdad, Mosul or Istanbul. The plays were staged at the boys' school or other public spaces as there were no purpose-built theatres in Kurdistan.[8] Direction did not play an important role in productions and actors relied on their own talents and followed their own instincts. Directors, who were usually schoolteachers, only gave advice on occasion and praised when it was due. In these early stages, theatre audiences were mainly male; however, women soon began to attend the performances.

The teacher/directors, who staged plays in schools and acted in them along with their students, began to emerge during the 1920s. This group of young men mostly encountered drama for the first time when they enrolled at the educational institutes in Baghdad or Mosul where they were introduced to theatre and became involved in acting. According to Ahmad Khaja, *Komeley Lawanî Kurd* (The Kurdish Youths Society) which had been established in Erbil in 1921 staged *Selahedînî Eyûbî* (Saladin) during the same year (Pirbal 2001, p. 70). This play, which was an adaptation of Sir Walter Scott's *The Talisman* (1825), was written by the Lebanese Najib al-Haddad. It was translated into Kurdish and directed by Danial Qasab (1913–2000), the renowned Jewish painter from Erbil, who contributed to many theatrical productions in Erbil with his paintings and scene design.[9]

The theatre movement in Kurdistan took off particularly in Sulaymaniyah as a result of the efforts made by schoolteachers, who included Mustafa Saib, Salih

---

[7] This has continued well into the recent decades. I have yet to encounter a Kurdish play that is divided into acts and then further divided into scenes.
[8] *Holî Gel* (People's Hall), Kurdistan's first proper theatre, was built decades later following the 14 July Revolution and the creation of the Republic.
[9] Like elsewhere in the Middle East, non-Muslim minorities have played a significant role in the early stages of theatre in Kurdistan. One example of their contribution is cross-gender acting which was made inevitable due to social stigma surrounding female acting. Non-Muslim actors in Erbil took on female roles in productions such as Saladin (1930) in which Bacchus Toma, Sarkis Toma and Wahbi Agop played the female roles (see Pirbal 2001, p. 73).

Qaftan and Fuad Rashid. Fuad Rashid had, at the age of nineteen, graduated from the Baghdad House of Teachers (1923–58), where he had been an active member of the school's theatre group. Upon returning to Kurdistan, Rashid brought the first Kurdish play on stage in Sulaymaniyah. This play, which was entitled *Îlm û Cehl* (Knowledge and Ignorance), was adapted by Rashid from a play performed by the Egyptian George Abyad Troup who had visited Baghdad in 1926. Later the same year, Rashid directed *Îlm û Cehl* which was performed by his students for three days in the house of Bahiya Khan, Sheikh Mahmud Barzanji's wife. The play depicts two brothers, one of them idle and the other hard-working. Their lives parallel Aesop's fable of the ant and the grasshopper, with the crucial difference coming at the end of the performance, when the hard-working son bails his brother out of difficulty. The performance was followed by two comic skits, one about a clever and cunning servant and the other about a schoolteacher, with Rashid himself assuming the leading role.

The tickets for the performance sold for three, five and ten rupees and were only bought by the town notables. According to Tanya, those in attendance predominantly viewed it as an opportunity to socialize (Tanya 1985, p. 53). The newspaper *Jiyan* reported that the profits from the performance were given to the students of the school. The first proper Kurdish play was therefore staged for the benefit of the upper classes, with a view to raise funds for a boys' school and thus ultimately promote literacy in a city (Sulaymaniyah) where illiteracy was widespread.

*Nîron* (Nero) or *Zulmî Qeyser Nîron* (Emperor Nero's Tyranny) was another play that had been presented by the George Abyad Troupe before being adapted by Rashid, who also played the role of Nero's wife (Pirbal 2001, p. 71).[10] As one of the first plays that was staged by *Zanistî*, *Nîron* was performed for two days in Sulaymaniyah in July 1927. Again, the profits made from its staging were distributed among the students.[11] In addition, they also helped purchase

---

[10] Pirbal mentions an older theatrical performance – *Aqa w Aqajin* (Aqa and His Wife, 1926) – in which Rashid assumed the female role thus becoming the first Kurdish cross-gender actor in Sulaymaniyah (Pirbal 2001, p. 71).

[11] *Nîron* was also staged in Rawanduz in 1931 (see Figure 3). The play, which was directed by Fuad Rashid, went on stage for two days for male audiences and one day for female audiences. The money that was raised was used to purchase sports equipment for the boys' school. According to Pirbal, the governor of Rawanduz, Reza Beg, had 'ordered' everyone to attend the performance (Pirbal 2001, p. 76).

musical instruments for the first Sulaymaniyah music group that Rashid had co-founded in the same year. Pîremêrd's report in *Jiyan* suggests that the play depicts the Roman emperor's tyranny and his fall in the hands of 'the Roman patriots' who, in the view of Pîremêrd, 'liberate their nation' (cited in Barzanji 2007, p. 50). When Pîremêrd praised this performance in his newspaper, his comments were the first piece of theatre criticism that had been published in Iraqi Kurdistan. He wrote,

> [T]his art has a great impact on the nation's morality, the customs of the country, and the minds of the individuals . . . Theatre teaches those who carry the virus of despotism and dictatorship a moral lesson and serves as a reminder of history. (pp. 18–19)

As Janelle Reinelt (2008, p. 228) notes, this kind of theatrical discourse pretends that the nation exists by addressing – or even implying – the audience as a national citizenry. This feature was also evidenced in the following decade when the Kurdish elite called on their 'nation' to support theatre as a service to their 'homeland'.

During the 1930s, but only sporadically and usually on the Eid of Ramadan, the Kurds' Literary Society continued to stage plays to collect money for poor students and support the Kurdish school of *Zanistî*. Among the plays staged by the society were *Dildarî w Peyman Perwerî* (Love and Faithfulness, 1933) and *Serbazî Aza* (The Brave Soldier, 1935). The former was a short story that celebrated love of family and country by depicting a hero who avenged his father's murder and voluntarily turned himself in to the authorities, therefore sacrificing the prospect of a happy married life to his fiancée for the sake of honour. Its author, A. B. Hawri (1915–1979), wrote that his intention was to teach the Kurdish youth the virtues of faithfulness in love and conveying the importance of the family unit in 'elevating their poor homeland' (Hawri 2002, p. 13). The hero of the story emphasizes this point at the end of the play when he puts the country above his love for his fiancée by saying: 'I will not exchange her with anything. But I cannot say I will not exchange her with the homeland because homeland is a man's pride, life and honour' (p. 26).

The latter play, *Serbazî Aza*, was upheld in *Jiyan* for nurturing the traits of bravery and courage in the battlefield in the hearts and minds of Kurdish youth, who would, when the time came, happily sacrifice themselves for their

**Figure 3** *Nîron* (Rawanduz, 1931). *Source*: Karwan, no. 64, 1988, p. 62.

land (Barzanji 2007, p. 40). The reports in *Jiyan* were written by Pîremêrd who had become the first theatre advocate and critic in Kurdistan. His writing offers valuable insight into the early Kurdish theatre in Sulaymaniyah. On the production of *Serbazî Aza,* Pîremêrd wrote an article in *Jiyan* entitled 'Temsîl, Serguzeştenimayî' in which he documented that the performance took place on the days of the Ramadan Eid by the students and teachers of the *Zanistî* school (p. 39). It is also noteworthy that Pîremêrd describes the performance as *tamsīl* and also devised the word *serguzeştenimayî* (performing narrative) as a Kurdish synonym for it, making it clear that the word *şano* had not yet entered the literary discourse at the time.[12] In further demonstrating his attentive engagement he notes that, on the first night of the performance, the hero of the story (who was played by Shakir Efendi, the teacher of the *Zanistî* school) showed weakness and desperation when he was captured but this defect was 'corrected [on] the second night' (Barzanji, p. 39). This contribution clearly demonstrates that Pîremêrd, and perhaps other spectators, attended the theatrical performances more than once.

---

[12] As has already been noted, the word *şano* entered the literary discourse in the 1950s after Goran used it in his poetry.

In addition to the Kurds' early attempts at theatre, several foreign troupes also visited Kurdistan during the 1920s and early 1930s. In 1923, Bishara Wakim (1890–1949), the Egyptian director and actor, staged several plays in different Kurdish cities and towns (Pirbal 2001, pp. 72–3, 78). Haqqi al-Shibli (1913–1985), the Iraqi actor and director, visited Erbil and Sulaymaniyah in 1929 and 1932 (pp. 72–3, 78). During his first visit, he acted in and directed three plays; he staged eight plays during his second visit, with *Selahedînî Eyûbî* (Saladin), the story of the Kurdish-Muslim commander's heroism, being staged every time (pp. 72–3, 78). The Egyptian Fatma Rushdi and her theatre group also visited Erbil in 1934, when they staged *an-Nasr is-Saqeer* (The Short Victory), with the male protagonist being played by Fatma herself (p. 79). In his writing on theatre in Erbil, Fayzi mentions that Egyptian and Lebanese theatre groups had also visited the city in the early and mid-twentieth century (Fayzi 2006, p. 147). A number of British and Indian theatre companies also performed in Baghdad during the British mandate in Iraq (al-Mufraji et al. 1998, p. 105) and reports in *Jiyan* newspaper suggest that they also visited Kurdistan in 1927 (Fayzi 2006, p. 71).

Under exceedingly challenging social and economic circumstances, theatre struggled to gain a strong foothold in Kurdistan. Despite all difficulties, Kurdish intellectuals and the intelligentsia continued to promote literacy and education by raising funds for schools through theatre. During the 1950s and 1960s, a group of theatre enthusiasts, which included actors, painters and musicians, embarked on creating a society for fine arts and committed themselves to the difficult task of making theatre in Kurdistan. At the time, there were no technical sound equipment or complicated stage designs. A microphone on a stand was sometimes the only sound equipment while stage design was simply limited to scenic paintings and basic furniture (see Figures 4 and 5). Voice training did not exist and sometimes the actors could not be heard due to the noise by the audiences. The actors mostly had to shout, with the exception of those who could sing and thus make the audience more attentive.[13]

---

[13] Rafiq Chalak, for example, not only had a beautiful voice but wore a microphone on his costume which would immediately silence the audiences. Some of his popular songs are those that he sang on stage – these include *Xaley Rêbwar* in *Gilkoy Tazey Lêyl* (see Ahmadmirza 1983, p. 50).

**Figure 4** Rafiq Chalak in *Gilkoy Tazey Leyl* (Leyl's New Grave, 1956). *Source*: Barzanji 2007, p. 84.

**Figure 5** *Bûkî Jêr Dewarî Reş* (The Bride under the Black Tent, Sulaymaniyah, 1961). *Source*: Barzanji 2007, p. 100.

Music was a popular part of early theatre performances and important to the overall theatre experience. In the history of theatre in Kurdistan, theatre and music were conjoined in symbiotic union, a feature which reflected the fact that many theatre actors were also musicians or singers. We may also be right to assume that music was needed in order to attract an audience who were not familiar with theatre or were not interested in it. The Kurdish Society for Fine Arts, which was founded in 1957, and the Sulaymaniyah Theatre and Music Group, which was founded in 1969, both exemplify this collaboration between theatre artists and musicians.

Painters were another group of artists who not only painted scenery and provided stage decorations but directed and acted in several productions. Danial Qasab, Jawad Rasul Naji (1922–1975), Anwar Tovi (1925–1994), Khalid Saeid (1927–1996), and Azad Shawqi (1930–2002) were among the painters who contributed significantly to early theatrical productions in Kurdistan. Their contribution was mainly through scenic art but also involved more technical aspects such as lighting. For example, in a 1940 production he directed in Erbil, Qasab experimented with lighting by adjusting its intensity on different areas of the stage (see Pirbal 2006, p. 97). During the early 1950s, Jawad Rasul Naji, a student of Qasab's and a graduate of House of Teachers in Baghdad, directed and acted in several theatrical productions including *Othello* (p. 110). Anwar Tovi, a graduate of Baghdad House of Teachers, acted as director and set designer for a number of productions including *Othello* (1956) and *Mem û Zin* (1958) (pp. 121–2). *Pîskey Terpîr* (1957) was the first theatrical production in Iraqi Kurdistan with an elaborate stage design. This was accomplished by Khalid Saeid, who had studied scenography at the Academy of Fine Arts in Rome, along with Azad Shawqi, a graduate of Baghdad College of Fine Arts.

The fact that theatre events usually took place during the Ramadan Eid is reminiscent of traditional Kurdish storytelling which took place in coffee houses during Ramadan. Theatre replaced traditional storytelling in both providing entertainment and teaching moral lessons. It also resembled the traditional storytelling in that Ramadan provided an opportunity for the lower-class (students) to collect money from the upper and middle classes. However, unlike traditional storytelling, theatre was more concerned with serving the community than with providing mere entertainment. The elite who sought to promote theatre did not seek to defend it upon the basis of its intrinsic virtues, but instead sought to accentuate its utilitarian, didactic and moral functions. Theatre was a means to fundraise for schools and victims of natural calamities. It combined the entertainment value of the performing arts with the ability to highlight important issues that related to community development. Theatre taught the populace the values of hard work, education, women's rights and condemned the despotism of kings and feudal lords.

The Kurdish theatre between the 1930s and the late 1960s, as Kurdish critics attest, was not based on any academic understanding or knowledge of theatre or the art of playwriting (see Aziz 2013, p. 21). It was the passion of a small educated elite who aspired to spread education and bring about change in the Kurdish society. For example, Sheikh Nuri Sheikh Salih, who wrote a play in 1930, was one of the members of the Kurds' Literary Society and also a newspaper editor, activist and poet. He was related to Sheikh Mahmud Barzanji under whose reign in 1922 Salih became the editor of the Persian section of the *Bangî Kurdistan* (The Call of Kurdistan) and the editor in chief of the *Rojî Kurdistan* (The Day of Kurdistan) newspapers. The former was owned by the retired Ottoman general and Kurdish nationalist, Muhammad Pasha Kurdi, and the latter was the nationalist mouthpiece of Sheikh Mahmud himself (McDowall 2004, p. 174). The writing of dramatic stories that would be performed by school theatre groups closely aligned with the goals of nationalism, as it promoted changes necessary for the development of Kurdistan. It also clearly demonstrates the seriousness with which the elite committed themselves to the theatrical endeavour, having come to see it as a legitimate and valuable cultural tool that offered engagement with national concerns.

In his study of Irish nationalism, Hutchinson argues that cultural nationalism in Ireland was essentially an educational and a modernizing movement that sought to regenerate the nation through scientific advances. 'By education rather than by machine politics', cultural nationalists aspire to create 'an integrated, distinctive and sovereign community, capable of competing in the modern world' (Hutchinson 1994b, p. 51). Likewise, theatre in Kurdistan mainly emerged as a means through which literacy and education could be promoted in the highly illiterate city of Sulaymaniyah. It became the means through which each of these goals could be simultaneously achieved. In the 1930s, the educated elite of Sulaymaniyah started to contribute to the process of Kurdish national identity-building by supporting theatre and using it as a means to promote education for children. Although untrained in the art of playwriting, they created texts for live performance with Pîremêrd's adaptations of folktales and local history being the most notable of them.

## Pîremêrd's *Mem û Zîn* and the beginning of a distinct Kurdish theatre

In 1934, Pîremêrd wrote the oldest printed Kurdish play in Iraqi Kurdistan, *Mem û Zîn*. This play, which was inspired by the famous Kurdish epic of the same name and the folkloric narrative of *Memê Alan*, was staged in 1935 by the Kurds' Literary Society in order to raise funds for the school run by the Society. This, along with other plays written by Pîremêrd in the 1930s, marked the beginning of a distinct Kurdish theatre in Sulaymaniyah. Pîremêrd suggests that earlier performances by foreign travelling troupes in Kurdistan had a limited impact and resonance 'because their stories were not about this land and because not everyone spoke their language' (Barzanji 2007, p. 50). It was only after Kurdish youth staged *Mem û Zîn and* other Kurdish stories, Pîremêrd claims, that the Kurdish public started to show passion for theatre (p. 50).

Pîremêrd considered *Mem û Zîn*, which was performed during the four days of Ramadan Eid in 1935, to be the first instance of serious theatre in Kurdistan (Barzanji 2007, p. 50). *Mem û Zîn* was based upon an old Kurdish folktale and was performed by well-trained actor-students. It is significant that the first instance of serious theatre in Iraqi Kurdistan should be based on a folktale that inspired the seventeenth-century epic of the same name, which is also one of the most frequently quoted texts in the Kurdish nationalist literature. Written by Ahmadi Khani (1650–1707), this tragic tale of love draws on one of the best-known stories of Kurdish oral literature amongst the Kurds.[14] Khani's version differs from the oral tradition in that he had a political objective in mind when he wrote his adaptation of *Mem û Zîn*. His purpose, as his introduction to the poem clearly establishes, was to construct a literary

---

[14] Both Chyet and Hassanpour agree that *Mem û Zin* existed in the oral tradition before Khani composed his literary version.

tradition in Kurdish that would rival those of the surrounding peoples, such as the Arabs, Persians and Turks.

Khani's decision to write his epic in Kurdish represented a conscious and intended rejection of Persian, which was the dominant literary language, and clearly signalled his intention to 'raise the standing of Kurdish culture in the eyes of the Kurds' neighbours' (Bruinessen 2003, p. 42). He presented his decision to write in Kurdish in the following terms:

*Da xelq-i nebêjitin ku Ekrad*
People won't say that the Kurds,
*Bê merifet in, bê esl û binyad*
Have no knowledge and no history;
*Enwaê milel xwedan kitêb in*
That all nations have their books,
*Kurmanc-i tenê di bê hesêb in*
And only the Kurds are negligible.

Khani believed that the Kurds had the makings of a great nation but suffered from a lack of unity which prevented them from establishing their own government and having patrons who would revive the Kurdish culture and language. Likewise, Pîremêrd believed that his nation was capable of progress if only it had not fallen victim to the tyranny of the feudal landlords and the ruling regimes and had patrons who supported public education. He believed that education for the masses was the key to a better future for the Kurds and Kurdistan. The establishment of the Kurd's Literary Society was a key step towards this end.

Pîremêrd's *Mem û Zîn* was written at a time when the municipality had cut the budget of the Kurds' Literary Society (one hundred and fifteen rupees) and the directors of the society were in dire need of money to support their school. Pîremêrd's play was staged in order to raise funds for the society during this difficult time (Barzanji 2007, p. 44). The income of the performance was later published in detail in *Jiyan* newspaper under the title 'We Are Accountable to the Nation', again illustrating the fact that for Pîremêrd and other intellectuals who had formed the Society, the Kurds were already a nation. Pîremêrd therefore viewed *Mem û Zîn* as a national work which served the interests of the nation by both celebrating its cultural heritage and providing financial support for the education of children. Pîremêrd had, prior to the staging of the play, written: 'Anyone who declines this invitation (to attend the performance) lacks national commitment' (cited in Barzanji 2007, p. 41).

Strohmeier stresses that Khani's *Mem û Zîn* constituted the backbone that Kurds are a nation capable of attaining a high level of civilization and possess a language which can yield great literature (Strohmeier 2003, p. 27). Whereas Khani viewed writing a *mathnawi*[15] in Kurdish as a form of *bid'et* (dissent) against tradition (Hassanpour 1992, pp. 86–8), Pîremêrd viewed writing plays in Kurdish as a *bid'et* which simultaneously promoted theatre in Kurdistan and supported public education. In the absence of a patron, and like his predecessor, he sought to raise the standing of Kurdish culture, and in so doing, strengthen claims to national identity and liberty. Pîremêrd's *Mem û Zîn* was a plea for public education that sought to contribute to the development of Kurdistan. As attested to by Pîremêrd, the public came and paid to witness the performance of *Mem û Zîn* and invested in it heart and soul (Barzanji 2007, p. 43), thus making it one of the first successful plays that was performed in Kurdistan. According to Pîremêrd's report in *Jiyan*, during a four-day run, *Mem û Zîn* sold 328 tickets of different values: 180 thirty-fils tickets, 103 fifty-fils tickets, 33 hundred-fils tickets and 12 two-hundred-and-fifty-fils tickets (p. 51). Its success clearly demonstrated that Kurdish language could be the medium of theatre, just as Khani's *Mem û Zîn* had demonstrated that Kurdish could be the medium of *mathnawi*.

Pîremêrd's writings in *Jiyan* also shed light on the condition of the early Kurdish stage actors and demonstrates how the establishment of the *Zanistî* School contributed to the rise of theatre in Kurdistan. 'We are proud', Pîremêrd writes, 'that these young boys, the children of *Zanistî*, who performed this art, were among the illiterate who a few years ago were working in bakeries and groceries in the bazaar. Now, thank God, they write their own speeches and songs for the stage and even correct the original play by Pîremêrd' (Barzanji 2007, p. 43). While the young actors were unschooled in drama and Pîremêrd was similarly inexperienced in drama criticism, his celebration of this art form and praise for the actors, along with the enthusiasm of his reports, clearly renders the honest

---

[15] Long narrative poems that consist of many distichs, each with its own rhyme.

excitement of a sensitive viewer who sees, for the first time, the possibility of creating a national drama.

Pîremêrd continued to draw on folktales and the history of the region as material for his plays. In doing so, he drew on his knowledge of the Kurdish folktales which he had heard as a child. He himself notes that when writing the story of *Dwanze Swarey Merîwan* (The Twelve Riders of Mariwan), he had no sources or documents to base his story upon apart from what he remembered from his father's narration of the old *beyt* (cited in Rasul 2010, p. 30). His historical plays include *Mehmûd Aqay Şêwekel* (Mahmud Agha Shewakal, 1936), which he printed in 1942 under the title 'A True Historical Play Which Has Happened in Our Own Country' (Malakarim 2009), and *Şerîf Hemewend* (Sharif Hamawand, 1936). The former is about the enlightened ruler of Sharbazher[16] who is betrayed by other Kurdish tribal leaders and ultimately killed by the Ottoman governor of Sulaymaniyah who is suspicious of the relations between the Kurds of Sharbazher and Baneh, a Kurdish town in Persian territories. The latter play is based on the historical tale of the title character, a fearless and renowned warrior of the Hamawand family, who wages war against the mighty Ottoman Empire for the control of the Baban principality in the aftermath of the Babans' fall (Amin 2008, pp. 15–16). This reckless but heroic action ultimately leads to his death. *Şerîf Hemewend* was staged in 1936, again partly to raise money for Kurdish schools.[17] It was also reportedly banned at the time when it was staged (p. 29), which clearly demonstrates the impact that Kurdish theatre could make, even in its early years, and also reiterates how the public representation of a national Kurdish hero who rebelled against the central authority could create significant unease within the Iraqi government.

Pîremêrd's plays serve to define the national community by reminding it of its history, heroes of the past and their noble ideas for the development of the nation. This is an important feature of cultural nationalism which, as Hutchinson (1987) observes, seeks to inspire communities to higher stages of development by invoking their past and providing 'authentic' national models

---

[16] A district in Sulaymaniyah Governorate.
[17] Izzeddin Mustafa Rasul notes that, in contrast to *Mem û Zîn* and *Mehmûd Aqay Şêwekel*, no printed copies of this play exist.

of progress. Much in the same way, Pîremêrd's plays revived national histories of local Kurdish rulers and heroes as part of a larger process of the moral regeneration of the national community.

In *Mehmûd Aqay Şêwekel*, the patriotic Mahmud Agha believes the main reason behind the underdevelopment of Kurdistan to be political instability and internal wars. In his view, the heads of great families are too self-centred to think of the future of their nation and what they can do to contribute to its development. It is the pettiness and greed of these families that ultimately results in Mahmud Agha's death. The play's preface makes it clear that Pîremêrd intended his play to be read in directly political terms. He sets out six lessons which are inherent to the play, one of which is that 'greed and schism within a nation leads to the loss of their great men' (Malakarim 2009, p. 55). However, despite his call for Kurdish unity, Pîremêrd makes it clear that he is not calling for Kurdish independence. In the final scene of the play, Mahmud Agha is poisoned by the Ottoman governor of Sulaymaniyah and is on the verge of death; however, he advises his friends not to take action against the governor because 'one cannot serve the [Kurdish] nation without the support of the [central] government' (p. 90).

While this conclusion may show a clear preference for cultural (as opposed to political) nationalism, it would be a mistake to categorize Pîremêrd and other members of the elite simply as cultural nationalists: the Kurdish elite who initiated nationalist cultural activities in Iraqi Kurdistan had already directly participated in the political and cultural nationalist movement in Turkey. The Iraqi-Kurdish elite who engaged in promoting theatre, including Sheikh Nuri Sheikh Salih and Pîremêrd, were already, by virtue of their association with Sheikh Said and Sheikh Mahmud, implicated in politics. Therefore, one can conclude that in early twentieth-century Iraqi Kurdistan, cultural and political nationalisms overlapped to the point where they appeared to be almost synonymous.

## Early Kurdish theatre and education for women

The Kurdish historian, Muhammad Amin Zaki Beg, who was the then minister of public works and transportation, played a central role in founding the first school for girls in Sulaymaniyah in 1926 (Barzanji 2007, p. 22). Four years later, the school teachers, Gozida Khanim Yamulki and Fatima Muhyuddin, having been inspired by the boys' school and their theatrical performances, wrote a play for their students that was entitled *Însan Ewe Eyçinê Ewe Edirwêtewe* (One Reaps What One Sows) (p. 26). They also asked the Kurdish poet Sheikh Nuri Sheikh Salih (1896–1958) to write a play for them in verse (p. 26). The play by Yamulki and Muhyuddin emphasized the importance of education for girls and therefore, by being directed towards girls rather than boys, offered an important variation upon a theme that had been advanced by *Îlm û Cehl* a few years prior (pp. 27–8). Meanwhile Sheikh Salih's play, which was entitled *Dayk* (Mother), sharply criticized the beliefs and habits that resulted from women's lack of education and illiteracy. Both plays were performed by students in the school for three days to an all-female audience (Pirbal 2001, p. 74). These advances in public education were welcomed and supported by the Kurdish elite who steadfastly advocated for women's rights and participation in society through their theatrical productions.

For a long time the two performances mentioned above seem to have been the only instances of female acting in Kurdistan; a fact that had resulted in male cross-dressing in early Kurdish theatre. During early theatre events, the schoolboys and their teachers took on both male and female roles, as it would have been a social disgrace for girls to flaunt themselves in the arena of public performance. During the 1935 production of *Mem û Zîn*, the role of Zin was played by a male actor named Sheikh Nuri Sheikh Jalal, who had assumed female roles in several performances. His cross-gender acting was not without difficulties as, like many other patriarchal societies, the Kurdish society has a rigid gender system which looks down on men who show feminine traits. Sheikh Jalal and the actor who assumed the role of Zin's maid were subject to scorn and humiliation and were even refused female costumes (Barzanji 2007, p. 44).

Pîremêrd's witty remark about cross-gender acting is a clear indication of the difficulties that were encountered in finding suitable male and female actors who would perform female roles. Writing about *Serbazî Aza* in 1935, he stated: 'Nazdar, the hero's fiancée was not *nazdar* (beautiful) at all! Even so, I admire and thank him for taking on this role as this noble craft is still seen as a disgrace (*neng*)' (Pirbal 2001, pp. 108–9; see Figure 6). This statement also serves to show that male acting itself was held in very low esteem by society at the time.

**Figure 6** *Serbazî Aza* (1935). *Source*: Barzanji 2007, p. 38.

As part of his nationalist project, Pîremêrd fought outmoded traditions, especially those that hindered the participation of women in public spaces. He was a staunch critic of outmoded customs and beliefs in the Kurdish society which had, for long, hindered women's freedom and participation in public spheres, including theatre. Pîremêrd advocated education for women by writing 'if the fair sex is recognized as equal to man and if women work hard for their education they won't fall short of men' (Ashna 2009, p. 26). He also criticized the forced and arranged marriages of girls by stressing that choice (of who to marry) was one of the preconditions of a healthy marriage (pp. 26–8) and even endorsed punishing fathers who forced their girls to get married (p. 27).

He had voiced feminist sentiment in his play *Mem û Zîn* where, in the final scene, Zin's heart-wrenching and impassioned monologue over Mam's dead body concludes with a plea for an end to the forced marriage of girls; a practice that was common in Kurdistan at the time. The concluding lines of the monologue read,

> *Ax bo dengxoşê le jûr serînman*
>
> How I wish there was someone who would sing at our grave
>
> *Be beytî kurdî bida telqînman*
>
> A Kurdish beyt to mourn us

*Bilê ax dilî dilxwaz meşkênin*

And say 'don't break the lovers' hearts

*Be zoremilî kiçan memrênin*

And don't force the girls to their demise.' (Pîremêrd 1968, p. 31)

Pîremêrd's concern for women's rights found expression in his next play, *Mehmûd Aqay Şêwekel*. While this play's plot revolves around Mahmud Agha, the forced marriage of girls and their lack of education are important themes within the play. In speaking through Parichihra, the female character expected to commit to Mahmud Agha in an arranged marriage, Pîremêrd complains: 'They think women are created for the pleasure of boys who lust after them like they are sweets and make them feel unsafe. I wish God hadn't created women or I was an illiterate girl, without any noble thought or feeling, whose mind was nurtured by old wives' tales' (Malakarim 2009, p. 67). Parichihra's commitment to women's rights extends beyond arranged marriages to engage women's lack of education and even her aspiration to play *oud* and sing. She is also critical of outmoded traditions in Kurdish society and extends strong criticism towards 'village' women who even refrain from calling their husbands by their first names and harass an enlightened girl who considers herself equal to her husband (p. 74).

According to Pîremêrd, the education of women in Kurdistan had traditionally been achieved through Qur'an recitations at home – this meant that they were not required to leave their homes and were predisposed to think and act in religious terms. They were not taught how to read or write, as this prevented them from reading the boys' love letters and responding to them. If they wore make-up, they were accused of immorality. Their confinement to their homes and their lack of education, Pîremêrd believed, contributed to poor parenting and the bad upbringing of their sons (Ashna 2009, p. 26). In expressing his exasperation with these outdated customs and practices, he wished 'for an educated class of girls and women who raise the sort of children who can serve their nation and homeland' (p. 26).[18]

---

[18] When the first school for girls was opened in Sulaymaniyah, it was celebrated as a great step forward in the progress of the Kurdish 'nation'. One year after the foundation of the school, one of the students wrote an open letter to 'our fathers and brothers' in which she asserted that if the importance of education for girls had been appreciated at an earlier point, oppression would not be an ongoing concern because 'there would have been thousands of women and men who would sacrifice themselves for their homeland and serve the nation and its sciences' (Barzanji 2007, p. 25).

## Theatre as a national fundraising tool

Kurdish theatre, which had begun partly as a means to support schools, continued to serve the immediate needs of the community when an earthquake struck the town of Penjwin in 1946. In response, a number of theatre artists in Sulaymaniyah staged a translation of the Arabic play *Fī Sabīl it-Tāj* (For the Homeland; Figure 7) with the intention of raising money for the victims of the earthquake. The play raised two thousand dinars in Sulaymaniyah and was followed by an operetta that was based on Goran's *Gulî Xwênawî* (Blood Red Rose). The operetta, which Thomas Bois compared to Shelley's *Ode to the Skylark* (Jwaideh 2006, p. 25), depicts a conversation between a boy and a girl (whose role was played by a male actor). The girl dares her lover to pick red and yellow flowers for her from the king's garden, which is surrounded by enemy forces. The boy risks his life only to find yellow flowers in the garden. He returns to his beloved who disdains him for having failed to bring her red flowers. The boy pulls down his collar and shows a gun wound to his shocked lover and asks if she will accept the redness of his blood instead. These two plays were also performed in the city of Erbil and thus became the first Kurdish plays to go on the road in Iraqi Kurdistan. The participants in these plays were celebrated in a poem by Pîremêrd who wrote,

> *Êsta emane hatûne jêr balî êmewe*
> Now these [survivors] have come under our protection
> *Hawxwênekan xoyan exene malî êmewe*
> Our flesh and blood take refuge in our homes
> *Lawan be jarê kewtûne çoş û xroşewe*
> The youth have stirred up
> *Temsîl û barbûyane be hewl û peroşewe*
> They stage plays with passion
> *Awatekem ebînim ewa hate dî be çaw*
> I see my dream has come true
> *Destey koran be meş'elî firyawe kewtne naw*
> The young men carry the torch of altruism. (Ashna 2009, p. 136)

**Figure 7** *Le Rêy Niştimanda* (1946). *Source*: Barzanji 2007, p. 58.

## Theatre after the Second World War

When the Second World War broke out, cultural life in Kurdistan deteriorated to the point of near extinction. Theatre only reappeared in 1945, as the War moved towards its concluding phases. Interestingly, the first play that was staged in 1945 was an adaptation of Khani's *Mem û Zîn*. While this performance is not documented, it is not difficult to understand why this old Kurdish masterpiece was the first choice for the stage. The Second World War had revived and intensified Kurdish nationalist activity (Jwaideh 2006, p. 272). The growth of a Kurdish town population whose commitment to nationalist values and ideas superseded tribal loyalties, along with the emergence of a Kurdish intelligentsia based mainly in Baghdad and Sulaymaniyah, established the basis for the growth of a national consciousness.

Mulla Mustafa Barzani (1903–1979), whose attacks on government forces had begun in 1943, had, within two years, established himself as the champion of Kurdish people and the embodiment of their cause (Jwaideh, p. 231). He demanded the creation of an all-Kurdish province run by Kurdish officials and the adoption of Kurdish as an official language. He allied with the new left-leaning political parties that had emerged in the cities of Sulaymaniyah and

Erbil. The Kurdish *Hîwa* (Hope) Party, which had initially been formed in 1935, was resurrected in order to support Barzani's rebellion. The programme that the party adopted during its first meeting clearly demonstrated that the unity of Kurdish tribes was still the primary concern for Kurdish nationalists who sought to form an autonomous Kurdish state (p. 239). The revival of Khani's *Mem û Zîn* was a reassertion of Kurdish national heritage and the legitimacy of Kurdish political demands. In incorporating Khani's national and political discourse, the play could also echo Khani's call for the Kurdish tribes to unify and fight against the oppressive foreign yoke.

## Theatre and the rise of leftist-nationalist sentiments

In the aftermath of the Second World War, the Kurdish political leadership underwent a fundamental change. While Kurds' loyalties previously resided with their family, tribe or religious sheikh, they now aligned with the nation, political party and its leaders. As political parties and intellectual cadres began to become more prominent, demands were no longer focused upon the local level, but were instead 'scaled up' to focus upon autonomy, federation or self-determination. The new leaders were urbanized professional intellectuals (although they were sometimes obliged to share power with traditional leaders). As urbanization progressed, social movements (artists, peasants, workers, women, students and teachers) began to grow. Their demands were increasingly articulated within the vernacular of modernization and therefore focused upon priorities such as land reform, women's rights and social welfare programmes.

The first generation of secular, educated and urban Kurds, who hoped for a degree of independence, began to emerge during the 1930s. In the absence of a Kurdish party, many of these young nationalists joined the Iraqi Communist Party (ICP); others joined *Al-Ahli*, which sought social reform for urban and rural workers (McDowall 2004, p. 288). In Sulaymaniyah, left-leaning Kurdish nationalist groups, including *Komeley Birayetî* (Brotherhood Society, 1937) and *Darkar* (Woodcutters, 1937), began to emerge. *Hîwa* the nationalist party which emerged from *Darkar*, was formed in Kirkuk in 1940. Led by Rafiq Hilmi, *Hîwa* brought together left-leaning intellectuals who supported Barzani's revolt against the Iraqi government and the Iranian

Kurdish nationalists in Mahabad. *Hiwa* dissolved in the aftermath of Barzani's exile, establishing the basis for *Şoriş* (Revolution) and *Rizgarî Kurd* (Kurdish Liberation) to emerge in 1945. The latter's nationalist and leftist objectives were clearly stated in its national manifesto, in which it instituted the unification and liberation of Greater Kurdistan while taking the opportunity to clarify its dislike of imperialist and reactionary governments (Jwaideh 2006, p. 241).

The Communists also played a role in leading and guiding peasant uprisings. Since the British Mandate and Hashemite rule, feudal landlords and notables had grown in strength. Due to the questionable loyalty of the army, which was 'led increasingly by officers of middle or lower middle class origin with little affection for the monarchy' (McDowall 2004, p. 297), the regime was forced to collaborate with tribal chiefs (*aghas*) in order to ensure the security of Kurdish countryside. Landed gentry were consequently well represented in parties and parliament. The abject rural poverty that resulted from corruption and changing social circumstances culminated in the first peasant rising in Sulaymaniyah countryside in 1947 (pp. 297–300).

The mistreatment of the peasantry by the *agha* class provoked solidarity demonstrations in Sulaymaniyah which had become the main centre of communist activity in Iraq as the younger generation increasingly oriented towards communist ideas (p. 298). Jwaideh explains the different factors which contributed to Sulaymaniyah's rise as a centre of communist activities:

> Sulaymaniyah, for many years a citadel of Kurdish nationalism, had a long tradition of opposition to Baghdad. This strongly developed anti-government sentiment, coupled with the fact that Sulaymaniya was more literate than any other Kurdish center, made it a promising field for communist proselytization . . . Furthermore . . . Sulaymaniya was conveniently located near an international frontier. Contacts with Communists in Iran and beyond were easy and unhampered. (Jwaideh 2006, p. 271)

The plays that were performed during 1946 clearly attest to the leftist-nationalist sentiments that were in the ascendancy within Iraq at the time. Anti-imperialist and nationalist themes predominated in *Manga* (The Cow) and *Cwamêrî Kafir* (The Infidel's Bravery). The latter, which addressed the workers' struggle against feudal lords, was performed by Sulaymaniyah students in Penjwin in 1946 (Barzanji 2007, p. 59). *Manga* addressed meetings between the Allies

(UK, France, the United States and Soviet Union) in the aftermath of the war, in which they decided upon the fate of the nations. Barzanji suggests that the play was performed in Arabic in order to appeal to the Arab population of the town; except, it concluded with Goran's *Demî Raperîne* (It Is the Time of Uprising), his famous patriotic poem which became the anthem of revolution by calling on Kurds to unite and rise up to claim their right to independence (p. 59). The poem, which has been a key component of the musical repertoire of Kurdish revolutionaries reads,

> *Demî raperîne demî raperîn,*
>
> Now is the time to rise up;
>
> *Hetakey be sistî w be pestî bijîn?*
>
> To end this life of weakness and servitude.
>
> *Pelamarê, ey kurd, ereq riştinê*
>
> Kurds, chanrge forward,
>
> *Le dil kirmî nakokî derkirdinê*
>
> Break free from the scourge of disunity.
>
> *Be yek bûne gişt, pitew bûnî pişt;*
>
> Come together as one;
>
> *Be yek bûn ebê, gelit pêşkewê*
>
> Only united can your nation progress. (Malakarim, 1980, pp. 403–4)

By the late 1940s, Sulaymaniyah had become a hotbed of dissent, in which both Kurdish communism and nationalism appeared as predominant ideological influences. In 1946, in a significant event within the development of the Kurdish political system, the Kurdish Democratic Party (KDP) was established. In operating under the leadership of Ibrahim Ahmad, a leftist intellectual, KDP adopted a leftist programme and in 1953 called for agricultural reform and the recognition of peasants' and workers' rights. The party enjoyed significant support among students and intellectuals, but it was less popular among tribal leaders (Farouk-Sluglett and Sluglett 2001, p. 30). The leftist KDP grew as economic conditions deteriorated. As oil wealth increased over the 1950s, peasant unemployment and landlord wealth grew in roughly equal proportion, with the consequence that class divisions became increasingly pronounced.

Growing support for the KDP and the communists within rural regions was one symptom of this general development (McDowall 2004, p. 299).

In January 1948, the Anglo-Iraqi Treaty of Portsmouth, which effectively made Iraq a British protectorate, sparked *al-Wathba*, a massive urban uprising led by students in Baghdad. Although the Portsmouth Treaty was annulled by the king of Iraq, the *al-Wathba* revolt was violently crushed by the government. The police fired onto the crowd of demonstrators and killed hundreds, and many communist leaders were imprisoned. Kurdistan was not unaffected by these political developments in Baghdad. It was in this context that the leadership of the Kurdish masses gradually passed from the feudal lords, sheikhs and older nationalists to the intelligentsia, who used theatre, as one among a number of devices, to promote their leftist ideals.

It should be noted that members of political parties saw theatre as an important means to spread their party doctrines and therefore encouraged theatrical performances and even directed or participated in them. Among those political activists were Jalal Talabani (1933–2017), Khalid Saeid (1934–1978), Rostam Hawezi (1913–1999), Osman Awni (1914–1992) and Mustafa Khoshnaw (1912–1947) (Hamadbeg 2007, p. 29). More often than not, the plays that were staged by these activists had political and revolutionary messages. For example, *Kawey Asinger* was performed during the Newroz celebrations of 1941, 1943, 1945, 1947 and 1948 in Koya.[19] The 1948 Newroz celebrations were the most elaborate as the communists (*Hizb al-Taharrur al-Watani*) and the KDP both planned several events including theatrical performances of *Kawey Asinger* which was staged by both parties (Pirbal 2001, pp. 88–9). A large number of guests from across Iraqi Kurdistan attended these Newroz events in Koya including the poet Abdullah Goran whose operetta, *Blood Red Rose* was staged by Koya students. One of those students, Jalal Talabani, played the role of Kawa's son in KDP's production of *Kawey Asinger* (Hamadbeg 2007, p. 34).

The Newroz and the legend of Kawa both exemplify how the Kurdish myth of origin has become a key element of the Kurdish national identity and an essential component of Kurdish nation-building projects (Bozarsalan 2003;

---

[19] The 1941 play was co-authored by poets Awni and Hawezi who were members of *Tîpî Şanoy Millî Koye* (Koya's National Theatre Group). Formed officially in 1952, this group rehearsed and staged their plays in a casino and therefore were known in Kurdistan as The Youths of Saeidi Mela Ahmad's Casino (*Tîpî Şanoy Lawanî Gazînoy Seîdî Mela Ehmed*) (Ahmadbeg 2007).

Hirschler 2001). Celebrated by several nations across the Middle East, Newroz has been reconstructed by Kurdish nationalists to stand for the victory of the oppressed over the oppressor and thus symbolize the contemporary nationalist movement. What was an ancient festival has therefore been transformed into an influential and modern ideological tool in the political arena, with a view to assisting the construction of Kurdish identity (Aydin 2014).[20] In Iraq the theatre groups played an important role in constructing the myth of origin and resistance around the Newroz festival and the legend of Kawa by utilizing them as symbolic representations of Kurdish unity against foreign dictatorship. In Koya, *Kawey Asinger* was staged every year throughout the 1950s by *Tîpî Şanoy Lawan û Qutabiyanî Koye* (Koya Youths and Students' Theatre Group) (Hamadbeg 2007, p. 38). This represented a continuation of the springtime folk festival which, as explained in Chapter 1, was traditionally held in the villages of Iraqi Kurdistan, with amateur actors performing the legend of Kawa.

The government swiftly clamped down on theatre, after recognizing the potential for this art form to propagate subversive ideas and sentiments. May 1948 saw the first instance of the interruption of a Kurdish theatre performance and the arrest of its participants by government forces. The play called *Têkoşanî Rencberan* (The Toilers' Struggle), told the tale of a group of working-class men who rebelled against the monarchy. This play, which went on stage twice a day for fifteen days,[21] was stopped on the last day by government forces who arrested some of the participants including the director of the play, Rauf Yahya (Barzanji 2007, p. 61). Tanya states that *Têkoşanî Rencberan* was based on a short story by Ibrahim Ahmad entitled *Menûçer* (Manuchar) which depicted the struggle of poor farmers in Iraqi Kurdistan against their feudal masters and the Iraqi monarchy (Tanya 1985, p. 59). *Menûçer* expresses this point by engaging with a wider national anxiety, in which class struggle overlapped with the struggle for national independence (Amin and Danish 2009, p. 50).[22]

---

[20] The myth of Newroz and the legend of Kawa had also contributed significantly to the Kurdish nationalist movement in Turkey, where Kurdistan Workers' Party (PKK) thinkers promoted shared myths of common ancestry, territory and history with the intention of countering Ankara's assimilationist policies, which had been pursued over the course of decades.
[21] According to Tanya, the play was staged for nine days.
[22] During the 1940s and 1950s, this overlap was a key component of the opposition movement as almost all manifestations of opposition by organized labour during this period were directed against British-owned and British-controlled concerns (Farouk-Sluglett and Sluglett 2001, p. 41).

Government clampdown failed to stop theatre's engagement with politics. This is most evident in Koya where, on the day of Iraqi Parliamentary election on 17 January 1953, *Tîpî Şanoy Mîllî Koye* (Koya's National Theatre Group) staged *Election*, a play whose lead actor, dressed in the Islamic white burial shroud (*kafan*), along with other actors and spectators, started marching through the streets after the performance. The crowd, which were joined by the women of Koya, protested the election by shouting slogans, throwing stones, taking down the Iraqi flag from government buildings and breaking the ballot boxes (Hamadbeg 2007, p. 37).

The theme of struggle against injustice is a thread that runs through numerous plays of the 1950s, which include *Kilolan* (Les Misérables, 1952), whose success resulted in its English film version being shown in the local cinema, and *Brûske w Şîrîn* (Bruska and Shirin, 1954), which depicted the love of a peasant boy for the daughter of a despotic landlord (Barzanji 2007, pp. 62–3, 66–8). *Elî Efenî* (Ali Efendi, 1958), which engaged the corruption of rich landlords who lacked principles or moral scruples, offered a further variation upon this general theme.

The anti-feudal sentiment found a strong advocate in Shakir Fattah (1914–1988), who was the governor of Chamchamal in the late 1940s. Fattah sought to revive the city's theatrical tradition by staging plays such as *Mem û Zîn*, *Niwîşte w Cadû* (The Spell and the Magic,1948), *Minim Mîkrofon* (It's Me, Microphone, 1949) and *Gulî Xwênawî* (Blood Red Rose, 1952). It is interesting to note that, when he was in Akre, Fattah had to stage *Mem û Zîn* in Arabic because the locals could not fully understand the Sorani dialect. Fattah continued to promote Kurdish theatre in Akre where he revived the local theatre group and staged several plays between 1955 and 1956. Most of Fattah's plays attacked feudal lords and conveyed narratives of suffering and oppression. This required considerable courage because, as Tanya notes, at the time, 'even speaking unfavourably about the feudal landlords was punishable; let alone criticizing them publicly on a theatre stage' (1985, pp. 60–1).

When the plays did not attack the landlords directly they would expose the ills of the society caused by poverty and the lack of education. *Kar Kirdinî Bekelk* (Fruitful Endeavor, 1952) and *Afret û Niwîşte* (Women and Magic, 1956), two plays whose texts have survived, clearly convey the educated elites' frustration at the underdeveloped state of Kurdish society, along with the miseries that the lack of education had inflicted upon the masses. In *Kar Kirdinî Bekelk,* a poor village is plagued by a disease which is caused by inadequate hygiene standards. The local mullah, who is a quack doctor, takes advantage of the situation by trading his pills in exchange for his poor patients' chickens or calves. His mendacity is exposed when a doctor is sent to the village who cures the disease and tells the villagers to burn the piles of cow dung and manage the waste water to prevent the spread of infections. *Afret û Niwişte* resembles *Kar Kirdinî Bekelk* in its criticism of prevalent superstitions, along with the tendency for local people to trust clergies with important matters in their lives. Not long ago, Muslim clergies used to write hexes, love charms and spells for a fee such as a goat. In this play the belief in a cunning mullah's magical abilities leads to three women's comic humiliation at the end of the play. Gelas, Hama Wafani's wife, who desperately wants a child, and her two friends, Galawej and Askol, who both have domestic problems, are visited by the local mullah at Gelas's home. The Mullah asks them to put their heads in three pots and be quiet while he writes their spells. He then steals their gold and departs. Hama Wafani returns home and shocked at the sight of the women, with their heads in pots, yells at them and swears to divorce Gelas if she does not come to her senses and renounce such superstitious practices.

## Kurdish Society for Fine Arts (1957–63) and the first female actors

In the 1950s, an increasing number of European plays which had been adapted into Arabic started to make their impression on the Kurdish stage. These plays, which were mainly social satires, included Nikolai Gogol's *The Government Inspector* (*Cinabî Mufetiş*, 1954), Shakespeare's *Othello* (*Oteyl*, 1956) and *The Merchant of Venice* (*Bazerganî Vînîsîa*, 1956) and Molière's *L'Avare* (*Pîskey Terpîr*, 1956). Income from these and (other plays), were, as per standard practice, distributed among students from low-income families.

In 1847, the Lebanese Marun al-Naqqash (1817–1855), had written and produced the first play in Arabic entitled *al-Bakhil* (The Miser), which was an adaptation of Molière's *L'Avare* (Badawi 1988, p. 43). *Pîskey Terpîr*, the Kurdish adaptation of *al-Bakhil* that was directed by Rafiq Chalak in 1957, played an important role in bringing the public closer to theatre, cultivating sympathy for actors and making Chalak's charismatic character and stage presence known to a larger audience. Although *Pîskey Terpîr* was based on a foreign play, it was Kurdified to the extent that 'if Molière was brought to life and witnessed the play he would fail to recognise it as his own' (Bekas 2008, p. 9).

Rafiq Chalak, who was born in Sulaymaniyah in 1923, graduated from House of Teachers in 1941. When the Allies established a radio station in Jaffa, Palestine, during the Second World War, Chalak, along with Goran, moved there to present a Kurdish-language programme. During his time there, Chalak met several Arab artists including the Egyptians Youssef Wahbi and Bishara Wakim whose works contributed immensely to his understanding of acting, directing, scene design, make-up design and other areas of theatre production. Upon returning to Iraq in 1945, he joined the Baghdad Kurdish Radio. However, he was expelled after only one month when he wrote a revolutionary piece called *China's Song of Freedom*. He returned to Sulaymaniyah where he became a teacher. He was expelled again – in this instance due to a public speech he made in 1947, when the leaders of the Republic of Mahabad were executed. He returned to Baghdad Kurdish Radio in 1950 and continued to work there until 1956. During this period, he presented several Kurdish radio plays which established his reputation as a great artistic figure in Kurdistan.

It was Chalak's production of *Pîskey Terpîr* that turned Chalak into a popular public figure in Kurdistan. According to Sherko Bekas, who had been made prompter by Chalak during the production of *Pîskey Terpîr*, he usually diverged from the text of the plays and extended his dialogues from two paragraphs to two pages! He was an eloquent speaker, was never short for words and was possessed of an agile body and a sharp mind. Having experienced defeat in the political realm, he devoted his life to acting, writing and singing (Bekas 2008). Bekas describes Chalak's impact upon the Kurdish culture during the 1950s and 1960s in the following terms:

> Before Rafiq Chalak, theatre was not alive, it was weak and cold. Rafiq Chalak was the first to warm it up. Also, it was him whose voice in Baghdad radio introduced the love of drama into every house in Kurdistan in the 1950s when people waited impatiently to hear his voice . . . We cannot talk about Kurdish radio plays and poetry recitations and presenters of those times without mentioning Rafiq Chalak. Neither can we talk about Kurdish

music or journalism. He covers twenty-four years of our theatre history. He was the pathbreaker at a time when there was no cultural movement or support for such movements in this land. (KNN TV's Special Programme on Rafiq Chalak)

In 1957, following the success of *Pîskey Terpîr*, Chalak, along with his friends, founded the first Kurdish Society for Fine Arts (1957–63) which he himself chaired. This was the first society of its kind in Kurdistan. It was made up of three groups of actors, painters and musicians. Among the members were the musicians of *Tîpî Mosîqay Mewlewî* (Mawlawi Music Group), painters Azad Shawqi and Khalid Saeid, and actors Nuri Washti, Rauf Yahya, Taha Khalil, Kawa Ahmadmirza, and Sherko Bekas, among others (Ahmadmirza 2011, p. 22). In 1957, the Society held musical and theatrical fundraising events in Sulaymaniyah, Erbil and Koya to help the victims of flood in Sulaymaniyah

**Figure 8** Actors Taha Khalil, Salah Muhamad Jamil and Fuad Omar with artists Khalid Saeid and Azad Shawqi in dressing room for *Pîskey Terprîr* (1956). *Source*: Barzanji 2007, p. 69.

(Tanya 1985, p. 67). The success of the events indicates, once again, the public's support for Kurdish art, especially when it served national interests.

The theatre movement established by Rafiq Chalak and others developed further when the Society for Fine Arts called upon women to join the theatre. In 1958, the Society successfully staged the classic tale of *Mem û Zîn* and notably, for the first time, an actress assumed the role of the heroine. Prior to each performance, Golzar Omar Tawfiq, who played Zin, would address the audience members and read from a paper – which had ironically been written for her by a man – that contained various insights upon women and theatre. She challenged the assumption that actresses were lacking in moral standards and conduct. In portraying Zin, a folkloric Kurdish character, she demonstrated the nobility of her profession by honouring Kurdish tradition and cultural heritage. Her appearance on stage was welcomed by the Kurdish elite who celebrated the performance upon the grounds that it simultaneously revived a national heritage and introduced women to acting (Barzanji 2007, p. 96).

Narmin Nakam's role in a stage performance entitled *Tawanî Çî Bû* (For What Crime Was She Punished?) in 1958 provided another instance of women's

**Figure 9** *Mem û Zîn* (1958). *Source*: kurdipedia.org.

participation in Kurdish theatre. The play depicts the life of Halo, a young man who is expelled from school as a result of his political activism. He then has to join the army and leave his hometown where his lover Shawbo lives. Shawbo marries an army officer and by chance they move to the same town where Halo is serving. Halo and Shawbo meet and engage in a conversation about their lives. When Shawbo's husband witnesses this, he immediately draws his gun and shoots her dead. The title of the play clearly demonstrates that *Tawanî Çî Bû* was another attempt by Kurdish theatre artists to attack the rigid patriarchy in Kurdish society which senselessly justified violence against women and inhibited their active participation in society in general and in theatre in particular. Nakam's body language in the photos from her performances in both *Tawanî Çî Bû* and *Emrekey Begim* (My Lord's Command) clearly depict the submissiveness of her character while the body language of the male characters in the same photos portrays their authority, dominance and even hostility (see Figures 10 and 11).

The records show that Narmin and Golzar were not the only female actors in Kurdistan in the 1950s. Haji mentions the names of other actresses in different Kurdish towns, who included Najati Mahwi in Sulaymaniyah, Pakiza

**Figure 10** Narmin Nakam in *Tawanî Çî Bû* (1958). *Source*: Barzanji 2007, p. 87.

**Figure 11** Narmin Nakam in *Emrekey Begim* (1958). *Source*: Şano, no. 14, 2009.

and Shukriya in Rowanduz, Suheyla and Nasrin in Erbil, Farida and Nazanin in Kirkuk and Mari in Koya (Haji 1989, p. 97).

Although women actors gradually stepped onto the stage over the course of the late 1950s, the stigma associated with female acting remained strong even a decade later. Omar Ali Amin's account of his group's difficulties in finding, or rather keeping, female actors clearly attests to this (Amin and Danish 2009, p. 51). In 1969, the more relaxed political atmosphere enabled theatre groups such as *Tîpî Nwandin û Mosîqay Silêmanî* (Sulaymaniyah Acting and Music Group) to appear. This group staged a play entitled *Serînî Badarî* (A Pillow for Joints Pain) in which a girl named Runak Hama Rashid participated. According to Ali Amin, Runak's parents clearly expressed their unhappiness with their daughter's decision to appear on stage. The group therefore had to, in a manner which clearly recalled the practice of asking for a girl's hand for marriage, approach Runak's parents and ask for their permission before she could perform in the play (p. 51). Even then, her mother would always accompany her to the theatre and even to other cities where the group performed. Perhaps unsurprisingly, this was Runak's only acting experience as she gave up the profession entirely soon after (p. 51). These social restrictions against women's participation meant that cross-gender casting in Kurdish theatre continued up until the early 1970s. Omar Chawshin is the actor who is perhaps most widely recognized for his cross-gender roles in the 1960s and

1970s, with memorable performances both on stage and on TV such as in the TV drama, *Mame Xeme*, produced in 1971 for Kirkuk TV.[23]

## The 14 July Revolution and Kurdish theatre after Qasim

In 1958, a coup put an end to the Hashemite monarchy which had ruled Iraq since its creation in the early 1920s. This coup followed the Egyptian Revolution of 1952 which ended the British occupation of the country and inflamed Arab nationalist and anti-imperialist sentiments across the Middle East. The Hashemite monarchy, which was seen as the stooge of British imperialism, was overthrown by Brigadier Abdulkarim Qasim and his fellow Free Officers.

The Republic of Iraq was established promising a better future for Kurds as Qasim pledged to establish a democratic republic with freedom and equality for both Arabs and Kurds. Indeed, the ensuing provisional constitution explicitly affirmed that 'Arabs and Kurds are partners in the Homeland, and their national rights are recognised within the Iraqi entity' (McDowall 2004, p. 302). Barzani and hundreds of exiled Kurds returned to Iraq from the Soviet Union. The Kurds were allowed to broadcast in Kurdish and to publish books and periodicals. Elementary schools in Kurdish-speaking areas were allowed to use Kurdish as the medium of instruction. *Holî Gel* (People's Hall), Kurdistan's first proper theatre, was built. Kurdish departments were also established in some Iraqi universities. In Kirkuk, theatre groups such as *Tîpî Hunerî Xebat* (Khabat Art Group) and *Tîpî Lawanî Kerkûk* (Kirkuk Youth Group) were formed.

The optimism of the post-revolution era was clearly evidenced in theatre activities across Kurdistan at the time. In Kirkuk, *Tîpî Lawanî Kerkûk* staged a play entitled *Şewî Kotayî* (The Deciding Night) on the anniversary of the 14 July Revolution. This play, which had first been staged in Sulaymaniyah, depicted a corrupt monarchy that was oblivious to the ills of the nation. It accordingly glorified the Free Officers who overthrew and killed the king in the final act of the play. Abdurrahman Hakim, who played King Faisal in the

---

[23] A video recording of this drama can be found in the archive of Sulaymaniyah's Old Pictures on Facebook. See https://www.facebook.com/Slemani.Photos/videos.

(a)

(b)

**Figure 12** Kurdish delegations showing support for the 1958 Revolution.
*Source*: **Galawej 2009.**

Sulaymaniyah production of *Şewî Kotayî*, narrates that in the final act he was actually beaten badly by Taha Khalil, who played the role of a revolutionary. Anti-monarchy sentiments were so high at the time that the artists involved in the play had to sneak a picture of King Faisal into the theatre that they used as a basis for their make-up (Barzanji 2007, p. 98). Another play that went on stage at the time and celebrated the fall of a despotic king was *Kawey Asinger*, the hero of the old Kurdish legend. The story, which described the victory of oppressed people over a monstrous king who lived off the brains of the youth, attracted large crowds in Sulaymaniyah, who attended the performance over nine days (p. 99). The poet Goran, who had spent several years in Iraqi prisons and was only freed after the 1958 coup, also wrote an operetta entitled, *Encamî Ejdehak* (The Fall of Ajdahak) that was to be performed on the occasion of the Kurdish New Year in 1959. Although the Society for Fine Arts was not able to stage it, the *Beyan* periodical published the first act of the unfinished operetta during the same year (Goran 2005, p. 262). This act reveals not only the anti-monarchist but the nationalist overtones of the work, when Kawa calls for revolution to free Kurdistan and predicts the decades-long guerrilla struggle that ensues in Kurdistan's mountains:

> *Cûle be zistan etezê*
>
> Winter has slowed us down
>
> *Serma wekû mar egezê*
>
> The cold stings like a snake
>
> *Ta gulale deşt sûr neka*
>
> Until the red tulips cover the land
>
> *Piyaw asan xwar û jûr neka*
>
> And men move around freely;
>
> *Destdanî şoriş girane*
>
> An uprising will be costly
>
> *Lem wilatî Kurdistane . . .*
>
> In this country of Kurdistan
>
> *Hat û pelamar ser nekewt*
>
> If the attack fails

> *Mil enêyn bo şax û eşkewt . . .*
> We'll go to the mountains
> *Birakanim! Emro rojî dan bexoda girtine . . .*
> My brothers! Today we need to exercise restraint . . .
> *Eger dilsozî rastîn, ebê hergiz newestîn*
> If we are real patriots, we must never rest
> *Asin bikotîn be asin, das drûst keyn û gasin*
> Let's pound iron against iron, make sickles and ploughs
> *Şemşêr û tîr û xencer, firya xeyn bo şorişker*
> Swords, arrows and knives, to help the rebels.
> (pp. 267–8)

While Goran was optimistic about the consequences of the 14 July Revolution for the Kurds, it did not take long before relations between the Kurds and the central government deteriorated. During the early 1960s, Qasim showed no intention of making concessions to Kurdish autonomy. Months went by without any serious attempt to implement the promises implicit in the temporary constitution. Kurdish disillusionment was further exacerbated by Baghdad's growing refusal to recognize any Kurdish rights. The KDP was declared illegal, some of its members were arrested and several newspapers were closed down. Fighting broke out in July 1961 with Kurds enjoying a series of victories at the start of the war. Qasim retaliated with air operations which inflicted great suffering upon the civil population. When the full-scale war began in September 1961, the government's brutal attacks unified Kurdish political opinion and gave the revolt the character of a national uprising known as *Şorişî Eylûl* (September Revolution).

Qasim was overthrown after a coup by the Baath party in February 1963 which also crushed pro-Qasim rebellions across the country. The Baathist coup was then followed by several months of indiscriminate murder and terror, during which the National Guard rounded up Communist party members and sympathizers and killed them in their homes.

> Many thousands were arrested, and sports grounds were turned into makeshift prisons to hold the flood of detainees. People were killed in the streets, tortured to death in prison under atrocious conditions. The killings, arrests and torture

continued throughout the Baathists' period ... almost every family in Baghdad was affected. (Farouk-Sluglett and Sluglett 2001, p. 86)

Autonomy negotiations between the Baathist government and Kurdish representatives also stalled, and hostilities resumed:

On 5 June Baathi troops surrounded Sulaymaniya, imposed a curfew and began rounding up wanted men. When martial law was lifted three days later the population found the streets littered with dead people and a mass grave containing 80 bodies. Many others had also disappeared. A few days later the Kurdish delegates in Baghdad were arrested and an offensive towards Amadiya, Rawanduz and Koi-Sanjaq was launched. (McDowall 2004, pp. 314–15)

The Baath government was overthrown in November; however, new governments were no better disposed towards the Kurds. They launched successive attacks upon the Kurds and even deployed chemical weapons and napalm. These attacks were ultimately unsuccessful and in 1968, the Baath, which had resumed power after a successful coup, decided to reach an agreement with Barzani whose success in guiding the Kurdish rebellion forced the Iraqi regime to sit with him at the negotiation table. After years of fighting against central governments, autonomy in Kurdistan was finally recognized with the establishment of the Kurdistan Autonomous Region, which encompassed the governorates of Duhok, Erbil and Sulaymaniyah. This formed the basis of the March Agreement of 1970.

Despite the efforts of the educated elite in Kurdistan, cultural activities in general, and theatrical performances in particular, declined substantially over the course of the 1960s, in large part due to continued political instability. Kawa Ahmadmirza suggests that the Kurdish theatre archives do not contain any records pertaining to the existence of any theatrical activities in Sulaymaniyah between 1961 and 1968 (Ahmadmirza 2011, p. 30). He attributes the declining role of theatre during this period to the sociopolitical conditions that emanated from the September Revolution (p. 30). Meanwhile, Jawad Hamadbeg states that the last play performed in Koya was staged during the Newroz of 1963 when the KDP and government representatives were holding negotiations. After that, arbitrary mass executions and arrests, destruction of villages and death or displacement of the elite population of Koya resulted in the demise of theatre until August 1969 when *Tîpî Şanoy Kekon* (Kakon Theatre Group) revived Koya's theatre (Hamadbeg 2007, pp. 48–52). The establishment of the Autonomous Region created an environment in which theatre activities resumed with greater force and Kurdish plays reappeared in print.

## Kurdish theatre during the Autonomous Era, 1970–4

The early 1970s is considered to be a golden period in the history of the Kurdish national movement in Iraq (Stansfield and Resool 2006, p. 102). The establishment of autonomy in Kurdistan in March 1970 led to drastic and visible changes in people's lives. The Kurdish cities were governed by Kurdish authorities and Kurdish was spoken in schools, universities, media and courts. The traditional Newroz festival was celebrated in all Kurdish cities with extremely large crowds enjoying dance, music and theatre performances (Zangana 2002, p. 48).

Autonomy also ushered in a honeymoon period for Kurdish cultural life, which experienced a renaissance with the establishment of a Kurdish television channel, cultural centres, publishing houses, a university and several theatre troupes including *Komeley Huner û Wêjey Kurdî* (The Society for Kurdish Art and Literature), *Tîpî Pêşrewî Şanoy Kurdî* (The Progressive Kurdish Theatre Group), *Tîpî Hunerî Hewlêr* (Erbil Art group) and *Tîpî Nwandinî Silêmanî* (Sulaymaniyah Acting Group). The Newroz of 1970 also saw the first Kurdish drama on Baghdad's television.

*Tîpî Nwandin û Mosîqay Silêmanî* (Sulaymaniyah Acting and Music Group) was the first official Kurdish theatre group which began its activities in February 1969 in Sulaymaniyah. As its name suggests, this group was made up of two separate groups of actors and musicians who soon parted ways to form their independent groups. In September of the same year, the actors formed *Tîpî Nwandinî Silêmanî* – this marked the start of efforts to establish serious Kurdish theatre as an independent art form which was not reliant upon music for its popular reception. Significantly, during their first dramatic performance, the group distributed leaflets which stated its intention to serve Kurdish art and called upon educated women to join their group and not be afraid to refute ignorance 'in the service of the nation and the homeland' (Ahmadmirza 2011, p. 55). This demonstrates that the founders of the first official Kurdish theatre group, like their predecessors, had to rely on nationalism in order to justify the validity of their art and to draw women to the theatre.

A further step towards the enhancement of women's role within society was taken in 1970 with the establishment of a theatre group called *Hawrêyanî Gezîze* (Gaziza's Friends). The group was formed by Omar Ali Amin who named it after his young daughter Gaziza, its only female member who had become a popular actor both on stage and on TV. While financial difficulties meant the group lasted less than two years, Gaziza's talent and acting abilities won her the hearts and minds of the Kurdish public, who still fondly recall her performances in the early 1970s ('Hawrêyanî Gezîze' 2009, p. 49). Its legacy was resurrected three decades later when Gaziza, who graduated from Baghdad Academy of Fine Arts in 1988, revived *Hawrêyanî Gezîze* in 2004, this time in the form of an all-female theatre group.

*Hawrêyanî Gezîze*, like other theatre groups, drew on Kurdish folklore as material for its performances. A number of theatre groups also sought to construct politically charged messages from national myths and legends. The new wave of Kurdish theatre groups that were established during the autonomous era also thrived within an environment that enabled them to openly engage political topics. Their works largely celebrated the fall of despots and sought to bring forth the spirit of revolution. During the four-year period of relative peace and autonomy in Kurdistan, many plays presented by Sulaymaniyah Theatre Group engaged with patriotic themes and the history of Kurdistan.

Theatre artists' contribution to Kurdish national identity can clearly be seen during these years. Every year on Newroz, the legend of Kawa was dramatized by different theatre groups in such performances as *Kawey Asinger* (Kawa the Blacksmith) and *Dwarojî Zuhakî Zordar* (The Fall of the Tyrant Zuhak). *Kotayî Zordar* (The Fall of the Tyrant), which was directed by Qazi Bamarni, is another play that was produced in the aftermath of the autonomy agreement that drew on Kurdish folklore to celebrate the independence struggle. The play told the story of Mir Muhammad Kor – meaning blind, as the prince was blind in one eye – the ruler of Soran principality who assumed power in 1814

**Figure 13** Gaziza's Friends Theatre Group. *Source*: kurdipedia.org.

and gained control of much of Iraqi Kurdistan by 1833. For probably the first time in the region, some form of centralized government was established as Mir Muhammad successfully subdued the local tribes and went so far as to mint his own coins. His brutality notwithstanding, Mir Muhammad was able to create a genuine administration, establish law and order, secure trade routes and levy excessive taxes by local notables. His rule would have presumably heralded a 'Golden Age' had he not surrendered to the Ottoman forces before being killed in 1837 (see McDowall 2004, pp. 42–4). His fall marked the onset of instability in the Kurdish principalities and the end of Kurdish semi-autonomy. Despite his fall, Mir Muhammad's success in creating the first genuine Kurdish 'Kingdom' catapulted him into immortality as Kurdish nationalists would later discover stories of *Mîrê Kor* in folklore and elevate him to the status of a national hero. Bamarni's description of his aim in directing *Kotayî Zordar* exemplifies such nationalist interpretations of wars fought by Kurdish princes:

> At all times, the literatures of nations testify to the existence of those nations. Although we are staging a true historical tale, our aim is to tell our thoughtful audience to free themselves from the chains of the dark past and

strive to achieve their. It is upon us to sacrifice to any measure so that we do not suffer under a brutal merciless enemy. Therefore, our youth should look up to their ancestors and follow our national heroes in the struggle for justice. 'Muhammad Pasha Kor' of Rowanduz is the best example of such heroisms. (Ahmadmirza 2011, p. 67)

Bamarni was one of the graduates of Baghdad Fine Arts Academy who, along with Ahmad Salar, Talat Saman, Farhad Sharif, Badea Dartash and others, played an important role in developing Kurdish theatre in the 1970s and later. He was born into a nationalist peasant family in the village of Bamernê. After the Kurdish uprising of the early 1960s, Qazi joined his uncle who was a prominent intellectual exiled to Nasiriya in Southern Iraq. Bamarni graduated from Baghdad Academy of Fine Arts in 1969–70, the year when autonomy was recognized in Kurdistan. He returned to Duhok where many Arabs from Mosul and a considerable number of Baathists resided. Qazi who was raised in his uncle's Marxist, Kurdish nationalist school of thought, found it impossible to work in Duhok. He therefore took the decision to move to Sulaymaniyah, which was home to many Kurdish artists, intellectuals, poets and politicians from all parts of Kurdistan (Bamarni 2011, p. 85).

In Sulaymaniyah, Bamarni became the head director of the student guild and taught drama and acting classes. He directed several performances for Sulaymaniyah Theatre and Music Group including *Nirxî Azadî* (The Cost of Freedom), one of the group's most successful performances (Bamarni 2011, p. 85). This was based on the play *Montserrat* (1948) by Emmanuel Roblès (1914–1995), the Algerian-French author. The play was set during the Spanish occupation of Venezuela in 1812 and it told the story of a Spanish officer who, repulsed by the atrocities committed against the natives, stood up against his commanders and refused to provide information about the location of the Venezuelan revolutionary leader, Simon Bolivar.

The Kirkuk branch of Kurdish Art and Literature Society opened during 1970–1. Among their performances were *Mereze* (Rice) and *Beharî Dizraw* (The Stolen Spring, 1972) which they staged in a school called Şoriş (Revolution) (*Şano*, no. 11, 2008). The latter is a political play about social injustice which depicts a callous landlord and his poor tenant, Rostam, whose wife the landlord covets. The landlords' sons, Wurya and Biland, are political activists in an underground anti-government organization. Biland is arrested by the police while distributing leaflets but escapes with Rostam's assistance. Rostam is, however, attacked and killed in a plot by Biland's father. Prior to his death, Rostam tells the young revolutionaries: 'At some point we will prevail and drive the foreign invaders out of our land and live in freedom.' The play ends with Wurya singing: 'Our spring was stolen, our moon was stolen, our stars were stolen' to the background accompaniment of drums (Zangana 2002, pp. 52–3). This play exemplifies the nationalist thinking at the time that the Kurdish upper class, particularly the *aghas*, were unpatriotic and complicit with the regime. Therefore, damning depictions of them were a common feature that united most nationalist plays of this period.

There are several other plays that demonstrate the artists' concern with social injustice and the poor living conditions of workers at the time. The play *Lanewazan* (The Homeless), for example, depicts the lives of those who live in cheap pension housing. Rafiq works for the owner, who treats his workers inhumanely, and accuses them of stealing his money. Rafiq cannot bear this treatment and therefore quits his job and joins an underground organization, with a view to building a new house that can benefit all; a clear metaphor for a fair and equitable society. Like *Beharî Dizraw*, *Lanewazan* highlights the existence of socialist and nationalist underground organizations and advocates for them.

World events, and specifically the Vietnamese liberation movement, were a key preoccupation for Kurdish writers such as Dilshad Mariwani (1947–89). During his short life, Mariwani was imprisoned and tortured several times for his activities in underground organizations. He joined the 1961 uprising and between 1962 and 1966 worked in the Society for the Revival of Kurdish National Resources (*Komeley Bûjandinewey Samanî Netewayetî Kurd*), which he had cofounded. This underground literary and artistic society distributed resistance works by several Kurdish writers, along with translations of Arabic, Persian and European resistance poetry. He joined the 1975 uprising and lived the life of a peshmerga in the mountains of Kurdistan between 1983 and 1985. He was finally executed in 1989 after several years of publishing essays, poems and political plays. His resistance works include a play entitled

*Çawî Vietnam* (Vietnam's Eye, 1973) which was staged in Kirkuk. In the play, Mariwani demonstrates how the oppressors fear the eyes of the nation and therefore gouge out the eyes of those freedom fighters they capture. The fight for freedom, however, as the play depicts, goes on despite all tyranny (Zangana 2002, p. 54).

The Kurdish struggle for freedom found a platform in the first Kurdish art festival, which was held in Baghdad in 1974. The festival's organizing committee held their first meeting on 3 February 1974, during which they determined the festival's motto ('for an original contemporary Kurdish art, peace and fraternity, and autonomy for Iraqi Kurdistan'). In addition to the main motto, four other mottos were also written upon posters before being distributed. These included the following:

- Our songs, our dance, our theatre is in the service of the Kurdish nation's wishes.
- Art is a means of revolution and a mirror of civilization.
- Kurdistan is a love song for artists.
- Give me bread and theatre, and I give you a free and thoughtful nation.

(Ahmadmirza 2011, p. 73)

These mottos clearly demonstrate that theatre artists had fully endorsed and incorporated nationalist discourse; furthermore, they also reiterate that the festival organizers viewed the event as the means through which nationalist ideas could be promoted and dispersed. The political nature of the festival is also reflected by the eleven plays performed in it – most engaged with themes such as freedom fighting, martyrdom and political oppression, along with other themes relevant to Kurdistan's political life at the time. These dramas included *Pirdî Wilat* (The Bridge of the Country, which was performed by the Progressive Kurdish Theatre Group), *Nirxî Azadî* (The Cost of Freedom, which was presented by the Sulaymaniyah Acting Troup), *Teqînewe* (The Explosion, which was presented by Kirkuk Art and Literature Society), *Şaxewanî Mezin* (The Great Mountaineer, which was written by Qazi Bamarni and presented by Sulaymaniyah Acting Group) and *Dîwar* (The Wall, which was based on a story by Jean Paul Sartre and presented by Sulaymaniyah Society For Kurdish Art and Literature) (pp. 73–84).

## Conclusion

Smith (2009) and Hutchinson (1987) observe that intellectuals play a central role in generating and analysing the concepts, ideology, myths and symbols of nationalism; as such, they assume a central role in generating cultural nationalism and the ideology, if not the initial leadership, of political nationalism. The cultural nationalism propagated by intellectuals provides a new rationale and justification to the intelligentsia who fill new occupational positions created by the rise of science, thus providing opportunities for their skills to be used and rewarded. The early Kurdish theatre is consistent with these theories of cultural nationalism because it depicts how the educated elite promoted modernization, and as part of it, the construction of an indigenous theatre.

At a time when Kurdistan suffered from a high culture which was prerequisite to the achievement of political independence, the small circle of Kurdish elite invested in and exploited culture, and specifically theatre, with a view to establishing a collective identity that could compensate for the lack of a state. They ran schools with Kurdish as the medium of teaching, wrote local history (including the biographies of Kurdish notables) and sought to enrich the local language by translating Kurdish literary works into Sorani. Individuals founded printing houses, published journals and commissioned literary works in Kurdish. This was never an end in itself but was instead a preliminary that was undertaken with the intention of establishing the foundations of a national identity. Members of the intelligentsia and intellectuals engaged in these cultural activities in order to spread the sense of belonging among the masses. The ultimate aspiration was always the achievement of political independence.

Despite the failure of political attempts to create an independent Kurdistan and the official annexation of this region to Iraq in 1932, the Kurdish elite consistently stressed the role that theatre could play in serving the Kurdish 'nation' and 'homeland'. The evocation of the name of the nation, is one of the techniques through which a national identity is constructed (Hutchinson 1994b, p. 46). Kurdish elite frequently deployed this technique when they called upon their community to support the burgeoning art of theatre. They stressed that theatre could demonstrate the high moral standards of their common ancestry, preserve their history and folklore and revive their great literature (Barzanji 2007, p. 86). They stressed the value of theatre in asserting that 'a city without theatre is like a graveyard' and that 'theatre is the nation's school' (p. 86). The writers of the *Şefeq* periodical called upon the Kurds to support the arts as a means of revival which should be respected by all. Loren Kruger observes that this rhetoric 'rests on the assumption that the nation-to-be-created is already present, singular, and distinct in the minds of those creating it, even though its actual absence from their lives suggests that its distinctive character is as yet imagined – or invented' (Kruger 2008, p. 37).

In materially representing shared cultural elements, the Kurdish stage affirmed national identity and promoted national consciousness and solidarity. Despite the manifest lack of a Kurdish state, Kurdish nationalism continued to shape theatre productions in Kurdistan. Pîremêrd's *Mem û Zîn* (1935), *Şerîf Hemewend* (1936) and *Mehmûd Aqay Şêwekel* (1936), along with Goran's nationalist poetry, exemplify how the educated elite used theatre as a site to construct national cultural identity and retrieve national cultural heritage – particularly by the staging of folklore, myths, legends and history. Theatre served as a tool of nation-building and also contributed to the advancement of leftist political campaigns in Iraq. In staging anti-feudalist and anti-monarchist plays, Kurdish theatre represented and legitimized the wider political movement that had resulted in the creation of ICP and leftist Kurdish groups in Kurdistan over the course of the 1930s. During this decade, Kurdish theatre shifted from folkloric tales to sociopolitical themes that were more closely aligned with the political realities of the 1940s and 1950s. Most of these plays were aligned with revolutionary leftist sentiments that ultimately culminated in the overthrow of the Iraqi monarchy. The significance of these 'serious' plays was attested to by the government's violent interventions against theatre performances.

Although drama had already become established as a tool for modernizing the society and highlighting social and political issues during previous decades, theatre was still mainly a school event confined to special occasions such as the Ramadan Eid. Due to difficult social and political circumstances, it had ceased to exist for a substantial part of the 1960s. During the 1970s, the establishment of Kurdish autonomy and the resulting stability created a vibrant sociopolitical atmosphere in which theatre groups started to form.

It was only then that, for the first time, a small group of theatre graduates started to work in Kurdistan. Their small number was attributable to the social stigma associated with acting, a stigma which often resulted in families refusing to allow their children to study drama (Karim 2013, pp. 75–6). In spite of tremendous social and financial difficulties, the theatre artists of the early 1970s managed to turn drama into a serious and popular medium by relating it to contemporary political issues and rooting it within a strong sense of nationalism. Nationalist messages were expounded with unique vigour during the free era of Kurdish self-rule. As the following chapters demonstrate, even after the loss of autonomy, the socialist-nationalist trend of the Kurdish theatre continued into the 1980s in defiance of the Baathist dictatorship.

3

# Kurdish theatre and resistance, 1975–91

This chapter examines the political developments during the second half of the 1970s and the duration of the 1980s. It then relates these developments to Kurdish theatrical outputs from the period with a view to demonstrating that the political struggle to cast off the Iraqi rule was synonymous with the growth of radical performance culture during this period. Scholars of Kurdish nationalism generally agree that 'the hardships suffered by the Iraqi Kurds in the second half of the 1970s and the duration of the 1980s was of catastrophic, even genocidal, proportions' (Stansfield and Resool 2006, p. 103). This period is however a source of some nostalgia for scholars and artists who view it as a 'Golden Age' of Kurdish theatre in Iraq (see Rauf 1995; Karim 2009; Karim 2011). It was a period when theatre was a popular medium in the cities of Erbil and Sulaymaniyah. The audiences were made up of not only the educated elite but also the lower classes, who were willing to spend their meagre income on tickets which sometimes equalled the total earnings of their day (Muhammad, interview, 8 October 2013).

Allison argues that 'in the authoritarian states of the Near and Middle East, where written material is rigorously censored, points of view which contradict the government are usually by necessity expressed orally' and oral communication 'is often the vehicle of minority discourses, of tendencies deemed to be subversive' (Allison 2001, p. 5). Kurdish theatre under the Baath rule is a clear case in point. Despite the censorship of dramatic texts prior to their public performance, Kurdish dramatists managed to maintain the nationalist tone of their works through the use of oral tradition and its reserves of folklore and mythology which fuelled revolutionary fervour.

It is safe to say that it was through theatre that cultural nationalism made one of its greatest – if not the greatest – impacts in Iraqi Kurdistan in the 1970s and 1980s: the impact that theatre made was not through print, which had a small readership, but rather through live performance, which was accessible to all. In fact, most Kurdish plays that were staged in the 1970s and 1980s were only printed after the establishment of autonomy. Those which were printed in journals such as *Karwan* and *Beyan* did not have a large readership either, in large part due to the obstacles faced by the Kurdish press. Printing in Kurdish has largely been insulated to the intelligentsia and, even for this group, access to Kurdish print materials was not easy until very recently (Sheyholislami 2011, p. 83). To the end of the 1980s, the Kurdish press was characterized 'by the absence of enduring dailies, low circulation, poor distribution facilities, dependence on subscription and single copy sales, lack of or insignificant advertising revenue, poor printing facilities, shortage of newsprint, and limited professionalization and specialization' (Hassanpour 1992, p. 276). While it was therefore unlikely that printed materials would make an impact upon Kurdish society, live theatrical performances drew large crowds to the theatres.

During the 1970s and 1980s, theatre became increasingly politicized in nature and nationalistic in tone. After a decade of conflict and political turbulence, Kurdish theatre began to reflect the growing sense of Kurdish nationalism and the wider socialist movement in Iraq. Anti-monarchist themes gave way to Kurdish nationalist and socialist themes which continued to appear in Kurdish theatre productions even under strict censorship. Some consider the late 1970s and 1980s to be the golden years of theatre because of the artists' strong sense of commitment to the nationalist struggle which often necessitated grave sacrifices. For these individuals, these sacrifices were made easier by the belief that theatre was as important as the peshmergas' armed struggle (Karim 2013). It was not coincidental that many theatre artists had in fact been directly involved in the guerrilla movement at one point or another.

## The collapse of the Kurdish national movement

Soon after the First Kurdish Art Festival, negotiations between the central government and the Kurdish politicians reached an impasse. Many Kurdish men, including theatre artists such as Ahmad Salar and Simko Aziz, along with members of their theatre groups, went to the mountains to join the resistance.¹ Baghdad launched an offensive against the Kurdish region in April 1974 and won the war immediately after signing the Algiers Agreement with Iran in March 1975. The withdrawal of Iranian support for the Kurds left the resistance in shatters. Mulla Mustafa Barzani was forced to abandon the fight and, along with over 100,000 Kurds, including fighters and their families, crossed into Iran to join the 100,000 Kurdish fighters already there. Thousands of others surrendered to Iraqi forces and the uprising ended within a short time (McDowall 2004, p. 338).

After the collapse of the Kurdish movement in 1975, the Iraqi government sought to placate the Kurdish public by issuing amnesty to the guerrilla fighters and implementing economic development projects. These projects, which resulted from the oil boom of the 1970s and Iraq's subsequent economic growth, sought to placate segments of Kurdish society that had not directly experienced government repression. At the same time, however, the Iraqi government started a massive campaign of Arabization, Baathization, cultural suppression, comprehensive mass deportations, arrests and large-scale executions.

The Arabization of the oil-rich districts of Kirkuk and Khanaqin, along with the border areas of Sheikhan and Sinjar continued as Kurds were deported and Arab peasants were settled in their stead, challenged only by sporadic and isolated resistance from Kurdish villagers. In 1976, the regime began to create a security belt which meant evacuating a zone of 10–20 kilometres along the Iran–Iraq border. In the north, too, government forces destroyed many villages, cutting down fruit trees and filling water wells with concrete. By 1978, at least 1,400 villages had been completely razed and their inhabitants had been evicted. Hundreds of thousands were deported to *mujama'al* ('collective' resettlement camps near to cities). These camps were 'drab townships located near major towns, with long wide avenues [that] permit[ted] control by armoured vehicles' (McDowall 2004, p. 339). Many others were sent to southern Iraqi cities of Afak, Diwaniya and Nasiriya. Over one million residents of the disputed districts of Khanaqin, Kirkuk, Mandali, Sheikhan, Sinjar and Zakho were deported and replaced by Arab Iraqi and Egyptian settlers (pp. 339–40). Kurdish civil servants, soldiers and police were transferred to the south of Iraq

---

¹ This theme will be engaged in more detail in the section on guerrilla theatre.

and replaced by Arab civil servants. Kurdish towns and villages were renamed in Arabic and Kurdish was, in different levels of education in some areas, either completely banned or mostly replaced by Arabic, a measure which sparked mass demonstrations in Koya and Sulaymaniyah (*Spark*, vol. 1, no. 12, December 1977). Further mass protests, which were strongly influenced by the underground Kurdish Students' Union, resulted in the release of 250 students and 70 teachers who had been arrested in October 1977 (*Spark*).

## Cultural suppression under the Baath Regime

After seizing power, the Baath party immediately co-opted and closed down Iraq's major newspapers and executed Aziz Abdel Barakat who was both the head of the Journalist's Union and the publisher of the independent *Al-Manar* (The Lighthouse), one of the most professionally run and widely distributed dailies in Iraq at the time (Isakhan 2012, p. 103). In 1969, the Baath party passed a publications law that resulted in a more controlled, monolithic and supine Iraqi media (Bengio 2002, p. 110). This meant that by the early 1970s, Iraq only had five daily newspapers, each of which was heavily influenced, if not completely controlled, by the state and almost completely stripped of any critical approach. The Baath's view on democracy and freedom of expression is made clear in its 1965 programme which declared,

> [while] the masses have the right of constructive criticism within the limits of the nation's progressive line of destiny . . . [such] criticism under the socialist revolutionary regime cannot become an end in itself, nor can it be allowed to proceed unchecked to the limit of undermining the nationalist socialist line itself. (cited in Thoman 1972, p. 32)

After the Baath party reasserted its power in Kurdistan, it sought to eradicate any traces of Kurdish nationalism in Kurdish political culture (Stansfield and Resool 2006, pp. 108–9). It reopened offices in Kurdish cities and towns and forced Kurds to join the Baath party and enrol in state-run unions and organizations, both social and professional (p. 109). Arabic became the official language in schools and Kurdish media, as in the rest of Iraq, became subjected to strict censorship.

After the amnesty that was granted following the 1974–5 uprising, most Kurdish theatre artists returned to their towns – however, their work was subject to strict monitoring. The freedom that had flourished during the autonomous phase came to an abrupt end in 1975, when the age of censorship started. Theatre performances had to be approved by the Ministry of Culture. Every literary publication, including all plays, had to be sent to the censorship office where each page was carefully scrutinized before being stamped 'approved' or 'not approved' (see Figures 14 and 15). During an interview, director Fattah Khattab described how the loss of autonomy affected theatre production in Kurdistan:

> From mid-1970s, one person would become in charge of giving permission and budget to theatre performances or TV shows. He would also become the leading manager of the theatre groups without having any knowledge about the art. Or he would become 'responsible for communications' which meant he would visit the secret service and participate in meetings which decided the fate of the dramatic texts . . . we wouldn't take the rehearsals seriously because they watched them and we feared they would ban them. (Khattab, interview, 4 August 2014)

Even with the prior examination and censorship of playtexts, the secret service agents would attend the performances and report on anything they deemed subversive. In an interview with Aso Sat, Nigar Hasib described that anything, from lighting to the colour of fabrics used in performances, could be interpreted as subversive and thus put the production at risk; as a result, the artists were constantly on lookout for government agents among the audiences and censored the dialogues on days they suspected their presence (Zakaryaei 2013). Indeed, the choice of red, yellow and green, the colours of Kurdish flag, for the costumes in *Ey Gelî Felestînî Rapere* (Rise Up, Palestinian Nation) directed by Badea Dartash demonstrates the subversive use of colour by Kurdish theatre artists during the 1980s (see Figure 16). This play, which was in Arabic, was staged at a time when the Iraqi regime had, for a short while, banned theatre in Kurdish. The ban was lifted after the regime realized that language was not an obstacle for the transmission of revolutionary messages of supposedly pro-Arab and pro-Palestinian plays.

**Figure 14** The Iraqi Ministry of Culture's approval for the staging of *Pîlan* in 1977 after the implementation of the ministry's alterations to the text.

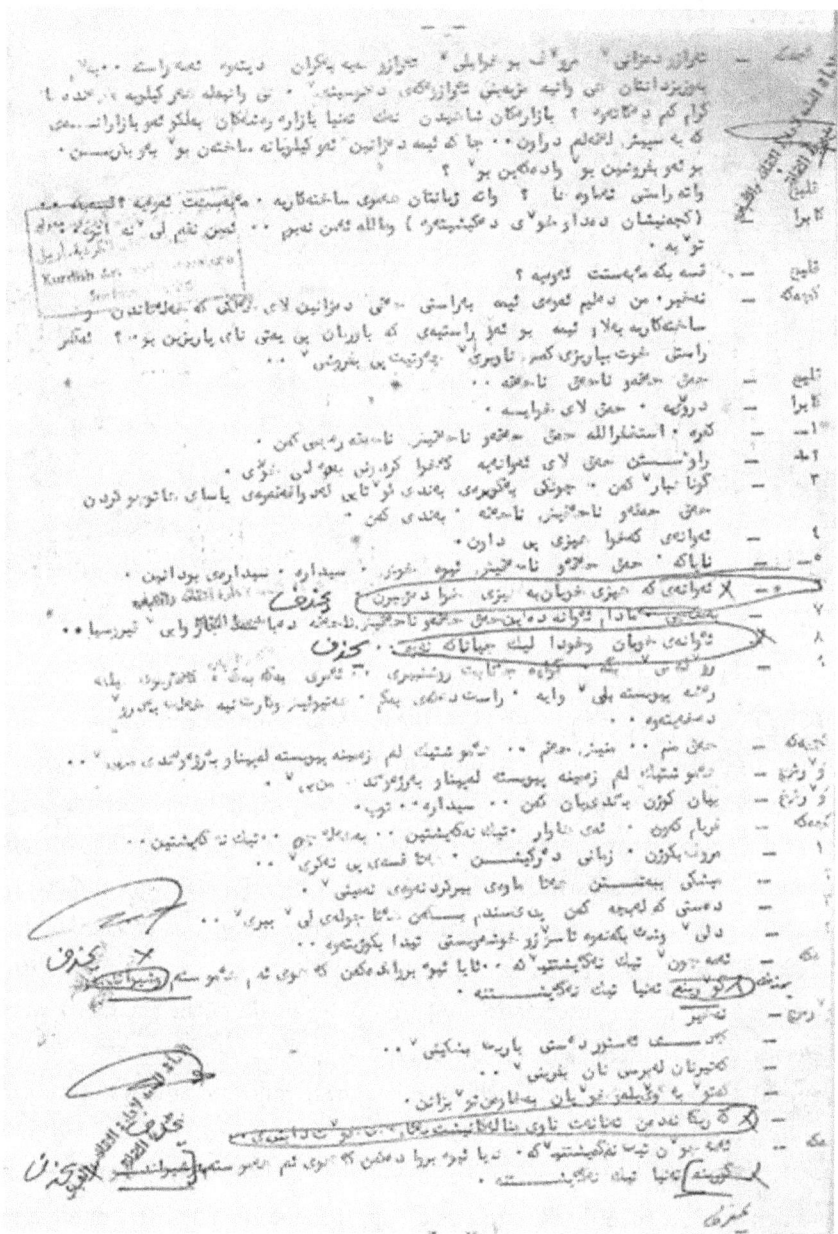

**Figure 15** A page from the play *Pîlan* shows the extent to which the Ministry of Culture controlled and censored dramatic texts. The circled parts with the Arabic word 'yahdhif', meaning delete, next to them are to be completely removed from the play.

**Figure 16** Badea Dartash in *Ey Gelî Felestînî Rapere* (1988).

In the Arabized cities of Kirkuk, whose name was changed to the Arabic *at-Ta'mim*, and Khanaqin, Kurdish theatre was banned and many theatre artists from Kirkuk, such as Mahdi Omid and Jalil Zangana, had to move to Erbil and Sulaymaniyah; others, meanwhile, opted for exile (Karim 2011, p. 147). It also became increasingly difficult to work in Kirkuk's TV station, *Ta'mim*. In 1976, Bamarni had, while working in Sulaymaniyah, directed a successful play called *al-Azrab* which was about the workers' strike, and which he had deliberately set before the rise of Baathism and Arab nationalism in order to avoid any association. At this point in time, the Baathists were determined to claim the leftist and communist struggle for themselves. During the initial phase of the Baath regime, it sought to cultivate an aura of radical political change by allowing several communist works to be translated into Arabic. In addition, it also sought to directly engage left-leaning intellectuals and activists. As such, Kirkuk television approached Bamarni and made him a generous offer for a TV production of his play. However, halfway through recording, Bamarni halted the production when he was told an order by the Revolutionary Command Council had ordained that all TV productions had to be accompanied by portraits of Ahmad Hassan al-Bakr, the president, and his deputy, Saddam Hussein, which were hung on the wall. Bamarni and his

Sulaymaniyah Acting Group protested this demand by arguing that it was inconsistent with the period when the play was set and returned to Kurdistan. Soon after, during October 1977, Bamarni went into exile to France where he stayed until Saddam Hussein's fall (Bamarni 2011, pp. 86–7).

As a result of strict censorship, Kurdish theatre had to veil its true targets and hide its political message behind symbols and allegories. The playwrights had to constantly tread a fine line, and explore which critical allusions would be allowed to pass and which would result in censorship and banning. The Ministry of Culture invariably demanded many alterations in the texts of the plays before they were allowed to be published or presented on stage. Despite these limitations, theatre became an important medium for representing the Kurdish history of resistance and motivating the Kurds in their struggle for liberation (Zangana 2002, p. 57).

## Kurdish theatre and the defeat of 1975

Despite encountering enormous difficulties, Kurdish theatre artists continued to persevere in their art and even achieved success on the national stage. In the spring of 1976, Salar, along with Simko Aziz and others, founded a theatre group in Sulaymaniyah University called *Tîpî Şanoy Zanko* (University Theatre Group). This group produced several successful works including *Dwa Goranî* (The Last Song), *Waney Reşbelek* (Dance Lesson), Othello, *Raport* (Report) and *Qulapî Çawekan* (The Hook of the Eyes). Their *Xec û Siyamend* (Khaj and Siyamand) won Salar the best director award in the First Theatre Festival for Iraqi Universities. The jury committee in the festival included great Iraqi theatre directors and professors such as Ibrahim Jalal, Ja'far al-Sa'di, As'ad Abdulrazaq and Fazil Khalil (Danish 2009c).

*Xec û Siyamend*, which was written by Fuad Majid Misri, was based on a folkloric tale that emanated from the Mukriyan region. It related the tragic fate of Khaj, the daughter of a feudal landlord, and Siyamand, a poor peasant, whose love for each other had no place within the feudal society in which they lived. After it was presented by the Progressive Kurdish Theatre Group in Sulaymaniyah in 1978, *Xec û Siyamend* was received passionately by the audience who saw an echo of their own national loss within this tragic love story. Hemin Mukriyani (1921–1986), the great Kurdish poet from Iran who lived in exile in Sulaymaniyah following the fall of the Mahabad Republic, was so overwhelmed by the performance that he burst into tears after the concluding lines. These lines, which are quoted below, resonated strongly with the audience, who saw in Khaj the image of their nation and in Siyamand, a hero who would save the nation from tyranny (Barzanji 2007, p. 229):

> *Eger be dil mebesttane*
> If you wholeheartedly desire
> *Xecî şeyda helnedêrin*
> To save lovelorn Khaj
> *Ba hemûman aşqî bîn*
> Let us all love her
> *Xec kîjêkî derûn û dil firawane*
> Khaj is a kind-hearted girl
> *Xec kabanî miskînane*
> Khaj is the lady of the poor
> *Xatûnêkî emekdarî hejarane*
> She is the lady of the wretched
> *Xec dulberêkî şeydaye*
> Khaj is a lovelorn beauty
> *Heta êstaş çawî le rêy siyamendêkî wiryaye*
> To this day, she is still waiting for a caring Siyamand
> (Barzanji 2007, p. 230)

Before *Xec û Siyamend*, a play entitled *Receb û Piyawxoran* (Rajab and the Man-eaters; Figure 17), which was performed by the Progressive Kurdish Theatre Group, expressed the Kurdish national despair in the aftermath of 1975. The play, which was written by Simko Nakam and directed by Ahmad Salar, told the story of how Rajab, a poor man, was tormented by Faysal, a neighbour and bully who coveted his house. In response, the members of a society that was established to 'help the helpless' (which was composed of a businessman, a court poet, an engineer, a lawyer and a thug) intervened with an offer to rescue Rajab from his neighbour – however, it later emerged that their intervention was guided by a desire to attain a winning lottery ticket,

**Figure 17** *Receb û Piyawxoran* (1975).

which they presumed to be in Rajab's house. At the conclusion of the play, Rajab dies in his house but there is the aspiration that his son, Mahdi, a blue-collar worker who lives in another town, will return one day to avenge his father's death (Barzanji 2007, pp. 218–22).

*Receb û Piyawxoran* is clearly a metaphor for the predicament of the Kurds in Iraq, and it represents the Kurdish artists' outlook at a time when Iraqi Kurdistan was plagued by disappointment and despair. This is reflected in the final scene of the play when the only character left on the stage is a sleepy policeman who arrests the wrong man for Rajab's murder; and the only sound that can be heard is an ambulance carrying Rajab's dead body. Although Rajab died at the hands of the bourgeoisie, a metaphor for the demise of Kurdish nationalist movement, there is still hope that his son, a metaphor for a new proletarian movement, will return to fight and defeat Rajab's oppressors. *Receb û Piyawxoran* heralded the revival of the Kurdish national struggle, which shortly emerged in the form of a socialist political party.

## The resumption of the Kurdish national struggle

The repressive measures carried out by the government against the Kurds after the Algiers Agreement led to the early resumption of guerrilla warfare. Several

Kurdish organizations were being established abroad. In May 1975, the Patriotic Union of Kurdistan (PUK) announced its establishment and intention to lead armed struggle against the Iraqi government. Former peshmergas who lived abroad or who were frustrated after they had accepted Baghdad's amnesty in 1975 made their way to Kurdistan and joined the movement (Bruinessen 1986). By 1977, the PUK's new uprising (şorişî nwê) was an ongoing reality, and clashes between the Iraqi army and Kurdish guerrillas were initiated.

The defining characteristics of the PUK were anti-feudalist, anti-tribalist, anti-bourgeois-rightist and anti-imperialist. It recognized the role of different social classes in the national liberation movement and sought to unite the peasants, the working class and the petit-bourgeoisie in the struggle. The party described the Kurdish liberation movement as an essentially socialist movement, in which the people and toiling masses would rise up against feudalism, imperialism and oppression and assert their right to self-determination ('Revolution in Kurdistan', 1977, p. 45). In keeping with its founding manifesto, the PUK declared its solidarity with the Palestinian Revolution and condemned all imperialist and reactionary plots that targeted their struggle. In its 19th congress, Kurdish Students Abroad (AKSA) held a pro-Palestinian congress in which it declared its full support for the Palestinian cause and, in so doing, reiterated that the Kurdish movement was a 'permanent ally of the Arab liberation movement and the Palestinian revolution' (*Spark*, vol. 2, no. 9, September 1978, p. 6). The Palestine Liberation Organization (PLO) representative, meanwhile, compared the Kurdish and Palestinian struggles and advanced the view that they shared common cause in their fight to retain their national identity and liberate their land; both were also united by a shared opposition to imperialism, Zionism and 'reactionary puppets' (*Spark*).

The PUK blamed the KDP for the downfall of Kurdish uprising in 1975 and condemned its leadership for what it saw as 'abandoning' the fourteen-year Kurdish struggle (1961–75). Since the establishment of the PUK, its leader, Jalal Talabani, was diametrically opposed to Barzani and his sons, and the two often appeared as the opposite poles of the Kurdish movement. While Barzani mainly depended on tribal support from the Kurmanji-speaking north (Badinan), Talabani enjoyed the support of urban, educated Sorani-speakers in the southern part of Iraqi Kurdistan (Soran). The PUK was strongest in the

Sulaymaniyah region where its support among the young urban population was, in large part, attributable to Talabani's radical and progressive political pronouncements (Bruinessen 1986).

## Socialist influence on Kurdish theatre

The influence of general progressive tendencies in Iraq upon Kurdish theatre in Sulaymaniyah and Erbil was clearly evidenced in the progressive and radical themes that were addressed by theatre groups. Kurdish theatre of the 1970s reflects the wider concerns with the liberation of the fatherland from imperialist yoke, along with the liberation of masses from feudalism, reactionary regimes and repressive bureaucracies of the ruling nations. Pro-Palestinian themes also feature prominently in both Arab-Iraqi and Kurdish theatre during the 1970s.

In order to escape the sharp blade of censorship, Kurdish dramatists resorted to symbolism in plays that had previously been produced by Arab Iraqi theatre artists. For its parallels with the Kurdish situation, the Palestinian struggle for freedom provided the best substitute for anti-regime and revolutionary expression on stage. Several pro-Palestinian plays were translated from Arabic and staged during this time – these included *Rizgarî* (Freedom), *Faylî 67* (File no. 67), *Felestîn Welatî Qesan Kenefanî* (Palestine, Qassan Kanafani's Homeland), and *Ger Felestînî Bûytaye Çît Dekird* (What Would You Do If You Were Palestinian?). These plays not only depicted the brutality of the occupation but also celebrated the fight for freedom, a theme which resonated strongly with Kurdish audiences. *Ger Felestînî Bûytaye*, a play based on Mamdouh Adwan's *Law Kunt Filasṭīnīan* (If You Were a Palestinian, 1977), emphasized the legitimacy of the armed struggle by referring to the sufferings of the Palestinians and their fight for liberty. *Faylî 67*, an adaptation of Ismail Fahd Ismail's novel, *Milaff al-Ḥādithah 67* (File of Case 67, 1975), which had already been performed by Arab theatre groups with great success, depicted the persecution of a Palestinian in Kuwait. While the wrongly accused and tortured Palestinian prisoner dies at the end of the play, *File no. 67* ends on a note of optimism when the narrator observes: '[T]he truth is . . . when a child is killed, another is born and so long as there is Palestinian blood in a mother's children, they will fight until they achieve freedom' (Chewar 1980, p. 95).

An example of how the close resemblance of Palestinian and Kurdish plight was used by Kurdish theatre artists to vent their internal trauma can be found in Badea Dartash's account of her performance as a mother of a martyred Palestinian boy in *Nexşey Xwênawî* (Bloody Map; Figure 18). One autumn day in 1976, on her way to Çalakî Qutabiyan Theatre Hall, where she would stage the play, she witnessed a funeral procession. A silent crowd of hundreds carried on their hands the bodies of Kurdish activists, Sheikh Shahab, Anwar Zorab and Jafar Abdulwahid, who had been executed by the Iraqi regime. Deeply saddened by the spectacle she had witnessed outside, Dartash delivered a strong performance that brought tears to the eyes of the audience. Her heartfelt wailing and copious tears at the sight of her young son's coffin were cathartic expression of real grief; this was not hidden from the audience nor the state officials who were witnessing the performance. Dartash was immediately reprimanded and banned from working as an actor or director. One year later, enough time had lapsed to allow her resumption of work on stage.

As *Nexşey Xwênawî* clearly demonstrates, the proximity of Kurdish and Palestinian situation was too close for the Iraqi regime to bear. Therefore, they finally put an end to the production of pro-Palestinian plays by Kurdish artists. In 1983, the successful production of *Faylî 67* was followed by harsh

**Figure 18** Badea Dartash in *Nexşey Xwênawî* (1976).

interrogations of the cast and the director, Talat Saman. Muhsin Muhammad and Ahmad Salar suggest that Baghdad was right to be suspicious of pro-Palestinian plays – in their view, these plays were only staged because of their similarity to the Kurdish situation. Palestine therefore served, to all intents and purposes, as a substitute which enabled the oppression of the Kurdish people to be depicted on the stage. Salar observes,

> Now we wonder how we could get away with staging those plays under those circumstances and the level of censorship. We used techniques that avoided direct expression. We sometimes referred to the Ottoman rule, British occupation of Iraq, or Palestine. Until one day they banned us from doing any work related to Palestine. 'You are lying,' they said. 'You are referring to yourselves through Palestine.' (Salar, interview, 5 May 2013)

Theatre artists continued to use foreign plays to implicitly comment upon the Kurdish situation and express their socialist ideals. These plays, which had previously been performed by Arab-Iraqi artists, were translated from Arabic. They usually dealt with the universal values of justice and freedom – relevant examples include Yaşar Kemal's *Teneke* (which was directed by Ahmad Salar) and Osvaldo Dragun's one-act plays, *A Toothache, A Plague, A Dog*, which had been translated into Arabic by the prominent Iraqi director, Qasim Muhammd (1936–2009). Original Arabic plays were also translated into Kurdish and staged, including *as-Sirr* (The Secret, 1968) and *al-Ijaaza* (The Holiday, 1977), both by Muhyuddin Zangana, and *al-Hisaar* (The Siege) by Adil Kadhim. While each of these political plays was staged with considerable success, the political situation in Kurdistan meant that theatre artists faced immense difficulties when they sought to obtain official approval for their production (Karim 2009, p. 97).

The translations of world and Arab theatre into Kurdish and the new dramaturgies of the Arab artists made a considerable impact upon Kurdish stage during the 1970s and the 1980s. Already in the 1960s, the Arab dramatists, with the Egyptians in the lead, had started to search for a specifically Arab drama that was based upon the indigenous folkloric theatrical tradition.[2] In the late 1960s, the Arab defeat in the 1967 war with Israel had directly contributed

---

[2] Badawi (1987) provides further insight into the attempts of Egyptian theatre artists to create an indigenous theatre by drawing upon local traditions of *al-samir* and *al-maqama*.

to a dramatic upsurge of political awareness among artists and intellectuals, and this found expression in a desire to raise Arab nationalist consciousness, strengthen national unity and fuel anti-colonial sentiments. It was in this context that a wave of Arab nationalist and anti-Zionist dramas emerged, including Alfred Faraj's *an-Nar waz-Zaytun* (Fire and Olives, 1970) and Yusuf al-Ani's *al-Kharaba* (The Wasteland, 1970).

The period gave rise to attempts to root an indigenous Arab theatre within local culture and history. This project first emerged in Egypt, where it was embodied in attempts to draw on the Arab performance tradition of *hakawati* (story-teller), along with the Arab world's legends and histories. The project soon extended to Iraq, where writers had traditionally shown an inclination to root their plots in local history, folklore, legends and myths. Through the combined influence of Egyptian and Western innovations in theatre, there developed in Iraq a similar search for specifically Arab drama based on traditional folk modes of entertainment. The Iraqi dramatists of the 1960s began their search by engaging with the ancient past and semi-legendary kingdoms. The echo of the past can be clearly identified in plays by Yusuf al-Ani, Adil Kadhim and Qasim Muhammad whose plays express hopes of unity for the Arab-Muslim community.

The growing interest in socialist ideologies in the Middle East also helps explain Brecht's popularity in theatres of Egypt, Iraq and Syria. Arab dramatists, inspired by the experiments of Brecht and Pirandello, drew on shadow theatre, the story-telling tradition and folk literature to comment on contemporary social and political reality. The Syrian Sadallah Wannous, a pioneer of contemporary Arab theatre, played a central role in introducing Brecht to Arab theatres. In his *Bayanat Li Masrah Arabi Jadid* (Manifestos for a New Arabic Theatre, 1970), Wannous spoke of the need for a 'theatre of politicization' – in his view, there was a clear need for a theatre that could provoke critical thought and thus catalyze social change. In order to do so, he addressed contemporary issues by using existing Arabic theatrical elements and traditional literary materials and adapting them to Brecht's theatrical techniques. The result is evidenced in *Elephant, the King of All Times* (1969), *The Adventure of Jaber's Head* (1970), *The King Is the King* (1977) and *Hanthala's Journey from Slumber to Consciousness* (1978), in which he introduced allegory, folktales, improvisation, live music, storytelling and direct interaction with the audience as methods to break the illusion of reality and create the Brechtian alienation effect (Verfremdungseffekt) thus stirring the audience to observe the play critically and reflect on the lessons to be learnt from it.

Wannous's plays achieved great success in Iraq where National Theatre Company produced many of his plays, along with those of Brecht. The Company also produced many successful works by Yusuf al-Ani, the Iraqi playwright who was heavily influenced by Brecht.[3] In Iraq, the works of theatre directors such as al-Ani, Ibrahim Jalal and Sami Abdulhamid marked the point at which Iraqi artists began to engage with Brecht. Abdulhamid notes that the majority of Iraqi intellectuals, including the theatre artists, believed in the Marxian dialectical materialist philosophy, thus providing an additional reason for their interest in Brechtian theatre (Abd al-Hamid 2010, p. 87). The Egyptian *al-Masrah wal-Sinema* (Theatre and Cinema) periodical served as an important source in familiarizing Iraqi theatre artists with Brechtian theatre. Jalal, who had just finished his studies in the United States, also played an important role in introducing Brechtian theatre to Iraqi theatre students in the early 1960s. *Furqa tal-Masrah al-Hadith* (Modern Theatre Group) that Jalal cofounded with al-Ani in 1952, was not only one of the first theatre groups in Iraq but also the first theatre group that used Brechtian techniques in its productions (p. 87).

Brecht's influence was evident in the way the Iraqi dramatists applied folk elements and vernacular dialects. The use of the classical Arabic narrator created the Brechtian alienation effect by interspersing the dramatic action with his remarks. The narrators, actors and choirs commented on events and linked the loosely connected dramatic images, an innovation which was popular in this type of drama. The Iraqi *hakawati*, who traditionally performed in cafés during Ramadan, appeared in al-Ani's *al-Miftah* (The Key) and *al-Kharaba*, as well as in Qasim Muhammad's *Baghdad al-Azal* (Baghdad the Everlasting)

---

[3] Al-Ani was the most prominent twentieth-century Iraqi playwright and one of the strongest voices in Iraqi theatre from the 1950s to the 1980s. His play *Shakir, I'm Your Mother* (1955), which portrays the misery of the Iraqi people in the period before the downfall of the monarchy, was staged several times in Kurdistan (see Tanya 1985, p. 71). The play depicts the persecution of political dissidents as Umm Shakir, the main character, witnesses the suffering and death of her children in the struggle for liberation. Despite her children's tragic fate, she remains steadfast in her belief in the nationalist cause.

and *Kan Ya Ma Kan* (Once Upon a Time). In *Baghdad al-Azal*, the narrator who also acted in the play is known as al-Muqazeli, the renowned Iraqi *hakawati*. In al-Ani's *al-Kharaba*, a chorus of five narrate the events and also act as different characters. The Arabic literary genre of *maqāma* and folk songs are used to illustrate the events of the Palestinian conflict. The stories of *One Thousand and One Nights* also inspired several plays, including Muhyuddin Zangana's *as-Su'al* (The Question) and Falah Shakir's *Layla Alf Layla wa Layla* (The One Thousand First Night).[4]

Ibrahim Jalal and Sami Abdulhamid, both of whom taught at Baghdad University at the time, introduced Kurdish drama graduates to these Brechtian influences and techniques. With regard to the Arab theatre, the influence of Brecht, along with other twentieth-century European dramatists, brought the Kurdish drama closer to the Kurdish performance tradition of storytelling. It achieved this by emphasizing drama's communal nature and obscuring the boundary between the performers and the audience. The use of folk elements, traditional Kurdish narrator, and actors and choirs (who commented on events and directly addressed the audience) appeared within the works of these early drama graduates who would later become Kurdistan's leading dramatists.

Their plays did not utilize act-divisions and were usually divided by scenes (*dîmen*) which were loosely connected dramatic images. In fact, there does not seem to be a clear differentiation between an 'act' or a 'scene' in Kurdish drama as both words translate as *dîmen* in Subhan's *Dictionary of Theatre* (2012). For instance, Saman's short plays *Qel û Rûte* and *Nefretlêkiraw* (The Damned) are, respectively, divided into two *beş* (literally 'part'; act) and three *tablo* (*tableau*), whereas his *Mem û Zîn* and *Heme Dok*, which are much longer, are divided into *dîmens*, with the latter consisting of twenty-five *dîmens*. Salar's *Nalî w Xewnêkî Erxewanî* and *Katê Helo Berz Defrê*, on the other hand, do not clarify any sort of division as the plays are narrated by different characters and music and dance provide a sort of structural fragmentation. In general, most Kurdish

---

[4] The late 1960s also marked the point when Expressionism, as embodied by the Theatre of the Absurd and the works of Beckett and Ionesco, began to make a great impact. The growing appeal of the absurd should be considered in relation to the bitterness engendered by the 1967 war with Israel and the intensification of political struggle in Egypt. Dramatists in both Iraq (Abdilmalik Nuri and Taha Salim) and Syria (Sadallah Wannous), whose plays depict faceless heroes, reduced to the abstract of man dragging his fate with utmost difficulty, evidenced a similar appreciation of the absurd, which was clearly rendered in their one-act plays.

plays are divided into *dimens*, if divided at all, as most of them are too short to need to be broken into acts.

It became customary for the plays to begin with a character who addressed the spectators, welcomed them to the theatre and introduced them to the story that they were about to witness. In *Şarî Evîn* (The City of Love), an actor welcomes the audience as 'the dear friends of *şano* (drama)' before relating the introduction of the story; meanwhile in *Heme Dok* (Hama Dok) a character welcomes the audience and introduces himself before narrating the life story of the title character. Developments in twentieth-century drama which had inspired new techniques in Arab theatre also brought Kurdish drama closer to the eclectic and hybrid nature of indigenous performance forms. This can be seen in the way the dramatists combined dramatic and narrative elements, and fused song and dance into performances. As we will see later, the fusion of song, dance and mimicry found its main proponent in Ahmad Salar who, in the 1980s, became the pioneer of *Şanoy Ahengsazî* (Ceremonial Theatre) in Kurdistan.

The influence of the Arab theatre on its Kurdish counterpart can be seen not only in the stylistic features of the plays produced at the time but also in its growing politicization. Saman observes that 'after the 1970s and the rise of the demand for democracy in the region, Brecht became the main influence [on Kurdish theatre]. These influences came through Arab literature, plays shown on the TV or the books translated into Arabic' (Saman, interview, 9 October 2013). In the late 1970s, Kurdish writers openly spoke of the role of theatre in addressing the sufferings of the nation. Osman Chewar, who adapted *File no. 67* from Arabic into Kurdish, wrote in *Beyan* that, 'now is not the time for theatre to be only a means to entertain. All artistic works must address the pain, the sufferings, the hopes, the dreams, the happiness and the misery of the people ... the end of all these works has to be to serve the people' (Karim 2009, p. 97). Kurdish theatre artists and critics not only promoted nationalist and socialist ideas in their works but also actively took part in political activities. The Kurdish Art and Literature Group, which was established in 1972 in Erbil, became a meeting place for members of different parties such as the Communist Party, the KDP and the PUK (Saman, interview, 9 October 2013).

Although strict censorship and government propaganda promoted a kind of theatre that conformed to the ideals of the Baathist 17 July Revolution and Saddam Hussein's pronouncements (Karim 2009, p. 96), Kurdish dramatists continued, over the second half of the 1970s, to – albeit in allegorical form – produce works which celebrated the Kurdish nationalist struggle and even called for a national uprising against the authoritarian Baath regime. Karim notes that one of the distinguishing features of Kurdish theatre from the late 1970s is that, in most plays, the hero is not an individual but the 'nation' itself. These plays were written about the people and for the people, a point which is evidenced in *Mem û Zîn* (1976) and *Pîlan* (Plot, 1977), both directed by Talat Saman. While the former is considered in extensive detail in the next chapter, the latter also exemplifies a modern nationalist interpretation of the *Mem û Zîn* love-story. In the final scene of the play, the chorus sings, 'Today Mam and Zin hold hands. Do not let go of each other's hands. Do not let go of each other's hands' (Saman 2010, pp. 114, 117–18), which is clearly a call for national solidarity and unity.

The last two years of the 1970s saw a significant increase in the number of printed plays. While between 1974 and 1977 only one Kurdish play was published, this rose to eleven in the period 1978–80. Karim believes that the reason for this sudden increase in cultural and dramatic production can be partly attributed to the Kurdish uprising in 1977 (Karim 2009, p. 102). He notes that while the 1975 defeat produced inertia in the Kurdish society in general and in intellectual circles in particular, the revival of the Kurdish nationalist struggle which took the form of *şorişî nwê* breathed new life into Kurdish society and provided it with a renewed sense of self and its national identity (p. 102). This period of cultural rejuvenation was simultaneous with the Iraqi regime's increasingly brutal policies in an effort to crush the uprising. Its failure in this respect is attested to by the fact that, as the government scaled-up its campaign of violence against Kurds in the countryside, city-dwelling Kurdish dramatists intensified their production of radical pro-revolutionary dramas. This dynamic would later become even more pronounced in the second half of the 1980s, when the government waged the genocidal *al-Anfal* campaign against the Iraqi Kurds.

## Iraq in the 1980s

The end of the 1970s witnessed the emergence of a new dictator in Iraq. After becoming the country's president in 1979, Saddam Hussein embarked on consolidating his power by eliminating Iraq's civil society and opposition movements. His presidency would come to be defined by both external and internal aggression. This included war on Iraqi society and a genocidal campaign against the Iraqi Kurdish population as well as attacks on the neighbouring countries of Iran and Kuwait.

The Iran–Iraq War brought about major changes in Iraq's policies towards Kurdistan. Bruinessen observes,

> Major military operations in the south forced the Iraqi army to relinquish its close control of Kurdistan and placate its population... many Kurds who had been deported to southern Iraq were allowed to return to Kurdistan where they were housed in camps. Thousands of them escaped to zones controlled by the Kurdish parties. (Bruinessen 1986, p. 19)

Iran scaled-up its financial and military support of the KDP and other guerrilla groups. In early 1983, Iraq admitted to 48,000 deserters, many of whom Kurdish and now in the mountains (McDowall 2004, p. 348). Faced with the mass desertions by its Kurdish soldiers, the Iraqi government amnestied the deserters and ruled that the Kurds could serve in Kurdistan rather than the dangerous southern front.

However, the state continued its repressive policies against the Kurds. The Kurdish student organizations voiced their opposition to these policies by organizing protests in major cities. In April and May 1982, mass demonstrations took place in Sulaymaniyah and Erbil, with thousands of Kurdish youth demanding autonomy and a halt to deportations (*Spark*, no. 1, 1982, p. 3). Several students were killed during these demonstration; however, this massive uprising forced the Iraqi government to release thousands of political prisoners and open negotiations with Kurdish parties (Stansfield and Resool 2006, pp. 118–19).

When the war reached Kurdistan in 1983 the KDP sided with Iran and received financial and military support in return. By 1986, the PUK was, like KDP, receiving weapons and financial support to fight against the Iraqi forces. This resulted in the growth of Kurdish-controlled areas, with the KDP expanding in the north and the PUK in the south.

The Kurdish revolt eventually ended when Saddam Hussein initiated his genocidal campaign during the period 1986–9. The Iraqi regime took severe reprisals against Kurds, and subjected the Barzanis to particular brutality. Eight thousand Barzani men living in the camps of Qushtapa and Diyana were taken to an unknown destination while relatives of Barzanis who lived in Baghdad also disappeared (Bruinessen 2000, p. 206). Summary executions, mass deportations and Arabization of place names continued. Thousands of peshmerga family members were arrested, herded into lorries and sent to camps in the south of Iraq.

In April 1987, Iraqi Air Force began dropping chemical bombs on villages and fields in the provinces of Erbil and Sulaymaniyah; this then escalated to bombing campaigns that lasted for an entire week, demolishing and burning entire villages and wounding and killing hundreds (*The Torch*, no. 7, 1987, p. 1). Between April and September 1987, 500 villages were razed in order to deny the peshmerga food and shelter (McDowall 2004, p. 353). As the Iran–Iraq War reached its conclusion, Iraqi forces seized the opportunity to suppress the Kurdish rebellion. The genocidal Operation *Anfal*, which killed 182,000 Kurds and created over a million refugees, began in 1988. The operation would later become synonymous with the Kurdish town of Halabja, where Iraqi government forces used chemical weapons and killed almost 5,000 of its residents in a matter of minutes.

## Theatre in the cities of Sulaymaniyah and Erbil in the 1980s

The Baathist government's strict censorship of media continued under Saddam Hussein, and the media increasingly came to function as an appendage of his regime – in the words of Isakhan, its essential purpose was 'to generate a complex matrix of discourses that served to obfuscate state tyranny' (Isakhan 2012, pp. 110–17). Iraq's entire media industry was subject to the authority of the government, and all journalists were required to declare their loyalty to the Baath party. Careful monitoring of the media ensured that all Iraqi papers became state-run propaganda machines, concerned with 'reciting official policy and praising governmental action' (p. 105). All papers and journals, including the Kurdish journals that are engaged in this volume, had to feature Saddam's photograph daily on page one and print his speeches in full (p. 105).

Theatre was also subject to strict state controls. Jaffar notes that during the Iran–Iraq War, several Kurdish artists were called before the committee of censorship upon the basis that they had endangered the Iraqi identity (Jaffar 2012, p. 127). The artists soon perfected a technique through which they could retain a veneer of Baathist loyalty while advocating the ideals of freedom and justice which had been denied to them. Foreign plays were an important resource in this regard. Increasing numbers of Western plays were translated into Kurdish during this period. Prominent examples included Shakespeare's *Merchant of Venice* and *Hamlet*, Chekhov's *The Seagull* and *On the Harmful Effects of Tobacco*, Clifford Odets' *Waiting for Lefty*, Gogol's *The Government Inspector* and Lorca's *Blood Wedding*.

However, the staging of foreign plays did not always guarantee the state's indifference. During the Iran–Iraq War, *Mangî Awa Bû*, a play based on John Steinbeck's anti-war novel, *The Moon is Down*, ran successfully for a month in Sulaymaniyah; however, it was banned in Erbil after only two days (Ahmadmirza 2011, pp. 99–100). The plays staged during the war clearly demonstrate that Kurdish theatre refused to become a state propaganda tool or legitimize the state's belligerence. This also confirms Isakhan's assessment that the brutality of the Iraqi regime was strongly opposed by a strong culture of clandestine dissent and opposition and a variety of counter-discourses.

In 1984, the first conference on Kurdish theatre took place in Erbil. During this five-day-long conference, several organs attended, including *Dezgay Roşinbîrî w Blawkirdinewey Kurdî* (Kurdish Culture and Publishing Organisation), *Emîndaretî Giştî Roşinbîrî w Lawan* (General Directorate of Culture and Youth), *Yekyetî Nûseranî Kurd* (the Union of Kurdish Writers), *Neqabey Hunermendan* (The Artists' Guild), *Komeley Hunere Cwanekanî Kurd* (The Kurdish Society of Fine Arts), *Tîpî Hunerî Hewlêr* (The Erbil Art Group) and the students of the Institute of Fine Arts (Abdurrahman 1984).

During the conference, the various challenges which confronted Kurdish theatre were discussed in depth – these included a lack of original dramatic texts, a lack of theatres and society's attitudes towards female actors. In a closing statement given by the host, the Kurdish Culture and Publication Organisation, Saddam Hussein was praised as a supporter of arts and theatre. He was also commended as a gracious leader who cared about the progress of Kurdish society and its cultural, intellectual and artistic life. The final words of the statement read: 'We hope theatre artists continue their activities to further the theatre movement and contribute to Iraqi people and the civilized society at the time of Iraq's victory and progress under our great leader, comrade Saddam Hussein, may God protect him' (Abdurrahman 1984, p. 87).

While Iraqi and Kurdish artists were forced by the state to praise and promote the Baathist ideology, they succeeded in using allegory, clever analogies, double-entendres and subtle imagery to expose the authoritarian and repressive culture of the Baath and force their fellow citizens to ponder alternatives such as democratic rule.[5] During the 1970s and 1980s, several plays were printed and published in *Beyan*, *Roşinbîrî Nwê* and *Rojî Kurdistan*. While all periodicals were obliged to commit their first pages to Saddam Hussain and extend eulogies to him, many of the plays they published indirectly challenged the status quo. For example, in *Cenabî Canewer* (Mister Animal, 1981), Hussein Arif, who has been celebrated as 'the greatest story-writer of his time' (Salar 2013, personal interview, 5 May), wrote about the general manager of a company which produced magnifying glasses. This was an allusion to the then Director General in the Ministry of Culture in Baghdad who was one of the oldest and most ruthless Baathists. Although a Kurd himself, he strongly opposed any expression of Kurdish nationalism and endeavoured to ensure that any books that conveyed these sentiments were burnt and destroyed. *Cenabî Canewer* is an account of Arif's experience as an employee at the Ministry where, along with other employees, he was routinely mistreated by its Director General (Salar 2013, personal interview, 5 May).

The 1980 opening of Sulaymaniyah Institute of Fine Arts (*Peymangay Hunere Cwanekan*) was an important development which established the basis for future theatrical endeavours. The Academy had two departments (painting and drama). The period of study was five years and at its conclusion students would receive a diploma in acting or directing. Shortly after its establishment, the Academy successfully attracted the attention of Iraqi theatre artists and critics by hosting an annual nation-wide theatre festival. The Academy's productions included *Julius Caesar* and *The Merchant of Venice* (both directed by Badea Dartash, Iraqi Kurdistan's first female drama graduate and

---

[5] For further insight, refer to my review of Talat Saman's *Qel û Rûte* (The Raven and the Pauper) in the following chapter.

professor)[6] and *Mem û Zîn* (directed by Farhad Sharif) – see 'Peymangay Hunere Cwanekanî Silêmanî (Sulaymaniyah Institute of Fine Arts', 2009).

The growing number of theatre groups was another important development. Upon returning to Kurdistan, Baghdad graduates brought a range of new insights and perspectives with them. This contributed to the establishment of several theatre groups over the course of the 1980s, including the Progressive Kurdish Theatre Group (*Tîpî Pêşrewî Şanoy Kurdî*), Salar Theatre (*Şanoy Salar*), Kurds' Fine Art Society (*Komeley Hunere Cwanekanî Kurd*) and The Experimental Theatre (*Şanoy Ezmungerî*). Kurdish-language television programmes also, despite continuing censorship, played an important role in promoting Kurdish drama.

During the mid-1980s, efforts were made to create a distinctly Kurdish theatre. Kurdish graduates of Baghdad University, having been influenced by the broader theatre movement in Iraq, sought to create an original authentic Kurdish theatre by drawing upon their cultural heritage. Folk culture provided a new form of expression and a code with which to raise political awareness. Ahmad Salar was the most prominent member of this group of Kurdish dramatists. He was particularly inspired by Abdelkarim Berrechid's *masrah al-ihtifali* (Festive or Ceremonial Theatre) which drew heavily on indigenous theatrical forms and alluded to local folk culture and history with the intention of addressing the problem of identity in the postcolonial Arab world. Having been strongly influenced by Berrechid's theatre, Salar relied on local historical characters and indigenous performance traditions to address the themes of Kurdish struggle for freedom. This was vividly illustrated by plays such as *Nalî w Xewnêkî Erxewanî* (Nali and a Violet Dream, 1987) and *Katê Helo Berz Defrê* (When the Eagle Flies High, 1988). As the later discussion demonstrates in more detail, these plays draw upon music, nationalistic poetry and traditional Kurdish tales to revive a sense of pride in Kurdish culture, strengthen a sense of national unity, as well as incite rebellion.

While Salar believed that it was necessary to write original plays in Kurdish in order to create an authentic Kurdish theatre (Salar 2012, p. 13), another group of young Kurdish artists sought to move away from text-based drama altogether. This new experimental theatre was pioneered

---

[6] For more information about Dartash, see Jaffar (2015).

**Figure 19** First drama professors at Sulaymaniyah Institute of Fine Arts: (sitting from left) Azad Jalal, Badea Dartash and Ahmad Salar. *Source*: *Şano*, 2009, no. 12.

by Dana Rauf, Nigar Hasib Qaradaqi, Midiya Rauf and Shamal Omar in the mid-1980s in Sulaymaniyah. Experimentalism, in Kurdish context, indicated the desire of the new generation of theatre artists to break with traditional forms of drama and create new ones. At first, they relied mainly on foreign texts and began by staging several modernist works such as Eugene O'Neill's *The Hairy Ape* (1922), which they staged in 1986 in both Sulaymaniyah and Erbil. They later performed plays such as *Waiting for Godot* (1948) by Samuel Beckett, *Marat/Sade* (1963) by Peter Weiss, *Black Stories* (1948) by Leopold Sedar Senghor, and *Zoo Story* (1958) by Edward Albee, amongst others. The main difference between these plays and the ones that had traditionally been performed in Kurdistan was in their modes of storytelling. For these writers, experimentation with style took precedence over ideological or thematic concerns. Their heroes were individualistic, and their experiences of life were accentuated. Experimental theatre disengaged from society and distanced itself from the didacticism of old theatre. This was only the beginning for the Experimental Theatre Group as they soon dispensed with narrative structure in their attempts to create an authentic Kurdish theatre.

The founders of the Experimental Theatre Group were all graduates of Baghdad University where they had been profoundly influenced by Salah al-Qasab's 'Theatre of Images' (Rauf 1995, p. 19). This approach to performance is associated with American avant-garde directors from the 1970s.[7] In turning away from an a priori text and language and instead relying on visual and aural sensory images, these directors sought to challenge conventional understanding of performance, which relied heavily on narrative structure. In contrast, they proposed that the imagination of the audience should be actively engaged in finding the significance of the performance themselves (see Marranca 1996). Having been inspired by 'Theatre of Images' and its substitution of tableaux and gesture in place of language, the young Kurdish graduates of Baghdad University sought to change the Kurdish theatre scene by instead focusing on body language. The emphasis accordingly shifted to abstract and distorted movement, costume and scenic elements. The boundary between actors and spectators was reduced with the intention of establishing the audience as direct participants in the performance, something that was achieved by intensifying the eye contact between actors and spectators. The main focus of the performance was no longer the meaning of the literary work, but rather its colour, image and sound.

In 1989, the Experimental Theatre Group took an important step towards applying these avant-garde performance methods to classic Kurdish texts when it staged *Le Çawerwani Siyamend* (Waiting for Siyamand, 1989), a play that was based on the Kurdish folktale of *Xec û Siyamend*. While clearly influenced by Fuad Majid Misri's modern adaptation of the folktale, the two female actors and directors of *Le Çawerwani Siyamend*, Nigar Hasib and Midiya Rauf, only retained the core idea of the play: they therefore dispensed with other elements, such as the traditional storyteller who narrated the story in Misri's play (Zangana 2002, p. 122). In relying on gestures and body language, Hasib and Rauf communicated the pain of Khaj's subjugation by men and the power

---

[7] Lee Breuer (b. 1937), Richard Foreman (b. 1937) and Robert Wilson (b. 1941).

of her resistance against their tyranny.[8] The fact that the characters of Khaj and Siyamand were both played by women, a feature clearly contrary to the traditional male dominance in Kurdish society and theatre, further reinforced the theme of resistance against outmoded traditional social structures.

Experimental Kurdish theatre's emphasis on form and style to the disadvantage of text and content (Qarib 2009), however, alienated those theatre-goers, who remained more beholden to classical narrative structures with a beginning, middle and end. The production of Western modernist plays were also criticized for failing to represent the realities of Kurdish pain and oppression, which could only be represented through original Kurdish texts (Zangana 2002, p. 116). Muhsin Muhammad maintains that the active support of the Iraqi government was a key contributing factor to the growth of Iraqi experimental theatre during the 1980s (Muhammad 2010). 'The Iraqi dictatorship,' Muhammad suggests, 'promoted experimentalism in theatre because they did not want theatre to become popular' (p. 73). He continued,

> This type of (experimentalist or modernist) drama has its own special audience. With regard to Kurdish theatre, as I have witnessed in the past twenty years, the intellectuals, artists, men of letters and journalists make up the special audience in Kurdistan. We were a small number…and we all knew each other. Many times one would see the same faces in Erbil theatres as he/she had previously seen in Sulaymaniyah theatres. (Muhammad, p. 72)

Dana Rauf, instead, defends the experimental theatre in Kurdistan on the grounds that it was a source of hope and excitement for a young generation deprived of both. He observes, 'We were a group of young people who dared to dream at a time when there was no joy; we believed in future at a time when we had no future' (Rauf 2010, p. 97). For Rauf, this form of theatre provided a welcome alternative to life under Baathist dictatorship and conscriptions during the Iran–Iraq War. He adds,

> We lived at the time of war, but we staged *Marat/Sade*; we had deserted the army and performed the *Zoo Story* and discussed the creation of an original Kurdish theatre. Those efforts were not only for the sake of theatre, but for

---

[8] See Zangana (2002, pp. 121–8) for a detailed analysis of the play which situates it within the wider context of the Kurdish resistance movement in Iraq.

**Figure 20** Midiya Rauf (right) and Nigar Hasib Qaradaqi in *Le Çawerwanî Siyamend*. *Source*: Rauf's personal archive.

the sake of survival. It was a way to emphasise our existence and our national and intellectual identities. (Rauf, p. 97)

For Rauf and other experimentalists, the production of avant-garde works on the Kurdish stage was itself an act of self-affirmation. While these plays did not command popular attention and remained within the limited orbit of intellectual circles, Rauf's assertion, which reiterates the importance of experimental theatre to theatre artists themselves, recalls the concept of 'beautiful resistance' developed by the Palestinian theatre group, *Alrowwad* (Thompson, Hughes and Balfour 2009, pp. 56–67). This concept asserts that theatre provides an environment in which those afflicted with daily experience of political oppression may develop self-esteem, self-confidence and self-expression. The translation of modernist plays into Kurdish and their production on stage similarly affirmed the national identity and intellectual capabilities of Kurdish youth who sought to assert their existence and their capabilities through modernist theatre. Experimental theatre also provided an escape from the bleak realities of war and destruction. These contributions, as Thompson, Hughes and Balfour note, quite clearly confound simplistic categorizations which render performance as aesthetic, escapist or political (p. 60).

In concluding this discussion of the 'Golden Age' of Kurdish theatre, it is worthwhile to review the reflections of the leading Arab theatre directors and critics who attended the Sulaymaniyah Fine Arts Institute's fourth theatre festival in May 1990. The Egyptian Kamal Eid (1931–2008), who was the first to introduce Chekhov, Gorki and Brecht to the Egyptian theatre, praised the Kurdish entries at the festival upon both artistic and technical grounds. He also suggested that the standard of critical debates exceeded Arabic theatre festivals of the same time (Karim 2009, p. 112). Fadhil Thamir, the Iraqi critic, also praised the Kurdish productions and asserted that, taking the festival as the unit of measurement, Kurdish theatre appeared to be at the same level of development as its Arabic counterpart (p. 113). The level of public engagement, as embodied in the number of spectators who awaited the performances from the early hours, also appeared to (positively) impact the perceptions of these Arab observers. Kamal Eid said the passion amongst the Kurdish audiences could not be found anywhere else in Iraq (p. 112). Likewise, Hasaballah Yahya, the Iraqi journalist who attended Erbil's first theatre festival, stated his amazement and pride when he encountered the large crowds waiting to enter the performance venues (p. 113).

## Guerrilla theatre, 1974–91

In *The Wretched of the Earth* (1967), Frantz Fanon argues that, when perceived from the perspective of revolutionary nationalism, 'cultural action cannot be divorced from the larger struggle for the liberation of the nation' (cited in Holdsworth 2014, p. 6). This conjoining of the cultural and political can be visibly witnessed in the Kurdish guerrilla theatre of the 1970s and 1980s – this is a rare case in which theatre was used by the guerrillas themselves.[9] Theatre by Kurdish

---

[9] Guerrilla Theatre in the Kurdish context should not be confused with the American Guerrilla Theatre that was initiated in 1965 by the American San Francisco Mime Troupe, who engaged in surprise performances in public spaces in order to draw attention to contemporary social and political issues. Guerrilla Theatre in the American context has been applied to theatrical events of the late 1960s through the mid-1970s which addressed the Vietnam war and capitalism; the agitprop theatre of the 1930s also provides a further example – for more information, see Doyle (2002). I have only come across one instance of theatrical performance that was actually, as in the case of Iraqi Kurdistan, performed by guerrilla fighters themselves – this was in Jane Plastow's study of the theatres of Ethiopia, Tanzania and Zimbabwe (Plastow 1996).

guerrillas can be traced back to the 1974 uprising when the urban artists who had gone to the mountains to join the uprising presented their works to the villagers of the liberated areas and to the peshmergas in the guerrilla camps.

As Stansfield and Resool (2006) point out, by March 1975, 'the vast majority of Kurds were involved directly or indirectly with some aspect of the Kurdish movement' (p. 103). The increasingly nationalist-minded urban centres of Kurdistan contained thousands of sympathizers who were willing to aid the peshmergas against the Iraqi government. In the space of days in March 1975, nearly 100,000 patriotic Kurds, mostly from the towns, left their jobs and ventured to areas of Kurdistan controlled by the peshmergas, thus swelling their ranks considerably (p. 103). This wave of volunteers from urban centres contained, among others, stage directors such as Simko Aziz and his Sulaymaniyah Acting Group and Ahmad Salar and his Progressive Kurdish Theatre Group. Salar presented several nationalistic plays including *Pirdî Welat* and *Çalî Cergî Pîrejin* (The Hole in the Old Woman's Heart). However, the 1974 uprising was short-lived. When the Iraqi regime issued an amnesty, guerrilla theatre groups soon dissolved and the artists returned to their hometowns.

It was in the 1980s, however, that theatre became an important propaganda tool for the guerrillas. During the Iran–Iraq War (1980–8), many Iraqi Kurds deserted the army and fled to the mountains to join the peshmerga. There, they engaged in cultural activities which included, among other things, theatrical performances. The revolutionaries in guerrilla camps were from diverse backgrounds, and plays were therefore written and performed both in Arabic and Kurdish. Most actors were amateur performers and educated young Kurds who had joined the peshmerga. Some were, prior to joining the peshmerga forces, drama students. Alternatively, they had previously been involved with school theatre groups or drama groups.

Some amateur groups were only established to perform at a specific event (e.g. Newroz), and were quickly dissolved after it took place. Solid theatre groups were however established by professionals who sought to adapt acting methods and align them with the realities of resistance in Kurdistan. The directors put great demands on actors and taught them acting techniques. This was not an easy task because the various daily tasks that were imposed upon the peshmerga left little time for practice. Zangana (2002) refers to Abu Arwa, a director who acknowledged the difficulties of teaching acting methods in guerrilla camps and yet continued to do so in order to convince his actors 'of the importance of art in resistance' (p. 81).

A lack of access to literary books resulted in some guerrilla theatre groups adopting themes directly from Kurdish life. Because there were hardly any libraries or bookstores in villages and books were difficult to obtain, these groups sometimes used their own personal experiences as material for their plays. Other plays thematized the suffering of people under the Iraqi regime, while others ridiculed and satirized Saddam Hussein and his followers (Zangana 2002, p. 76). Music also played a central role within guerrilla theatre by creating atmosphere, underscoring situations and accentuating the dramatic action. *Bilwêr*,[10] *duhol*, *keman*,[11] *senc*[12] and *oud*[13] were among the musical instruments that accompanied the songs. Music was one of the most effective and widely deployed means of cultural propaganda in the liberation struggle, in no small part due to its emotional resonance and adaptability. In addition to written slogans, liberation songs were sung with the intention of raising the audience's political consciousness and revive a sense of identity.

The performances took place wherever it was possible: in tea-houses, caves, or on mountain slopes. For security reasons, the venues had to remain secret until a few hours before the show. In case of an attack, the partisans had to protect themselves and also the audience – as a result, there was a constant state of emergency. The actors carried their weapons with them or hid them close at hand so they were immediately ready to fight against an unexpected attack (Zangana 2002, p. 86). If the performance took place in the open air, the peshmerga sought to find a location that would enable them to respond in case of attack. Performances usually took place late in the afternoon or in the evening when villagers were back from farm work and had sufficient leisure time. The risk of an aerial attack was lower at nightfall; even if it occurred, the camouflage worked better. The stage was lit by nothing more than an oil lamp in order to offset the danger of being discovered by the enemy. Electric generators or flashlights were used only at very large events (p. 86).

---

[10] An end-blown flute.
[11] A bowed, stringed instrument.
[12] A metallic percussion instrument like a cymbal but larger in diameter.
[13] A pear-shaped stringed instrument.

The peshmerga actors wore the costumes that were available in everyday life or whatever else that was available. The costumes also needed to be adjusted so that they would not prevent a quick response if/when a sudden attack occurred. The same applied to the props, which were all objects of everyday life and struggle – this included the pictures on the walls, the weapons or the shelves. A blanket was hung at the back of the stage and the props were handed to the actors from behind it. The stage was minimal because, if the group wanted to perform at a different location, everything had to be transported on animals (see Figures 21 and 22). When a play was performed in different villages, the march often took several hours. Taking the everyday dangers and stresses of life as a peshmerga, it is incredible that theatre groups believed so strongly in their work that they were willing to put up with the inconvenience of continual changes in location and the provision of additional security personnel (Zangana 2002, p. 86).

One of the theatre groups formed by the guerrillas was the Partisan Theatre Group. Founded by Fattah Khattab, the dramatist, director and literary critic, this group was made up of film-makers, journalists, musicians, painters, poets and theatre artists. According to Khattab himself, the Partisan Theatre Group was made up of peshmerga artists, intellectuals and writers who had not been co-opted by the regime (Khattab, interview, 4 August 2014).

**Figure 21** *Ragwêz* (Transfer), a play performed by PUK peshmerga fighters in the village of Bilekê in Saqez, Iran, 1989. *Source*: Sheikh Mahmud 2011, p. 63.

**Figure 22** *Tewbey Gurg Merge* (A Wolf's Penitence Is Death), a play performed by PUK peshmerga fighters in 1980. *Source*: Sheikh Mahmud 2011, p. 69.

The Partisan Theatre Group used the Living Newspaper, a technique that was developed in the USSR in 1917 to spread propaganda and which was later adopted by Piscator in Germany in the 1920s (Khattab, interview, 4 August 2014). The Living Newspaper was a method in which the news was acted out in a series of vignettes for the benefit of largely illiterate audiences. After it emerged in the United States in 1935 as part of the Federal Theatre Project, its supporters advanced it in the belief that it could be an instrument of social change and consequently presented a number of Living Newspapers on social issues of the day. This form of drama resembles the Brechtian epic theatre in its use of simple sets, props and costumes. It acknowledges audience members and engages controversial issues, dramatizes current events and offers appropriate suggestions for improvement.

For its agitprop style and its minimalist scenery, Living Newspaper was a convenient dramatic technique for the guerrilla theatre groups who found it perfectly adjusted to their needs and requirements. Khattab describes the guerrilla artists' search for an appropriate dramatic technique in the following terms:

> As early as the beginning of the 1970s, we . . . were aware that one day the doors of the state-sponsored cultural organisations will shut down on us because of the political mafia's monopoly on them which would not allow the expression of anything other than the Baath party propaganda . . . therefore, we searched for an artistic method that would suit our literary and artistic aspirations; a method that would allow for a dialectic educational theatre . . . since the 1970s we have been looking for a theatrical method immune to and independent of official supervision and financial support. This can be done through partisan theatre . . . an inexpensive theatre that is possible everywhere, in streets, teahouses, prisons, parks, libraries, villages or mosques. (Khattab, interview, 4 August 2014)

Khattab and his group found their ideal in the epic theatre of Brecht and Piscator; additional influences included Osvaldo Dragun, Gholam-Hossein Sa'edi, Sabah Mandalawi, Heiner Müller, Sadallah Wannous, Peter Weiss and the poetry of Sa'di Yusuf, Fazil Azawi and Muzaffar Nawab. Most of these dramatists and poets are united by a shared commitment to left-wing politics and social change. Sa'edi was a prolific Iranian writer whose plays, which combined minimalist stage scenery and props, simple language and political and social themes, were frequently staged by amateur and professional theatre groups in the 1960s and 1970s. Dragun's drama also engaged with international political issues such as the US coup against Jacobo Árbenz, the leftist Guatemalan president.[14] Yusuf, Azawi and Nawab were all Iraqi poets whose works reflected the contemporary politics of their country and the world. Yusuf and Nawab were imprisoned for their leftist beliefs while Azawi was forced into exile as the Baathist control over the country grew stronger.

Khattab suggests that it was a historical inevitability that Kurdish artists would follow in the footsteps of these venerable dramatists and poets. 'They showed us the way forward', Khattab says, 'in the process of founding a partisan theatre during our nation's struggle against the Iraqi regime' (interview, 4 August 2014). The leftist ideology that was pervasive in Iraq at the time, and which was actively promoted by the PUK, is clearly evidenced within Khattab's

---

[14] *La Peste Viene de Melos* (The Plague from Melos).

theatre productions from this period. It is immediately noticeable, for instance, that his foreign plays are more concerned with universal political and social issues than with the specificities of Kurdish struggle. However, the two were not necessarily diametrically opposed – Khattab suggested in an interview that he saw the Kurds as part of a larger world in which they shared dreams, goals and sufferings with other nations (4 August 2014).

The Partisan Theatre, according to Khattab, followed the techniques of the Living Newspaper drama which had previously been expounded by Peter Weiss. It appears that in this instance Khattab is referring to the German documentary theatre which emerged in the mid-1960s and which was embodied in the works of Rolf Hochhuth, Hiener Kipphardt and Peter Weiss. Their theatre used factual reality and historical documents as source materials for their plays, with a view to investigating the political driving forces that underpin historical events.

Erwin Piscator preceded Weiss's documentary theatre in many important respects. His agitprop productions incorporated film footage and scenes from recent history and political events, most notably the class struggles of the 1920s. In his productions, performances lasted for less than thirty minutes, scripts were straightforward and stage equipment was makeshift/moveable. His work, which engaged social injustice and issued calls for revolution, ultimately sought to raise audience awareness of the class struggle or clarify the official party line. This recalls Weiss's documentary theatre, which was more preoccupied with struggles between opposing socioeconomic forces and groups than with individual conflicts.

The legacy of documentary-style theatre, the Living Newspaper, the Brechtian epic and the one-act plays by the aforementioned dramatists inspired the Partisan Theatre in its direct engagement with the audience, its use of music and songs as a form of commentary to stage action and its minimal scenery, props and costumes and small number of characters. This group, along with other peshmerga theatre groups, staged its plays on political or national occasions which included celebrations of the 14 July Revolution, International Workers' Day and Newroz (Khattab, interview, 4 August 2014). During World Theatre Day, which was held annually on March 27, resistance theatre groups arranged large-scale celebrations and organized lectures on the history of Iraqi and world theatre (Zangana 2002, p. 84). During Newroz, they performed the folk play, *Kawa the Blacksmith*, to public in liberated villages (p. 84).

Political theatre, and especially documentary theatre, could be viewed as preaching to the converted – quite clearly, the individual would not expose himself/herself to this material if he/she was not already convinced of its value. Kurdish Guerrilla Theatre, however, was clearly different in this respect – its audience was composed of both the peshmerga and also the inhabitants of the liberated villages who voluntarily attended the performances and showed great enthusiasm. Theatre also enabled the peshmerga to communicate with civilians. This reduced distance, increased understanding and strengthened solidarity. More could be achieved through theatre than through a political speech. In addition, theatre also enabled Arabic-speaking members of the peshmerga to communicate with the Kurdish country dwellers through body language and mime (Zangana 2002, p. 73). A former Guerrilla Theatre director clearly conveys the potential contribution of the art form in the following terms:

> You, in your peshmerga costume, come to a place where no one knows you. But after the performance, the audience becomes interested in you and wants to meet you in person. Later they write you letters and visit you. They invite you back and bring you presents . . . Playing in the countryside, you see and feel the spectators' love for your theatre in their faces. You are touched by their invitations and their gifts and see the pure emotion that they feel for you. (Zangana 2002, pp. 73, 79)

As the above quote demonstrates, theatre was used by the peshmerga as a means of communication by helping to overcome many social boundaries and obstacles. It was customary for the peshmerga to gather villagers in one place and lecture them on politics. While these lectures were usually only attended by male adults, theatre was attended by men and women of varying ages, therefore reaching a wider public. However, drama's potential contribution in this and other respects was not always appreciated by the main military leaders in guerrilla camps, who underestimated the drawing power of drama. Political parties also sometimes demanded agitprop performances that advanced a specific party ideology. Zangana maintains that it was actually the ordinary civilians who had a better appreciation of the value of theatre as a means of resistance and social change.

## Theatre of the displaced

According to Salar, his troupe of forty actors not only staged plays in peshmerga camps in the mountains but also crossed the border into Iran where thousands of Kurdish refugees lived in camps. 'We had a stage we could dismantle in an hour, our own electricity and, in case of rain, a tent,' Salar said (interview, 5 May 2013). In the year after March 1974, Salar's theatre group performed in refugee camps in the Iranian provinces of Kurdistan, Kermanshah and Ilam. The plays staged in camps were all nationalistic plays. The actors sometimes adopted mime in response to the fact that the sheer size of the audience meant their voices could not be heard. In Haji Omran, the Progressive Kurdish Theatre Group presented Salar's *Çalî Cergî Pîrejin* and another play entitled *Katê Wêne Dêtewe Lam* (When the Image Comes Back to Me), which was directed by Omar Chawshin (Salar, interview, 5 May 2013). During this time, Salar's theatre troupe survived several bombardments. Salar was himself injured in Qaladiza when Iraqi government's forces attacked the region (interview, 5 May 2013).

The story of Kurdish displacement continued into the 1980s. Whenever a rebellion was crushed and towns and villages were destroyed, new waves of refugees, who included theatre actors, directors and teachers, were forced to flee across the border into Iran. Kamal Hanjira, the peshmerga director and drama professor, describes how he came to perform plays in the refugee area:

> I am a peshmerga fighter and can fight with a weapon. I am familiar with weapons because I fought for twenty years as a peshmerga. But my art, the theatre, was greater and more important to me than weapons. In theatre you can fight without weapons. I could not remain silent as an artist when I witnessed the harsh conditions in the refugee camps, the hunger, cold and misery. I chose the path of art to protest. (Zangana 2002, p. 88)

The theatre of the displaced was not only directed against the Iraqi government, but also against the foreign governments that supported it. Opposition parties were also sometimes criticized during the course of performances. In *Nêrgiz û Mergî Helebce* (The Daffodil and the Death of Halabja), the victims of the Halabja atrocity are depicted as ghosts who witness their demise become headlines for foreign journalists and objects of study for foreign scientists. The play, which is starkly factual throughout, directs the question of criminal responsibility to the international community and implicitly criticizes the PUK for its military and political alliance with Iran. This play, which can be described as a documentary drama, was written based on facts and details such as name of places that had been bombed and chemical products used in the bombing.

Thompson, Balfour and Hughes believe that performances in the aftermath of war present opportunities 'for the telling and witnessing of narratives of atrocity' committed against 'those marginalised, demonised or oppressed' by the dominant discourses and practices (Thompson, Balfour and Hughes 2009, p. 206). This statement certainly rings true in the case of *Nêrgiz û Mergî Helebce* which was performed at a time when the world was slow to respond to the atrocity in Halabja or to acknowledge that it was part of a more general campaign of genocide. The United States, in particular, was reluctant to accept that the Iraqi regime had used chemical weapons against its own population, and instead sought to blame Iran. *Nêrgiz û Mergî Helebce* therefore arose as a demand that this crime be acknowledged and recognized in its true significance 'so that lives are not forgotten and justice can be claimed' (p. 210).

During the performance of *Nêrgiz û Mergî Helebce* the spectators started to cry and remained long after the end and wept together. *Nêrgiz* offered audiences a chance to mourn and remember and focus on the losses they experienced in war. The re-engagement of that extremely traumatic event was so overwhelming for the spectators that they poured out their emotions in a collective act of mourning that enveloped and united them. Theatre of the displaced, therefore, not only highlighted the plight of the victims, but also became a therapeutic act for the survivors in the audience who shared common stories of loss and pain.[15]

---

[15] Zangana suggests that this form of theatre gave rise to a debate among theatre artists who sought to establish whether this art form should be used to make audience members cry or motivate them to fight. Kamal Hanjira was a strong opponent of performance-as-mourning until he witnessed a theatre performance which directly engaged with the events of Halabja. This performance is said to have taken place on the anniversary of the bombing of the town of Halabja. A large crowd gathered in Halabja's cemetery to witness a performance in which a doll was constructed from wood and the leftover belongings of the victims. A picture taken during the performance shows a Kurdish turban cloth, which is unique to the region, wrapped around the doll's head. The picture also depicts children's dress, a cradle, the belts of Kurdish men, prayer beads, scarves, schoolbooks, a woman's handbag and the colours of the Kurdish Flag – green, red and yellow. Daffodils symbolize the Kurdish New Year that had taken place four days before the Halabja atrocity. The performers, in a manner similar to the *çemer* tradition, marched through the cemetery, singing to the accompaniment of music (see Zangana 2002).

Theatrical performances in refugee camps continued in 1991 when thousands of people were displaced by war and forced to live in UNHCR (United Nations High Commissioner for Refugees) tents in the border regions which divide Iran, Iraq and Turkey. These performances usually took place on special occasions, such as the anniversary of Leyla Qasim's martyrdom or Newroz.[16] No records of these theatrical performances seems to exist, and they can therefore only be retrieved through further exploration of oral history, which gives a voice to those involved in theatre performances in guerrilla and refugee camps and provides further insight into the contribution of theatre to Kurdish nationalist struggle.

## Post-uprising Kurdistan

In the aftermath of Iraq's resounding defeat in the First Gulf War in 1991, Iraqi Shi'as and Kurds rose against the central government, an event which Kurds simply refer to as *raperîn* (uprising). The uprisings resulted in mass reprisals, and almost two million refugees fled the country. In order to protect the civilians, the Coalition established a no-fly zone over Kurdistan and the Kurdish opposition established the autonomous Kurdistan Regional Government (KRG) in what is known as Iraqi Kurdistan.

Due to its continued refusal to recognize and abide by relevant UN resolutions, Iraq was, for much of the 1990s, subject to sanctions that were imposed by the United Nations Security Council. These sanctions severely hurt the economy, medical services 'and not least the country's theatre and cultural infrastructure' (Al-Mufraji 1991, p. 104). Despite these ongoing challenges, Iraqi theatre continued to produce a large number of state-supported theatre companies over the 1990s. Branches of the Baghdad-based *al-Firqa al-Qawmiyya lit-Tamtheel* (National Theatre Company) also opened in smaller cities such as Baabil, Basrah, Karbala and Nineveh (p. 104).

---

[16] Zangana mentions a play entitled *Aştî Dexwazîn* (We Want Peace), written and directed by Kamal Hanjira, which was staged at a camp in Zêwe (a village near the border between Iraq and Iran) (Zangana 2002, p. 89). Another play called *Leyla Qasim* was performed by Ibrahim Hakim and others in Zêwe Refugee Camp on the occasion of her execution in May 1974.

Life in Kurdistan was very different to the rest of Iraq. It had been shattered by intermittent civil war since 1961, the eight-year Iran–Iraq War (1980–8), Saddam Hussein's *Anfal* campaign and the 1991 Gulf War (which resulted in a total of two million refugees fleeing to Iran and Turkey). The situation in Kurdistan only worsened following the looting of institutions by Iraqi Army in the short period of regaining control over cities of Kurdistan in late March and April of 1991, the withdrawal of Iraqi administration and services from Kurdistan in October 1991, Saddam's imposition of economic blockade against Kurdish areas and the UN sanctions against Iraq which included the free Kurdish areas (Sheikhmous, 'The Self-made Tragedy in Kurdistan', p. 2).

In 1994, rivalry between the KDP and PUK resulted in a bloody civil war which claimed the lives of between 3,000 and 5,000 fighters and civilians. Hostilities between the two parties simmered until 1998, when the two parties signed a cease-fire agreement in Washington. Since then, an uneasy political balance has prevailed, with the KDP administering Erbil and Duhok, and the PUK governing over Sulaymaniyah, Darbandikhan and the towns belonging to Kirkuk.

The chaos caused by war and its aftermaths resulted in the drastic decline of theatre in the early 1990s. Karim points to the following as the main reasons behind the decline of theatre in Kurdistan during this period:

- The loss of cultural organizations and the withdrawal of government administrations from Kurdistan due to war and the uprising.
- High inflation and cost of living due to strict economic sanctions imposed on Iraq and Iraq's economic sanction on Kurdistan. No cultural organization or group could afford the cost of staging a theatre production which was no less than ten thousand dinars.
- The high cost of paper and print which meant the writers were not able to publish their works many of which saw the light of day several years later.
- A large number of artists were forced by circumstances to seek other jobs to make a living and thus had no time for theatre.
- Many artists left the country.
- A number of artists were killed in the uprising and its aftermaths.
- A number of dramatists abandoned their profession to start a political career. (Karim 2009, pp. 137–8)

It was only in the latter half of the 1990s and with the establishment of the KRG, the Kurdish parliament and several cultural organizations in Kurdistan, that theatre started to regain some of its lost lustre. Under the auspices of the Ministry of Culture, cultural and theatre administrations, and also several theatre groups, were set up in different towns and attempts were made to renovate the old theatres and build new ones. The establishment of the Institute of Fine Arts, first in Erbil and then in Duhok, was also an important step towards the promotion of drama education. Budgets were also made available to fund stage productions and TV dramas that were produced for the growing number of Kurdish TV stations. Autonomy also produced an environment in which Kurds were increasingly able to speak openly of the suffering that the Iraqi regime had inflicted upon them. Various TV dramas further expounded this theme – important examples included *Firmêskî Reş* (Black Tears), *Erebane* (Carriage), *Gul Umer* (Gol Omar), *Pêlaw* (Shoe) and *Şehîdekan Em Hefteye Degerênewe* (The Martyrs Return This Week) (Karim 2009, p. 141). These dramas mainly recounted the story of the Kurds' struggle and resistance in the face of Iraqi oppression.

## Conclusion

Kurdish theatre under the Baath regime between 1975 and 1991 largely responded to the loss of autonomy in 1974 and the resultant collapse of national morale. It therefore sought to contribute to the healing process by asserting a distinct Kurdish culture and identity. The very act of staging Kurdish plays was important in that it celebrated the language and identity of a people who had continuously been defeated, denigrated and made invisible to the outside world. For Kurdish artists, writing and staging Kurdish plays was therefore an act of self-preservation against a history of loss and defeat that threatened to strip them of their identity.

Theatre not only contributed to asserting Kurdish identity and legitimacy, but also played a significant role in mobilizing the populace by courageously calling upon the Kurdish youth to join the resistance movement. In this sense, the Kurdish theatre of 1975–91 conforms to Mda's definition of Theatre for Resistance – this is a theatre performed with the overt aim of rallying or mobilizing the oppressed to fight against oppression (Mda 1998). Theatre in

Iraqi Kurdistan between 1975 and 1991 consistently opened up possibilities of resistance to the Baathist dictatorship. This resistance took various forms, ranging from folk forms to mythology, the re-enactment of oppressed histories and the revival of native history. Theatre was also deployed by Kurdish guerrillas themselves as a propaganda tool and a means of struggle.

At a time when the peshmerga were fully engaged in a mortal struggle, theatre artists believed that their profession was similarly important and therefore were prepared to sacrifice for it. Theatre artists received no financial support, with passion often being their main source of sustenance (Karim 2011, pp. 145–6). They were also fully aware that their work could come at the cost of their freedom or even lives. The state sought to impose a range of impediments – actors and directors were imprisoned and interrogated, the censorship department banned plays, theatres were closed down during performances. This commitment was most clearly evidenced in guerrilla camps and liberated villages, where performances took place in spite of grave risks to the lives of both performers and spectators.

It is important to note that the 1970s and 1980s saw the Arabization of Kurdish lands, and the banning of Kurdish in those areas. The several active theatre groups, whether in drawing upon Kurdish folk culture and literature or translating Modernist dramas into Kurdish, helped reassure the Kurdish people of their culture and identity. Theatre revived the spectators' sense of self-worth and reinforced a collective belief in their name, language, land, history of struggle, unity and themselves by both elevating the status of their language and also drawing on their folk culture and literature as valid sources of artistic inspiration and material for theatre. Following chapters will now consider the use of Kurdish folklore and nationalist myths and literature in the theatre of the 1970s and 1980s, particularly representative plays written and directed by Talat Saman and Ahmad Salar.

For their patriotism and courage in the face of dictatorship, theatre artists of the 1970s and 1980s are regarded by many Kurds as equals to the Kurdish guerrillas. In the aftermath of the failed 1974 uprising, while the resistance had been crushed, it had been replaced by theatre – and theatre artists had replaced the peshmerga as the most prominent advocates of patriotism (Salar, interview, 5 May 2013). This further proves the point that cultural and political nationalisms in Kurdistan were complementary responses; when the latter was blocked, the former functioned as a viable substitute.

4

# The construction of leftist-nationalist identity in Talat Saman's theatre

In order to better understand the Kurdish theatre of the 1970s and its role in promoting Kurdish nationalism and resistance against the Baath rule, this chapter examines two important plays that were directed by Talat Saman, one of the first graduates of drama from Baghdad University and the most successful director of the 1970s. Saman was the most renowned theatre director in Erbil at the time and his productions were frequently well received. This chapter will focus upon *Mem û Zîn* and *Qelay Dimdim* in close detail, as they both provide considerable insight into the politicization of Kurdish theatre during the 1970s. They also testify to the courage and commitment of Kurdish theatre artists who continued to produce nationalist works after the loss of autonomy in 1975.

## Talat Saman

Saman was born in 1946 in Erbil. He went to school in Nasiriyah in Southern Iraq, where his family had been relocated to in 1963. He attended *Dar ul-Muallimeen* (House of Teachers) but was expelled after one day after shouting slogans in support of Barzani during an anti-Kurdish demonstration. The intervention of his father, a police officer, ensured that he escaped punishment for this 'offence' (and also later ones). As a child, Saman was deeply influenced by the Kurdish Radios of Baghdad and Kermanshah and the plays and stories told by Shokrollah Baban and other radio presenters. He was also an avid film-goer who would watch at least one film a day in one of the two cinemas in his neighbourhood. Along with Qazi Bamarni, Saman was the first Kurdish drama student to graduate from Baghdad Academy of Fine Arts (1969–70) where he studied under Sami Abdulhamid, Ibrahim Jalal and Ja'far Sa'di. Upon returning to Erbil, he co-founded the Erbil branch of Kurdish Society of Arts and Literature (*Komeley Huner û Wêjey Kurdî*) in July 1972. This Erbil-based society would later make an important contribution to Kurdish culture, literature, music and theatre. Many of Erbil's actors, musicians, singers and writers worked in the society and benefitted from it. It also became a centre where political and revolutionary figures from different parties held meetings. Several of them lost their lives because of their political activities.[1]

In the Kurdish Society of Arts and Literature and later in the New Kurdish Arts Group (*Tîpî Nwêy Hunerî Kurdî*) which he co-founded, he directed several plays including *Qelay Dimdim*, *Şarî Evîn*, *Pîlan* and *Xec û Siyamend*. All the plays he directed commented on current sociopolitical issues; they either advocated struggle against the political dictatorship of foreign rulers or criticized the oppression of the lower social classes by the self-serving landed gentry. *Pîlan*, which was written by Muhamad Mawlud Mam, comments upon the arbitrary character of the borders that divide Kurdish lands between different nation-states. A dialogue between the representative of the state and a Kurdish man and woman (named Zerin) clearly conveys the absurdity of the arrangements put in place by colonial power:

**Officer:** Ho, ho, ho . . . they are on two sides . . . they are two villages.
**Zerin:** The two sides are one . . . they are one village.
**Officer:** He, he, he . . . they are two villages in two countries.
**Zerin:** This is one country and we all belong to each other.
**Officer:** They are two villages, foreign to each other.
**The man:** We are all related . . . you are the foreigners.
**Zerin:** Those who call us foreign are the foreigners. (Saman 2010, p. 109)

The hope for the reunification of Kurdish lands is symbolized by the marriage between Mam and Zin who are from these two villages and the play concludes with a call for unity between Kurds as the actors invite the audience members to chant with them: 'Do not let go of each other's hands' (Saman, p. 118).

---

[1] This paragraph derives from an interview with Saman (9 Oct 2013).

In Şarî Evîn, the foreign dictatorship is symbolized by a dragon (*ejdeha*) who resides across the borders of 'the land with tall mountains and green valleys', a tacit allusion to Kurdistan (Saman 2011b, p. 68). This dragon clearly recalls the mythical Zuhak, an evil king who lived off the brains of the youth and who was defeated by Kawa, a blacksmith. The invocation of this powerful nationalist myth did not escape the attentions of the Ministry of Culture, who forced Saman to change the title of the play from *Ejdeha*, which could be (mis)interpreted as a reference to the Iraqi dictator, to the more neutral *Şarî Evîn* (Saman, interview, 9 October 2013). It is however important to note that the play's criticism is predominantly focused upon, not the foreign evil, but the subjugation of the masses by the Kurdish upper class as embodied in the characters of Agha and Merchant, who benefit from the siege of the land by selling water to their desperate compatriots. It is no coincidence that it is ultimately a poor young man who risks his life to kill the dragon and free his people. The play ends when he is reunited with his fiancée, a similarly poor flower-selling girl. For its idealization of the lower classes and its condemnation of the corrupt bourgeoisie and gentry, *Şarî Evîn* is evidently a leftist work and a plea to all members of society to think beyond their selfish interests and act for the greater good of their community; only then can they liberate their land from foreign yoke.

The Iraqi Baathist dictatorship became the subject of ridicule in Saman's *Qel û Rûte* (The Raven and the Pauper), which has been called by Muhsin Muhammad 'the comedy of election at the time of dictatorship' (Saman 2010, p. 3). Written and directed by Saman, this play, which drew on folk tales, was first staged in 1979 in Erbil by the Kurdish Arts and Literature Group. At the time, Saddam had become the president and also the chairman of the Revolutionary Command Council (RCC), the ultimate decision-making body in Iraq during the Ba'ath's rule. Saddam changed and controlled the RCC by eliminating any manifestations of pluralism and punishing those affiliated with political parties other than his Arab Baath Socialist Party. In 1979, he accused dozens of party officials, including five RCC members, of treason and had them executed. This state of affairs is courageously satirized in *Qel û Rûte*.

Like many other Kurdish plays of the time and their Arabic counterparts, *Qel û Rûte* begins with a storyteller addressing the audience. He opens a big old book and starts reading out a story: once upon a time in an ancient city a new king was chosen to rule every year, not by the people but by the ravens. He, whose head the bird sat on, would become the new king. In this city, there was a poor, homeless, hungry man called Rûte, whose name literally translates as 'pauper'. The pauper dreamt of all the noble things that he would do if he became king: 'I'd cover the cold, I'd feed the hungry . . . I'd turn this city into a paradise . . . I'd distribute the lands among the peasants' (Saman 2010, p. 10). The narrator returns to stage, this time as another character called Dêwane (Madman), the Wiseman of folk literature. He promises the pauper to be the next king on the condition that he would abolish the raven-based system and replace that with the vote of the nation. However, the concept of democracy is so alien to the pauper that the idea of people electing their ruler baffles him. What follows is a series of questions and answers which end with a play with the rhyming words of *qel* (raven) and *gel* (nation):

**Wiseman:** How can the king be chosen by the raven?

**Pauper:** Then by what should it be chosen? You don't mean the stork, do you? I think the raven is wiser than the stork.

**Wiseman:** What stork?!

**Pauper:** Oh I see, you mean the falcon. Falcons are wiser and smarter.

**Wiseman:** No!

**Pauper:** Of course! You mean the rooster.

**Wiseman:** No!

**Pauper:** Simurgh?[2]

**Wiseman:** What?

**Pauper:** Simurgh. Yes, it must be Simurgh. Simurgh is the king of all birds, it's the biggest and strongest of them all . . . long live Simurgh and death to the raven . . . it's a shame that in this land, this important task is given to the raven . . . long live the Simurgh.

**Wiseman:** No!

**Pauper:** Not even the Simurgh? . . . then which bird is it?

**Wiseman:** It is the nation, the nation . . . it is the interests of the nation which are at stake here, not those of the raven. Who suffers if the king oppresses his

---

[2] A mythical bird which features in Iranian folklore and literature.

people?... who suffers when the king allies with the aghas, lords and nobility against the peasants and labourers?... the raven or the nation? (Saman 2010, pp. 20–1)

At the end, the Wiseman grants the pauper's wish and makes him king. The landlords and nobility who were confused and disgruntled by the election of a poor nobody as the new king soon realize that their simple-minded adversary is easy to manipulate. They begin to sway his authority by flattering and bribing him. Their ally in the court is the king's deputy who is in fact the main decision-maker in the realm. In his first service to the new king, this cunning figure changes the new king's name from Rûte to Tawfiq Pasha, the son of Shaswari Salim. Having fabricated a noble pedigree for Rûte, his deputy remarks: 'His one hundredth grandfather is from *Ser* (up) Khan family who are from the nobilities who are descendants of *Jêr* (down) Khan' (Saman 2010, p. 38). The only people who are admitted to Tawfiq Pasha's court by his deputy are the landlords and the nobility who grant him a hundred villages and palaces. Tawfiq Beg is told by his deputy that they should take good care of the ravens to ensure his re-election and long reign. Therefore, the deputy states, 'It is the king's order that anyone who kills a raven or destroys a raven's nest or commits any crime against a raven should be immediately executed... every household has to take care of one raven' (Saman 2010, p. 42).

The pauper is soon corrupted by his courtiers and loses sight of his old dreams and the promises he had made to the Wiseman. He not only fails to abolish the old regime but also strengthens the authority of the ravens, thus further weakening his already impoverished subjects. His reign ultimately becomes the worst in the history of his people.

Although *Qel û Rûte*, *Pîlan* and *Şarî Evîn* were all well-received, Saman's best-known stage productions are *Mem û Zîn* and *Qelay Dimdim*. The former was written in 1968, published in 1975 and staged in 1976 under the direction of Talat Saman and Farhad Sharif. What is significant about this play is that it was an overtly nationalistic work which was staged only one year after the Kurds' loss of autonomy during an era of strict censorship. 'From 1968 onwards,' said Saman in an interview, 'we dreamt of a greater Kurdistan and a leader to unite all four parts of Kurdistan. I described this in a love story' (Saman, 9 October 2013).

*Mem û Zîn* and *Qelay Dimdim* both belong to the Kurdish oral tradition and are the two most renowned *beyts* that were performed by traditional Kurdish storytellers for hundreds of years. *Mem û Zîn*, which later provided the basis for a tragic love poem by the seventeenth-century poet, Ahmadi Khani, is celebrated by Kurdish nationalists as a national epic, for reasons mentioned earlier. To the same extent, *Qelay Dimdim*, which renders the heroism of a small group of Kurds confronted by a substantially larger Persian army, is considered by many to be a great national epic, second only to Khani's *Mem û Zîn*.

As folktales that have long been drawn upon by Kurdish cultural and political nationalists, *Mem û Zîn* and *Qelay Dimdim* have inspired Kurdish poets and novelists, as well as playwrights (as the example of Pîremêrd showed). The continual retelling of these stories underlines their social and political significance and their already deep resonance with the national culture. These plays have both attracted dramatists who have sought to articulate national anxieties and preoccupations. Saman's *Mem û Zîn* and *Qelay Dimdim* are examples of modern retellings of these folktales in performance with emphasis on nationalist and socialist themes. To understand the construction of this leftist-nationalist identity in these two political plays, the following explores them in the historical context within which they were written, performed and received.

## *Mem û Zîn* (Mam and Zin, 1976)

The story revolves around Mam, a Kurdish prince from the House of Ardalan who, disillusioned by his family's subjugation of their peasants and lack of nationalist sentiment, abandons his hometown in search of a more progressive ruler. He ultimately finds his ideal in Mir Zineddin, the ruler of Bohtan, where Mam settles in and starts a new life. Without revealing his princely identity, he serves as Mir's secretary and becomes a close friend of Tajeddin, the son of Mir's deputy, Shaliyar.

During the feast of Newroz, Mir Zineddin's two young sisters, Zin and Siti, disguise themselves as men in order to wander among the crowds in the streets and identify the type of men they would like to marry. They take an immediate attraction to two girls they meet, who are actually Mam and Tajeddin in disguise. Mam falls in love with Zin but he lacks the courage to ask for her hand, as he now lives as a poor subject of Mir, not a prince of Ardalan. However, Tajeddin's decision to marry Siti gives Mam the courage to ask for Zin's hand.

Mir Zineddin, a kind but naïve ruler, is beguiled by Bakr, an Iago-like advisor, into imprisoning Mam for treason. Bakr conspires with the leader of the Ak Koyunlu (The White Sheep) Turkomans to overthrow the Kurdish principality in return for Mir Zineddin's throne. Made aware of his brother's imprisonment, Sarkhab Beg, the head of the House of Ardalan, sets off with his army to Bohtan, not to wage war but only to beg for his brother's release. Bakr, however, attempts to convince Mir Zineddin to unite with Bijan, the leader of the Ak Koyunlu Turkomans, against Sarkhab Beg by claiming that he is coming to conquer Bohtan. After Shaliyar and Tajeddin intercede and Sarkhab expresses his peaceful intent in writing, Mir changes his mind and decides to accept Sarkhab into his court. Sarkhab visits his brother in prison and discovers that he has wasted away physically and emotionally for weeks; he succumbs to his death moments later and the bedridden Zin follows soon after. At the conclusion of the play, Bakr confesses to his treachery and commits suicide; meanwhile, Sarkhab and Mir join troops to fight against the foreign invaders.

This play was written in 1968 but was first staged (in Erbil) in 1976. The story draws upon Ahmadi Khani's *Mem û Zîn*, which was itself inspired by the Kurdish folktale of *Memê Alan*, one of the most renowned stories of Kurdish oral literature. The story of *Memê Alan* enjoys extremely widespread circulation among the Kurmanji-speaking Kurds as well as their Armenian and Neo-Aramaic-speaking neighbours (Chyet 1991, p. 6). However, as Chyet's research demonstrates, no two versions that exist within the oral tradition recount the story in exactly the same way (p. 9). Saman's play more closely resembles Khani's adaptation which differs from oral tradition not only in both form and content but also in that it was written with a political objective in mind. It is to Khani's *Mem û Zîn* that Saman's play owes much of its political imagery.

Ahmadi Khani, who had been a secretary at the court of the Mir of Bayazid, wrote *Mem û Zin* during the conflicts between the Ottoman and Persian empires which had resulted in turmoil in Kurdish lands. The political events of the seventeenth century eventually determined the fate of Kurdistan as the 1693 peace treaty between the two empires set the boundary between the two and also divided Kurdish lands for centuries to come. It was in the Kurdish town of Bayazid, the point at which the two belligerent powers encountered each other, that Khani wrote his *Mem û Zîn*, in which he lamented the fate of his people in the following terms:

> Both sides have made the Kurdish people targets for the arrows of fate. They are said to be keys to the borders, each tribe forming a formidable bulwark. Whenever the Ottoman Sea [Ottomans] and Tajik Sea [Persians] flow out and agitate, the Kurds get soaked in blood separating them [the Turks and Persians] like an isthmus.' (cited in Hassanpour 1992, p. 53)

Khani maintained that internal divisions within the Kurdish political community were the main reason for their ongoing subjugation. He wrote, 'If only there were harmony among us, if we were to obey a single one of us, he would reduce to vassalage Turks, Arabs and Persians, all of them' (cited in Bruinessen 1992, p. 267). For its appeal to the 'disunited, rebellious and split (*bêtifaq, be temerud û şiqaq*)' Kurdish groups to unite, Khani's prologue to *Mem û Zîn* has become the most frequently cited text within Kurdish nationalist literature, thus contributing significantly to the formation of a Kurdish national identity. It played an important role in the early stages of Kurdish identity-building, particularly in Turkey and Iraq. In Turkey, it became a great source of inspiration for Kurdish nationalists in the early twentieth century.[3] In Iraq, Hajar's Sorani translation of *Mem û Zîn*, which was published in 1960, profoundly impacted upon the Kurdish movement (Bruinessen 2003, p. 53). Even today, this story continues to inspire Kurdish cultural activities in Kurdistan and other parts of the world.[4]

---

[3] In October 1941, Celadet Bedirxan published an article in which he described Khani as a prophet: '*Lê Xanî pêxember e ji; pêxemberê diyaneta me a milî, pêxemberê ola me a nijadîn.*' (Khani is a prophet; the prophet of our national belief, the prophet of the doctrines of our race.) (see Strohmeier 2003, p. 143).

[4] Fethi Karakeçili, a Kurdish choreographer and dance instructor, staged the first Kurdish ballet dance based on the *Mem û Zîn* love story in Toronto, Canada in October 2011. This eighty-five-minute performance focused on Kurdish culture but, with a view to engaging the Canadian audience, it incorporated contemporary elements to bring out an East/West balance in its costume, dance, music and staging. Karakeçili used three dance styles (ballet, contemporary and folk) that were performed by a diverse range of dancers and a live orchestra which included musicians from different parts of the world.

Saman's play closely resembles Khani's poem in several respects: first, it criticizes Kurdish rulers, to the point of promoting rebellion against their authority; second, it promotes the welfare of the working class and peasantry; third, it envisages a future in which a unified Kurdistan is ruled by a decisive leader who is concerned with the fate of his nation. However, Saman's *Mem û Zîn* differs from Khani's work in that, while the love story in that while Khani's political commentary is mainly the narrator's occasional reflections, in the former, the whole plot is focused upon the political. In Saman's play, Mam, the not-so-heroic hero of the folktale and the sufist martyr of Khani's *mathnawi*, articulates the most vindictive statements against the self-serving Kurdish rulers. Mam, in this play, is a leftist intellectual who blames the numerous Kurdish *aghas* and princes for all of Kurdistan's miseries. Their short-sightedness and greed, Mam believes, are evidenced in their servitude to foreign powers and their cruelty towards their own people. His character therefore advocates the complete obliteration of Kurdish principalities in the hope that the lower classes will finally be able to live in peace.

Saman's *Mem û Zîn* represents the leftist tendencies which were strong in the region at the time. During the 1930s and 1940s, communism and pan-Arab nationalism were the two most influential ideological currents. Many Kurdish intellectuals were influenced by the socialist ideas of the Iraqi Communist Party (ICP), which was founded in 1934. The conflict between these (educated and urbanized) leftist intellectuals and (conservative, feudal and religious) tribal leaders would concretely influence the history of Kurdish political parties for many years to come.

The division of political spheres of influence in Kurdistan between the KDP and PUK has already been discussed in Chapter 3. This split first emerged within the KDP between the traditionalist 'wing' associated with Barzani and more radical elements (the so-called KDP politburo) which were led by Ibrahim Ahmad, and Jalal Talabani, his son-in-law. Barzani further inflamed the division by talking 'freely, with a bitterness amounting to hatred, against the alleged inertia, cowardice, inefficiency and intellectual presumptuousness of the KDP politicians' (McDowall 2004, p. 306). Ahmad, on the other hand, sharply rebuked Barzani for his 'selfishness, arbitrariness, unfairness, tribal backwardness and even his dishonesty' (p. 306).

The 1960s proved to be a tortuous decade for the Kurds as the KDP struggled to maintain unity between Barzani and its leftist members. By 1964, simmering tensions between the two escalated into full-scale confrontation when Ahmad and Talabani attempted to eliminate Barzani from the KDP leadership. This conflict further intensified in 1964, when Barzani signed a ceasefire accord with Baghdad without informing the politburo. Ahmad and Talabani both criticized him, while Barzani reiterated his commitment to the peace agreement. Barzani would later emerge victorious when the Ahmad and Talabani factions were driven into Iran. McDowall observes,

> Kurdistan was rent with schism. On one side, Ahmad, Talabani and the KDP intelligentsia asserted an ideological position evolved over the previous 20 years, on the other, Mulla Mustafa was able to rally the conservatives, the tribal and religious leaders of Kurdistan. For these it was a contest between the religious and the secular, the primordial and the nationalist, tradition versus atheistic Marxism. (McDowall 2004, p. 316)

In March 1965, war broke out between the Iraqi government and Kurds under the leadership of Barzani, who was now the head of the KDP. In 1966, Ahmad and Talabani began to receive support from the central government to take up arms against Barzani, who was armed with heavy weapons by both Iran and Israel (McDowall 2004, pp. 318–19). The two main Iraqi-Kurdish parties, with the direct encouragement of two rival states, therefore fought each other for power and political influence in Kurdistan. In order to demonstrate their loyalty to their external benefactors, these factions sometimes conspired against fellow Kurds who fought for autonomy in other parts of Kurdistan. This internal scheming fuelled grievances and mutual suspicions that would erupt into open violence during the Civil War of the 1990s.

Between the writing of *Mem û Zîn* in 1968 and its staging in 1976, internal Kurdish conflicts and tensions had not abated; if anything, they had worsened, in large part due to the death of Ali Askari, one of the PUK's most capable and popular commanders, who was killed in a KDP ambush. This caused extreme anger among the PUK members; a fact that is reflected in the PUK publications at the time. *Spark*, the party's mouthpiece, denounced Askari's murder in strong terms by calling the KDP a 'treacherous and anti-people gang of US and Zionist stooges' (*Spark*, vol. 3, no. 2, November 1979, p. 1).

In acting thus, it maintained, this 'puppet gang' unmasked itself as 'the most vulgar, primitive, and barbarian political group in the world' (p. 1).

Already in 1975, students belonging to the PUK had condemned the KDP for several 'crimes' including its submission to the Shah's regime by opening a Kurdish branch of SAVAK (*Parastin*) within liberated areas, which murdered hundreds of progressive Kurds; its submission to US imperialism by functioning as its 'watch-dog' and its collaboration with the Zionist settler state of Israel and stabbing the Palestinian liberation movement in the back (Kurdish Students Society in Europe – UK Branch, 1975). Unfortunately for the Kurds, the accusations and the animosity between their political leaders were as rife in 1976 as they had been in 1968.

In *Mem û Zîn*, this intra-Kurdish conflict is represented as the only way to weaken and conquer the Kurds. At the beginning of the play, Bakr, the collaborator, informs the Turkoman messenger that schism is the only power that can defeat Bohtan. He states,

> At the time of war, especially against you, all citizens pick up guns . . . I assure you, no amount of force can conquer a handful of Kurdish soil. If you want to live in peace, shake hands with Zineddin, as Tamburlaine and Shahrukh did . . . Tell Bijan, he will not succeed even if he becomes Hulagu.[5] Even Hulagu lost two thousand men in Hewlêr (Erbil) and failed to conquer it . . . it helps if you read a bit about Kurdish history. A nation who has experienced freedom fights for it to its last breath. (Saman 2011a, pp. 13–14)

But, as Mam mentions, Hulagu finally succeeded in conquering Erbil with the help of a few traitors in the Erbil fortress (Saman 2011a, p. 31). Shaliyar compares the traitors to 'a snake which is hiding in your house and you don't notice it until it stings you' (p. 31). The problem is those 'snakes' are trusted and followed by the Kurdish society, which according to Mam, is 'gullible, honest and naive' (p. 31). These gullible Kurds can be easily manipulated by the like of Bakr, who is well aware of the weaknesses of Kurdish society and its rulers. The only way to conquer Bohtan, Bakr suggests to the Turkomans, is 'deceit, killing Kurds by Kurds' (p. 14). In order to make this happen, Bakr advocates peace with the foreign Turkomans. He tells Mir, 'we are all Muslims. How can we kill

---

[5] Hulagu Khan (1218–1265), the Mongol conqueror of southwest Asia.

each other? . . . it's time for peace . . . you, representatives of this poor nation, never know when to make peace and when to wage war' (p. 28).

While advocating peace with the enemies, Bakr tries to disgrace Mir's loyal servants, Mam and Tajeddin. He accuses Mam of trying to dishonour Mir's sister, Zin, and as proof of her flirtation with Mam, he shows Mir her necklace which she had dropped at their meeting place. Mir, who is made aware by Bakr of Mam's connection to the House of Ardalan, falls for Bakr's lies and suspects Mam and his brother of trying to disgrace his family and conquer Bohtan. The domestic turmoil which is created out of mistrust and suspicion leads Mir to entertain the idea of joining troops with the Turkomans against the Kurdish House of Ardalan. This is reminiscent of the Kurdish parties' alliances with foreign powers against each other. In fact, in the 1980s Saddam Hussein boasted that 'the Kurdish organisations would never be able to achieve anything since they were hopelessly divided against each other and subservient to foreign powers' (McDowall 2004, p. 347). This is clearly reflected in the exchanges between the characters in the play:

**Mam:** Our biggest problem is our naivety. We are honest, simple and gullible.
**Shaliyar:** That's why I always tell you not to trust the enemy's sweet words.
Outsiders are never our friends. (Saman 2011a, p. 31)

Shaliyar's lines also highlight the nationalist myth of common ancestry and descent that the play promotes. Smith (1999) explains that this myth, which is central to cultural nationalism, links all members of the present generation of the community as one nation with common forebears. It therefore provides a means of identifying one's friends as 'kinsmen' in opposition to unfriendly outsiders. The activation of national identity works insidiously through assumptions about participants in the performance and the spectators – as Michael Billig notes, 'the term "we" is unreflexively used as a signifier of "us" as members of the nation' (cited in Edensor 2002, p. 11).

While the myth of common descent entails the claim to a distinct national identity and a homeland, what stands in the way of Kurdish nationalism, as the play diagnoses, is the credulity of Kurdish leaders in believing their enemies' good gestures, as well as their lack of unity with and concern for other parts of Kurdistan. Mam represents a young Kurdish intellectual who dreams of unity between all Kurdish regions, and whose nationalist aspirations therefore extend beyond the borders of Iraqi Kurdistan. His dream is 'for Kurdish regions to unite and for leaders to think of a unified Kurdistan' (Saman 2011a, p. 52) and not to differentiate between parts of Kurdistan (p. 63). 'I like for Bohtan to feel the pains of Lorestan and for Soran to support Bidlis' says Mam (p. 67). What stands in the way of this unity is the selfishness of Kurdish princes. Mam abandons his hometown, expressing a profound sense of disappointment in Ardalan, Soran and other principalities. He goes to Bohtan hoping to find social justice, in the expectation that Mir would prove to be a progressive leader, independent from foreign influence (p. 88). However, Mir Zineddin proves to be yet another self-centred ruler with little regards for his subjects and no sense of nationalism. When he is warned by his deputy against enmity with Sarkhab Beg of Ardalan and is told to care about the fate of his nation, he exclaims, 'Nation! What nation? Cows, peasants . . . ? I am the nation; my army, my court, my family, my power, me. I destroy anyone who dares to oppose me' (p. 94). This is why Mam's wish for a unified Kurdistan is directly linked with his desire for equality and freedom for the nation. His last words call for a revolution that uproots the feudal lords:

> Principalities are like God's curse on our oppressed people . . . My brother, Tajeddin, if the princes do not come to their senses and start to think about the future of their nation, if they do not see all parts of Kurdistan as one, strike them with an iron fist. Go to villages, streets, markets, spread the idea of revolution . . . if the rulers cannot distinguish between friends and foes, if they are preoccupied with building palaces, if they continue to sacrifice the lives of our youths in their futile wars, destroy them Tajeddin, with an iron fist, this is my will, destroy them Tajeddin, with an iron fist. (Saman 2011a, pp. 109–10)

It is here that the play's characterization of Mam clearly diverges from Khani's narrative. In Khani's *Mem û Zîn*, it is the author himself who reflects on the nature and reality of Kurdish politics and political power in general. After Bakr successfully deceives Mir into suspecting Mam and Tajeddin, Khani takes the opportunity to give his verdict on politics when he states, 'The rulers externally and internally resemble fire . . . when they are compassionate they are like the sun, when they hate, they burn the earth, for goodness' sake don't trust them!

Even if they were your fathers, sons, or brothers' (Mirawdeli 2012, p. 331). Khani demonstrates his dislike and distrust of rulers on another occasion when he writes, 'The rulers are from the race of vipers, they have venom and beaded heads, when they show beads (smile), know it is poison, when they show compassion, know it is hatred' (p. 433).

Khani's dislike of princes is rooted in his sufist and philosophical worldview that all those who seek material power and entertain the illusion of eternal authority are prone to making wrong choices (Mirawdeli 2012, p. 330). Therefore, while he justifies social revolution against injustice and fighting evil in the world, he clarifies that 'as life is transitory and worldly power is insignificant, empty and ephemeral, it is only spiritual love that can ensure eternal happiness' (p. 224). This spiritual journey and transformation is represented through Mam and Zin, whose heroism resides in their ability to endure hardship and even die for the sake of love. This is evident when Zin visits Mam in a vision and their souls dissolve in each other – this supernatural event takes place in the prison and is witnessed by other prisoners who see rays of light mixing together and lighting up the whole building. Moments before her death, Zin tells her brother about her spiritual journey and inner happiness.[6]

Those contemporary scholars who have interpreted Khani's Mam as a symbol of enchained Kurdistan and the story of Mam and Zin as a general metaphor for the situation of the Kurds, have perhaps retrospectively projected their own nationalist beliefs onto the seventeenth-century poem. Hassanpour, for example, maintains that Mam and Zin represent the two parts of Kurdistan, with Bakr symbolizing disunion. Chyet echoes Hassanpour's interpretation and claims that Khani believed that the Kurds' biggest enemy was internal divides and divisions (Chyet 1991, p. 62) – hence he used the story of Mam and Zin as a metaphor for the Kurdish situation. The epilogue to

---

[6] Izzeddin Mustafa Rasul, the esteemed Kurdish scholar, has explored Khani's mystic and philosophical ideas and his vision of the world by examining the mystic terminology of *Maqāmāt wa ahwāl* – this implied a closer engagement with various stations and states, the attainment of *martaba* and elimination in God, the mannerisms of mystics, the pre-existence of soul, *nafs* and *rūh* (see Rasul 1979). Rasul and Mirawdeli (2012) both observe that the character of Bakr is the embodiment of evil; as such, he serves as necessary component of the various antitheses and contradictions on which the life of man, the operation of nature and the system of universe are based. Mirawdeli maintains that this philosophy, which views evil as a necessary counterpart of good, can be traced back to Zoroastrian origins (p. 318).

Khani's poem, however, calls into question such nationalistic interpretations by depicting Bakr in paradise, where, having been forgiven by God, he lives near Mam and Zin's palace. On the other hand, this epilogue further reinforces the mystic interpretations of Khani's work.

While Khani may not have intend his story to be interpreted as a metaphor for Kurdish situation, his literary work was written, as he himself states in the prologue, to revive a sense of pride in Kurdish culture and language. By describing Kurdish architecture, clothes, food, jewellery, medicine, music, utensils and types of calligraphy and writing, he clearly conveyed the distinct character of his people and their way of life and, in so doing, justified their liberation from the Ottoman-Persian yoke (see Rasul 1979). His choice of a quintessentially Kurdish folktale clearly establishes his ambition from the outset. All these distinctly Kurdish attributes, in addition to the poem's prologue (where the poet complains about the subjugation of the Kurds and their lack of unity) strongly influenced nationalist adaptations and interpretations, such as Saman's play.

Strohmeier asserts that Khani's assessment of the Kurdish situation has a clear application to contemporary circumstances, 'while lending a prophetic aura and historical legitimacy to the appeals of early proponents of Kurdish nationalism' (Strohmeier 2003, p. 29). Saman has similarly seen in Khani's work reflections of the Kurdish situation. He has made the characters of *Mem û Zîn* embodiments of weaknesses and strengths of Kurdish character. Bakr is the enemy within, the traitor, disloyal and self-serving, representative of what must be corrected or eliminated before Kurds can reach unity and prosperity. Tajeddin, on the other hand, is the nation's brave and honourable soldier, the peshmerga. However, his life could easily be wasted in an unnecessary intra-Kurdish war launched by the gullible prince.

There is no doubt that, in retelling Khani's *Mem û Zîn*, Saman's play sought to strengthen the Kurdish nationalist movement. It should be noted that the play was staged only one year after the collapse of the fourteen-year Kurdish armed struggle amidst bitterness and acrimony. The laying down of arms after the Algiers Agreement is referred to as *nisko* (setback) by the masses, while Barzani's opponents also describe it as *aş betal*, which literally translates as 'to desist'. This term, which denotes cowardice and weakness, reflects the extreme anger and frustration that, at least parts of, Iraqi-Kurdish society felt towards the KDP leadership. In fact, the Kurdish defeat of March 1975 was so complete that even the most optimistic observers did not expect the movement to regain its strength for many years (Stansfield and Resool 2006, p. 108). In Saman's *Mem û Zîn*, Muhsin Muhammad notes, culture becomes a means to describe this dark time of national crisis (2011).

In retrospect, it is hard to believe that a performance with such strong nationalist overtones was staged immediately after the collapse of autonomy and the Kurdish nationalist movement. Romantic descriptions of Kurdistan and references to its 'enemies' are abundant throughout the play. Mam states,

> Our nation longs for peace and tranquillity. Our land is rich and full of blessings. Everything in Kurdistan calls for love. If it wasn't for the poisonous sufferings inflicted upon us by the enemy, we would never exchange one *heyran*[7] or *lawik*[8] with thousands of unfitting conquests. (Saman 2011a, p. 32)

In this instance, 'nation' does not denote Bohtan but rather the Greater Kurdistan because Mam clarifies that he does not distinguish between different parts of Kurdistan (Saman 2011a, p. 63). The 'nation' and 'homeland' which are referred to several times throughout the play (see pp. 71, 83, 87, 94) are surrounded by enemies from outside: Ardalan has to fend off the Qizilbash[9] while Bohtan confronts the threat of the Ak Koyunlu Turkomans. However, Kurdistan is also threatened from within: Tajeddin bemoans a state of affairs in which Kurdish princes are misled by traitors; consequently, they lose sight of their common enemies and instead engage in wars of 'fratricide' (p. 83). The only way out of this bleak situation, Mam and Tajeddin believe, is the uprising of the masses against the princes, *begs* and *aghas* for whom the peasants are little more than fuel for their futile wars (p. 83).

It is only after the death of Mam and Zin that Mir Zineddin finally acknowledges his mistake and apologizes to Mam's brother, Sarkhab Beg of Ardalan. The tragic fate of Mam and Zin issues a clear warning to the Kurds

---

[7] A type of traditional Kurdish song usually unaccompanied by music.
[8] A type of long lyrical song.
[9] Qizilbash or Kizilbash (sometimes also Qezelbash or Qazilbash) is a general label that has been applied to the wide variety of Shi'i militant groups that flourished in Anatolia, Azerbaijan and Kurdistan from the late thirteenth century onwards, a number of which contributed to the foundation of Iran's Safavid dynasty.

and, as Shaliyar says, further reiterates the need for a stronger internal unity (Saman 2011a, p. 108). This unity is heralded at the end of the final scene when Bohtan and Ardalan swear allegiance to fight the 'outsiders' and 'to send them to hell' (p. 109).

For its condemnation of the feudalist society and its call for an uprising against Kurdish feudal lords and princes, Saman's *Mem û Zîn* can be categorized alongside Simko Nakam's *Receb û Piyawxoran* – both plays foretelling the revival of the Kurdish movement in the form of a socialist party. While the guerrillas fought their battles in the Kurdish countryside and mountains, it was Kurdish dramatists who, in producing nationalist works such as *Mem û Zîn*, undermined government suppression in the cities and brought the clandestine resistance to the public stage, thus encouraging the society to keep the revolutionary spirit alive.

## *Qelay Dimdim* (The Dimdim Fortress, 1982)

The fall of the Kurdish Dimdim fortress to the Safavid army during the reign of Shah Abbas is one of the most celebrated stories in Kurdish history and heroic folklore. It is well known among the Kurds in different parts of Kurdistan, with both Sorani and Kurmanji, and even Armenian versions of it existing (Allison 2010, p. 56). In many versions, the commander of the fort is referred to as *Xanê Lepzêrîn* (also *pelzêrîn*), or Prince Goldenhand, and the story is known by his name. An early version of this story was published in Kurmanji by Jaba in 1860 while the first Sorani version was published by Oskar Mann in 1905. Ordikhan Dzhalilov (Ordîxanê Celîl) collected these and other manuscripts and published a Russian translation in 1967.

Thanks to the Safavid Shah's historian, Iskandar Beg, and Kurdish sources such the poetry of Faqi Tayran (Feqîyê Teyran, 1590–1660), which provides the earliest literary record of the event, the accounts pertaining to the fall of Dimdim fort are recorded in written sources. This, according to Allison, is unusual for a Kurdish oral tradition:

> Many versions of the story contain enough details to link them with the siege and capture of a Kurdish fort commanded by Emer Xan, the ruler of Baradost, by the armies of Shah Abbâs in 1609 CE. The Shah wished to

curb the power of the Mukri and Baradost principalities and Emer Xan had fortified a ruined fort on Dimdim Mountain, some eighteen kilometres south of Orumiyeh in Iran. After capturing the fort and massacring the inhabitants, the shah settled a Turkish tribe in the area which further weakened the Kurdish principalities. (Allison 2010, p. 56)

Hassanpour (1996) observes that while Persian historians (e.g. Iskandar Beg) depicted the battle of Dimdim as a consequence of Kurdish mutiny or treason, Kurdish oral traditions, literary works (e.g. Dzhalilov 1967, pp. 67–72) and histories instead rendered it as a struggle against foreign domination. The story of Dimdim is considered to be a national epic second only to Ahmadi Khani's *Mem û Zîn*, and most of the collected *beyts* portray Dimdim's defenders as martyrs in a holy war (pp. 81, 97, 98).

Recounted differently in different areas, the long oral narrative of Dimdim was sung and performed for hundreds of years in Kurdistan by the *beytbêj*, who presented the siege of Dimdim as a Kurdish struggle against foreign domination. This nationalist rendering of the fall of the Dimdim fortress can be found in the Kurdish prince's final and heroic reply to Shah Abbas:

*Xelqî me nayê rayê*
Our people will not surrender
*Hêviya dijmine le meydanê*
Which is what the enemies hope for in the battlefield
*Mîna şêra ew şer dike*
They fight like lions
*Hertim dijmina let deke*
They destroy their enemies
*Me ne xofê eskerê te*
We are neither afraid of you
*Me ne xofê xanî tewrêzê*
Nor are we afraid of the khan of Tabriz
*Tacê te qibûl nakem*
I do not accept your crown (authority)
*Kurdistanê bênav nakem*
I will not bring shame to Kurdistan. (cited in Rasul 2010, p. 51)

The audience, unaware of written records, appreciated the narrative as 'a historical event fashioned into a romance, aesthetically pleasing and resonant with powerful themes' (Allison 2010, p. 56). In the oral versions of the story, the epithet of Goldenhand, who appears to be a popular figure and much older than Emer Xan (Amar Khan), is attributed to him. As Allison shows, while the versions of *Dimdim* published by Jaba and Mann differ in both plot and style, they all converge upon a common subject, which is the heroic resistance of a Kurdish prince against a foreign oppressor. For its powerful themes, *Dimdim* has inspired a range of modern novelists, poets and also playwrights, who found in this heroic epic inspiration for the expression of their own nationalist sentiments.

The Introduction to Saman's *Qelay Dimdim* clearly establishes that it is not drawn from the oral narratives but rather from several written sources, which include Iskandar Beg's *The History of Alam Aray Abbasi*, Oskar Mann's *Tuhfayi Mudhaffariyyah*, Erebê Şemo's *Dimdim* and Sharaf Khan Bidlisi's *Şerefname*. Also, unlike the oral versions of the story, which almost exclusively take the form of the long narrative poem or alternate prose and poetry, the play is written entirely in prose.

The play, which was staged in Erbil in 1982, is, as with most modern versions of the story (see Şemo 2007; Celîl 2011), an overtly nationalistic work which presents Dimdim as an allegory for Kurdistan and the plight of Kurds in the twentieth century. In representing national heroes and models of heroic conduct from the 'Golden Age' of Kurdish history, when men were 'heroes', the story of Qelay Dimdim provides its audience with an exemplar of virtue and heroism to guide contemporary regeneration and instill courage in those that witness it.

*Qelay Dimdim* clearly resonated with its audience as it was successfully staged for over twenty-five days. It should be noted that this play was staged during a period (Spring 1982) of sustained uprising, when demonstrations convulsed almost all of the towns and cities of Iraqi Kurdistan (Stansfield and Resool 2006, p. 118). Having been prewarned by informants, the government recognized the play's nationalistic overtones and informed Saman and his group that it could only be performed if required changes were made. While Saman's group ostensibly accepted the government's demand, they chose to ignore it on the day of performance. A recorded version of the performance made its way to the Intelligence Service in Baghdad, and Saman and his group were later interrogated by government officials (Danish 2009a).

The play begins with Prince Goldenhand standing trial for his rebellion against the central government. The play's nationalistic themes are clearly indicated from the outset when a chorus, inspired by Brechtian theatre, sings,

> *Ey qelaykey serbestî . . . ey serbestî*
> Oh the fort of freedom . . . oh freedom
> *Gerçî dujmin toy dawete ber top û agir . . . burjî rûxand*
> Even though the enemy has fired canons at you . . . destroyed your tower
> *Şwênewarit mezarêke le bîr naçêt . . . ta gel mabê*
> Your site is a mausoleum, never forgotten . . . as long as the nation lives
> *Swêndim bew xwêney rijawe . . . Swêndim bew burjey rûxawe*
> I swear to the blood that has been spilt . . . I swear to the tower that has fallen
> *Swêndim bew razey nêjrawe . . . Dûbare dîsan*
> I swear to the secret that is hidden . . . Once again
> *Dûbare hoş û bazû bixeme kar, we çing bihênim ew behare . . .*
> I will exercise my will and strength, to snatch that spring. (Saman 2011b, p. 9)

When the prince is asked about his age, he replies 'as old as the occupation of Kurdistan' (Saman 2011b, p. 10). He is described by a representative of the state as a vicious ruler who rules over a vicious people (p. 10). His nation is described as violent, ignorant, barbaric, disunited, ungrateful and unworthy of self-rule, almost everything the Kurds have historically been accused of by the ruling powers in the region. In a clear anachronism, Prince Goldenhand draws on ideals of democracy, freedom and national self-determination to justify his actions and those of his 'nation' (p. 24) – this makes it clear from the outset that Dimdim should be viewed as representative of the whole Kurdish nation. When his nation is accused of being lazy and ignorant, he cites the work of Khani along with the twentieth-century poets, Nali, Mawlawi and Goran, in celebration of Kurdish literary achievements. He cites the Mahabad Republic (January 1946–December 1946) as a tragically short-lived instance of democracy and the rule of law (p. 25). Prince Goldenhand rejects the charge of rebellion by claiming that he only protected his homeland from the occupiers, to which the court responds,

> Your homeland? Since when have you had a land of your own? Your land has always been parts of the Ottoman and Persian Empires and its protection is the duty of the Sultan and the Shah, not you . . . according to the modern law of the twentieth century if a land is not owned, it can be claimed and settled by anyone. (Saman 2011b, p. 37).

In return, the prince asserts,

> Damn your modernity . . . we don't bow to anyone . . . . we might fall at times but we always rise again . . . Kurds never bow but to God . . . I am a prince, I am Prince Goldenhand, I'm the leader of a nation . . . I fight to expel the occupiers and to achieve independence for Dimdim. (Saman 2011b, p. 39)

The play's social concerns move to the forefront when the trial scene is cut short to consider the events that led up to the trial. The first scene offers an idealized image of the Khan as a humble leader who is closely aligned with his people; the lower classes are then praised for their patriotism while the landed gentry are presented in unflattering terms. In this scene, the prince encourages the workers to finish the reconstruction of the Dimdim fort before the onset of winter. He demands help from Hamad Beg, a feudal lord who is surprised by the prince's sympathetic behaviour towards the labourers and who fails to fully comprehend why the prince seeks to renovate the fort. Hamad Beg is humbled by the workers who show a better sense of common purpose and citizenship. One worker states, 'Dear Hamad Beg, the lord of all lords, I am not a *beg* but I know what I'm working for . . . I'm not a *beg* but I know what's in Goldenhand's head. I'm not a *beg* but I know what's going to happen in future' (Saman 2011b, p. 12). A chorus then intercedes to further underline the scene's key message. It asserts, 'When a nation resorts to uprising . . . to end oppression, open the prisons . . . burn the gallows . . . everyone, from any side, any class . . . in any village, of any religion or belief, must put their selfish interests aside and unite for victory' (p. 13).

The play depicts common men and women as noble and loyal to their prince. While men are engaged with rebuilding the fortress and defending it, women are presented as the mothers and wives of fighters. The newly wed Golnaz is proud that she will soon be the widow of a man who sacrifices his life for the homeland (Saman 2011b, p. 44). An older woman insists upon enlisting her three sons into Goldenhand's army, in clear defiance of the rules that forbid the recruitment of underage boys (pp. 41–2). In a separate scene, a woman is informed by a fighter of the death of her second son. However, instead of mourning her son's death, she immediately calls upon her youngest son to join the prince's army. He leaves but not before his mother gives him and the messenger the last drops of water in the house (pp. 55–6).

The character of Goldenhand is sharply contrasted with the Shah of Iran, who is depicted as a self-indulgent ruler whose main concern is attending to his harem. Significantly, it is Budagh Khan, the Mir of Tabriz, who shows concern over the renovation of Dimdim and brings the Shah's attention to it. Shah orders the Mir of Tabriz to halt the reconstruction of Dimdim if he views it as being incompatible with the government's interest.

Prince Goldenhand is, in contrast, humble and devoid of any selfish motives, his only ambition being the restoration of his homeland. He is fair and tolerant of people from all backgrounds or beliefs as long as they serve Dimdim. He protects the alcohol-drinking Armenian who is in charge of making cannons, from the complaints and outrage of the Islamic teacher. He asserts that they are both respected as long as they care about Dimdim, which needs both the jolly Armenian and the sombre Muslim cleric. The most important priority, the prince maintains, is to protect Dimdim's independence – anything else should be subservient to this main cause (Saman 2011b, p. 34).

Both *Mem û Zîn* and *Qelay Dimdim* engage with the lack of unity among Kurdish leaders in their relations with central authorities, which is a recurrent theme in the history of Kurdish movement. Goldenhand is certain that there are spies within Dimdim's walls (Saman 2011b, p. 19) and Ahmad Beg's treachery confirms the validity of his suspicion. It is also significant that Abdal Khan, the prince of Mukriyan, is the only Kurdish prince that comes to his aid. In speaking to Goldenhand, he states,

> When the sense of nationalism overpowers all trivial concerns, the nation unite like an iron wall against the threat of the greedy enemies. I'm not here as the prince of Mukriyan, helping out the prince of Baradost . . . I'm here as a patriot, a soldier in the Kurdish army which Prince Goldenhand has the honour of leading at this age. (Saman 2011b, p. 48)

Goldenhand complains that 'we are short in numbers but their numbers never change . . . they always receive support and help each other out, unlike the Kurdish princes who instead of helping us, bow down to our enemies' (Saman 2011b, p. 48). The tragedy, according to Goldenhand's advisor, is that most of the enemies' soldiers and commanders are Kurdish (p. 47). The princes of Hakkari are said to be servants of the Ottomans, while Shawirdi, the prince of Lorestan, and Ahmad Khan, the prince of Ardalan, are said to be the servants of the Shah of Persia. Still, the play expresses hope for a better future:

> We are victims of selfishness and greed . . . as long as there are Kurds like Abdal Khan, we can hope that one day, from all four corners, young patriots will rush to our support, under one flag, for one cause, that is the independence of our homeland. (Saman 2011b, pp. 48–9)

Despite its glorification of Prince Goldenhand and Abdal Khan, Saman's *Qelay Dimdim* is strongly socialist and anti-feudal in its outlook. While common men and women are depicted as patriotic and self-sacrificing, the feudal lords are generally depicted as imprudent and greedy, Goldenhand and Ebdal being exceptions to this rule. In further reinforcing the play's socialist message, a chorus reappears on stage and addresses the audience directly, asking them to rise against those Kurdish princes who stand against Dimdim: 'The old and new princes of our history, have always been obstacles on Dimdim's way to freedom. Neither strong enough to succeed, nor smart enough to unite. They collaborate with the enemies' (Saman 2011b, p. 24).

Apart from the use of a chorus, the influence of Brecht and also Piscator can be seen during the final scene of the play when a montage of tragic images, which depict the martyrs of the Mahabad Republic, the Palestinian *intifada* and the African-American civil rights movement, appear to an accompaniment of gunshots, cannons, jets and human cries (Saman 2011b, p. 51).[10] This is also a reminder of widespread anti-imperialist sentiments which, combined

---

[10] Erwin Piscator's political theatre began in the early 1920s in Berlin, where financial depression, inflation, left-wing revolution and war resulted in an intense politicization of theatre. He introduced film into live stage action by projecting images onto a screen that filled the back of the stage-set. He later developed a documentary-style theatre that incorporated feature film, newsreels and other documentaries – this contribution would later have a substantial impact upon worldwide theatre, most notably upon Brecht's epic theatre. The latter shares many of the characteristics of Piscator's work – this is most clearly evidenced in its use of internal commentary and its undermining of the naturalistic fourth-wall illusion. In contrast to Piscator's use of complex machinery, Brecht's staging was minimalist, and this made it easier for Arab and Kurdish theatre groups to adopt.

with anti-feudalism, anti-tribalism and anti-bourgeois-rightism, defined the Kurdish intellectual circles at the time. The confluence of Kurdish nationalism with wider national, anti-racist and class struggles is clearly evidenced during Goldenhand's trial, when the UN's Declaration of Human Rights, which was adopted in 1948, is read out three times by a chorus. A TV reporter then reads Article Two, which states, 'Everyone is entitled to all the rights and freedoms set forth in this Declaration, without distinction of any kind, such as race, colour, sex, language, religion, political or other opinion, national or social origin, property, birth or other status' (p. 18). A chorus mocks the Declaration and its clear detachment from material reality. A man and woman then appear on stage and bemoan the fact that, thirty-three years after the Declaration came into force, various forms of discrimination – class, ethnic, racial and religious – are prevalent within many countries (p. 18).

In complementing other modern reiterations of Dimdim's story, Saman's play illustrates that, for Kurdish writers, Dimdim remains a national epic that describes Kurdish resistance and struggle in the face of foreign oppression. This is clearly evidenced in Goldenhand's final remarks, when he states 'we are a nation who never gives up; we never bow down to any power, sultan or shah' (Saman 2011b, p. 63). Prince Goldenhand symbolizes the ideal Kurdish hero – intelligent, noble, selfless and willing to die for the homeland. The average Kurdish men and women share the same patriotic ideals with their ruler whom they love and admire. In offering an idealized portrayal of the prince, Saman's *Dimdim* recalls modern versions of the story by writers such as Celîl who writes,

> *Bejn bilind bû ew Gefat û û mêrxas,*
>
> He was tall, brave and courageous,
>
> *Hebû merîfet rehm bû bêqeyas,*
>
> A man of honour, of unparalleled generosity,
>
> *Alîkar bû ew piştemêr bû Kurda,*
>
> Giving help freely, offering support to the Kurds.
>
> *Tezkirî bû ew nav eşîreda,*
>
> He was much loved among the tribes. (cited in Allison 2010, p. 61; trans. Kreyenbroek)[11]

---

[11] Celîl's version also resembles Saman's in its social concerns and implied criticism of class-based hierarchies, evident in the fact that Gulbihar, the Khan's wife, is the daughter of a simple shepherd (see Allison 2010).

The idealized description of the Kurdish hero in Saman's play is the continuation of the myth of 'Golden Age' which has been central to Kurdish cultural nationalism. In the myth of the heroic age, according to Smith (1999), old heroes show the qualities of courage, self-sacrifice and wisdom that are felt to be lacking in the present generation. The liberty enjoyed in the 'Golden Age', which is currently lost to oppression and neglect, entails the claim to autonomy in the contemporary era. The twentieth-century struggle for Kurdish autonomy is therefore rooted within a desire to recover the liberties and rights enjoyed in the mythical past. The myth of a heroic age provides the playwright with models of virtuous conduct in a community's past: these are then resources that he/she uses to inspire faith and courage in the face of oppression and to call for collective action (Smith 1999, pp. 67–70).

The 'Golden Age' of Dimdim is, like all other national myths, followed by the 'Age of Decline'. The community loses its grandeur and liberty mainly because individualism and self-interest win over collective ideals and communal solidarity (Smith 1999). In the absence of external support and internal solidity (having been betrayed by self-serving gentry), Dimdim cannot withstand the pressures of the ruling state, and the resistance ends with the fall of Dimdim and the massacre of its inhabitants – the pictures that portray the fall of the Mahabad Republic representing only one instance of a thread that runs throughout Kurdish history. But, in referring to the ideals of human rights and democracy and by showing slides that depict global struggles for rights and democracy (both the African-American Civil Rights Movement and the Palestinian resistance movement), Saman clearly conveys the essential point that Dimdim is not about the Kurds alone; rather, it is the story of all oppressed groups.

## Conclusion

Saman revived the nationalist heroes of folk literature, Mam and Prince Goldenhand, at a time when Kurdistan had lost its short-lived autonomy and fallen under the dictatorship of the Iraqi Baath government. His portrayals of heroic national characters from the past and images from national folklore was not just an assertion of the unique character of Kurdish culture; to the same (and arguably even greater) extent, it helped to disseminate resistance within a disillusioned Kurdish community that had just lost its freedom.

Hutchinson suggests that great artists are those who take and remould the raw material of the collective experience of the people, as preserved and embodied in historical legends, into lessons that have a contemporary resonance (Hutchinson 1994b, p. 45). Similarly, Saman's plays should not be read as mere duplications of old national folktales and myths. His *Mem û Zîn* and *Qelay Dimdim* are products of their time and, as such, can provide considerable insight into prevailing concerns and trends amongst theatre artists and the educated elite in general. Saman's emphasis on anti-feudal and socialist themes, along with the reception and resonance of his plays, should be assessed and understood in relation to major political and social circumstances of the time, which culminated in the emergence of the socialist PUK. The PUK played a central role in reviving the Kurdish political struggle in the aftermath of the defeat of the fall of the Autonomous Kurdistan Region in the mid-1970s. The PUK was ideally placed to assume this role because its political agenda overlapped closely with prevailing intellectual currents within the Kurdish society of the time. A review of Kurdish theatre productions of the 1970s confirms the leftist environment of that period and provides a deeper understanding of Kurdish society through its theatre.

5

# Ahmad Salar's theatre: The mythical 'Golden Age'

Iraqi Kurdistan in the 1980s was characterized by resistance, demonstrations, anger, grief and often a feeling of powerlessness. The people struggled with a political reality defined by arrests, executions, expulsions, ongoing war and violence perpetuated by state 'security' organs. By the end of the 1980s, Iraq's Kurdish policy became characterized by a systematic attack upon the Kurdish population, which was increasingly genocidal in nature (Stansfield and Resool 2006, pp. 117–18). Given the scale and scope of human suffering, it may seem surprising that this period is frequently celebrated as a 'Golden Age' of Kurdish theatre (see Karim 2009). This 'Golden Age' has become synonymous with the name of Ahmad Salar, the most prolific dramatist of his age and a pioneering director who sought to create an authentic Kurdish theatre based on Kurdish culture, folklore, history and literature. His theatre was not only aesthetically innovative but also highly politicized, in response to the increase in state brutality and the onset of the Kurdish genocide by the Baath regime in the late 1980s. In examining Salar's construction of a distinctively Kurdish nationalist theatre, this chapter places particular emphasis upon *Nalî w Xewnêkî Erxewanî* (Nali and a Violet Dream, 1987) and *Katê Helo Berz Defrê* (When the Eagle Flies High, 1988) to show that Salar's theatre acted as a site for the staging of national history, folklore and culture therefore strengthening a sense of national identity. But, perhaps more importantly, it served as a cultural medium that implicitly called for revolution by romanticizing the 'Golden Age' of Kurdish self-rule, which was epitomized by the reign of Baban rulers in Sulaymaniyah and glorifying the Kurdish national heroes and their struggles against foreign invaders. In so doing, his plays clearly contributed to the strengthening of national solidarity and reinvigorating the national spirit.

## Ahmad Salar

Ahmad Salar, the prominent Kurdish actor, director and playwright, is considered to be among the most influential and important experimentalist theatre artists of the 1980s. What distinguishes Salar from others, however, is his introduction of a distinctly Kurdish theatre based exclusively on Kurdish history, folklore, legends, music and myths. Salar was born in 1947 in Sulaymaniyah. Having studied drama under the likes of Sami Abdulhamid, Ibrahim Jalal, As'ad Abdulrazaq, Behnam Mikhail and Jafar al-Sa'di, he graduated from the College of Fine Arts in Baghdad University in 1971 (Salar 2013, p. 111). During the course of his undergraduate studies, Salar proved himself to be a gifted actor and won the respect of his teachers. He acted in several productions of Shakespeare's tragedies, and this profoundly influenced the poetic language of his future plays. He was especially influenced by Brecht's narrative style which had become popular among Arab theatre artists.

After graduating, Salar returned to Sulaymaniyah where he taught at the College of Fine Arts in Sulaymaniyah University. In 1973, he founded the Progressive Kurdish Theatre Group and wrote and directed a number of plays in Kurdish – these included *Dildaranî Baran* (The Rain's Lovers), *Pirdî Wilat* (The Bridge of the Country), *Waney Reşbelek* (The Dance Lesson) and *Werzî Nwê* (The New Season). He also directed several non-Kurdish plays by writers as diverse as Brecht, Chekhov, Gogol, Yaşar Kemal, Molière and Shakespeare, along with plays by Kurdish writers such as Hussein Arif, Fuad Majid Misri and Muhyuddin Zangana.

In 1984, he established and led the Salar Theatre Group, and in the late 1980s, he started to write and direct his plays in the school of Abdelkarim Berrechid's *masrah al-ihtifali* (Festive or Ceremonial Theatre or, in Kurdish, *şanoy ahengsazî*). Berrechid, who is generally recognized as the most prominent contemporary theatre theorist in Morocco and the Maghreb (Amine and Carlson 2011, p. 166), has devoted himself to finding a theatrical form that reflects Moroccan/Arab cultural identity, as opposed to the Western model (p. 166). His Ceremonial Theory is characterized by a rejection of the fourth wall, the dynamism of the dramatic text and the freedom of the actor (pp. 166–7). Ceremonality appears through creations that anchor themselves in and draw their material from popular memory, myths and literature (Berrechid 2008, p. 78). In addition to borrowing characters from folk narratives, the Ceremonial Theater, inspired by the Arab tradition of *hakawati* and *halqa*,[1] puts the characters into a theatrical setting and imbues them with attributes drawn from Arab culture and history (p. 78).

*Nalî w Xewnêkî Erxewanî* (Nali and a Violet Dream, 1987) was Salar's first attempt to engage Berrechid's festive methodology in theatre. It was a tremendous success in both Baghdad, where it was staged in Arabic, and Sulaymaniyah. While Salar had written four plays before *Nalî w Xewnêkî Erxewanî*, it was this experimental play that gained him national recognition. *Nalî* was first staged in March 1987 in Sulaymaniyah; soon after, it was performed in the Baghdad Academy of Fine Arts, where it received an enthusiastic reception from the audience (Zangana 2002, p. 119). After being performed in Baghdad University College of Fine Arts, it received standing ovations from drama professors who strongly commended it. Its impact was so strong that it even moved Salah al-Qasab, the great Iraqi director, to tears (p. 120).

In relating his inspiration for this play, Salar recalled,

> I was a drama teacher at the Fine Arts College in Sulaymaniyah. I was going to college one day when I saw a large number of lorries full of men and women, young and old . . . all pale and worn-down. I was told they were *Anfal*, people from the villages of Qaradaq who were being transferred to the south to be killed. I had no power. Only my pen and the stage. The same night Iranians were bombing Sulaymaniyah as well. In the midst of bombs and explosions, I sat down and vented out my anger in this play. (Salar, interview, 5 May 2013)

For its innovative use of Kurdish culture, history, folklore, performance traditions and its patriotic theme, *Nalî w Xewnêkî Erxewanî* has been hailed as a breakthrough moment and the beginning of an original Kurdish theatre (see Simo 2007, p. 126; Karim 2009, p. 259). The prominence of musicians and musical instruments such as *daf, ney* and *santur* within Salar's productions clearly attests to the influence of Arab theatre, particularly the Moroccan Ceremonial Theatre.[2] As a popular and effective means of cultural propaganda,

---

[1] A circular assembly of people surrounding a performer in a public setting usually in a marketplace or city gate.
[2] Zahir Jalal and Burhan Muhammad were the singers in *Nalî w Xewnêkî Erxewanî*.

folk songs, such as the one at the beginning of *Nalî w Xewnêkî Erxewanî*, were used to pass on contemporary political messages. In this way, tradition could be called upon to both reassert cultural pride and protect the playwright from state censorship. Therefore, in Salar's theatre, oral and written literature both served as important means through which artistic creativity could be reawakened and political awareness could be fostered.

Salar's next play, *Katê Helo Berz Defrê* (When the Eagle Flies High, 1988), repeated – and even exceeded – *Nalî*'s success. It sold out within two weeks. Even the corridors of the theatre were sold to an eager crowd who, in Salar's words, 'knew what they came for and understood the meaning of the play' (Salar, interview, 5 May 2013). On occasions, they would shout anti-government and pro-Kurdish slogans which resulted in police intervention and even the arrest of Salar himself. The arrest of actors could have fatal consequences as several members of Salar's theatre group were young army deserters who were hiding from government authorities. Salar recounted an event that reveals the brutality of the regime and his good fortune escaping an arbitrary death during these difficult years. He recalled,

> It was Newroz and my group was staging a play at the Labourers' Syndicate Hall. The communist party members had written a large slogan on top of Saddam's picture which was hung on the wall. The Baath forces saw it and came to arrest me. Right there and then the Baathist commander ordered his soldiers to shoot me. My wife and child started to cry. The man took pity on us and told his soldiers to lower their guns. I asked permission to speak and explained that I had nothing to do with the place and was only there with my theatre group for a short time. (Salar, interview, 5 May 2013)

Summary executions were commonplace during Saddam's rule, especially during the Iran–Iraq War when any perceived threat to national unity was deemed treasonous and was punished accordingly. The Baathization of state institutions also continued as Baathist teachers were sent to Sulaymaniyah University and students were pressured to join the Baath party. Many students refused to join the army during the Iran–Iraq War. Salar claimed that from a class of eighteen he would end the term with only four, 'the others were arrested, killed or escaped' (Salar, interview, 5 May 2013).

The end of the Iran–Iraq War marked the onset of a genocidal campaign against Kurds in rural areas. The history of Kurdish theatre clearly demonstrates that the city of Sulaymaniyah did not remain silent in the face of those massacres. Theatre revived the spirit of rebellion and reminded the city's inhabitants of their national heritage and a 'Golden Age' of self-rule that was now lost and needed to be restored. Salar's plays, which were written in the late 1980s, clearly demonstrate the commitment and dedication of theatre artists to their national cause. During an interview, Salar emphasized that the thirty plays he had written up to that point, 'all dealt with the Kurdish question' (Salar, interview, 5 May 2013). Given the strong sense of national commitment displayed by Kurdish intelligentsia, it came as no surprise when, four days before the 1991 uprising, the Ministry of Intelligence ordered the arrest of a number of Kurdish artists and writers, including Ahmad Salar, for their 'subversive activities' (cited in Salih 2006; see Figure 23).

## *Nalî w Xewnêkî Erxewanî* (Nali and a Violet Dream, 1987)

*Nalî w Xewnêkî Erxewanî* has been described as a quintessentially Kurdish play (Kamal Qambar considers it to be the first truly Kurdish play in all its features – see Karim 2009, p. 254). The narrative style, allusions to local historical figures and the use of folk music and dance clearly demonstrate the impact Arab theatre and Salar's education at Baghdad University had made upon his artistic work. Having been inspired by Brecht to create an authentic progressive theatre, Arab playwrights had drawn upon indigenous theatrical devices such as *hakawati* and other folk forms. By the mid-1960s Brecht's influence had begun to manifest itself in the work of Arab directors and playwrights. Storytelling emerged as the dominant theatrical form for articulating national identity and political aspirations. Soon it became common to destroy dramatic illusion by making use of a narrator who addressed the audience directly or other characters that stepped out of their roles to draw the attention of the audience to some point or another. All these influences are evident in *Nalî w Xewnêkî Erxewanî* with several characters drawn from Kurdish folk culture and history appearing on stage to relate and comment on the dramatic action.

**Figure 23** Letter by the Ministry of Intelligence demanding the arrest of the listed Kurdish intellectuals including Hussein Barzanji, Fuad Qaradaqi, Fuad Majid Misri, Rauf Hasan, Ahmad Salar, Karim Kaban, Sherzad Hasan and Taha Khalil.

Before the audience enters the theatre, the stage is set with several *dafs* placed round it. A tray containing lit candles is placed in the middle of the stage and the whole theatre becomes infused with the scent of incense. An actor uses a sprinkler to splash rosewater on spectators who enter the theatre hall. A musician plays *santur* as the actors gradually enter the stage. The lighting then dims. When the stage is lit again the actors have each picked up a *daf* and walk around the stage singing a famous song by Dervish Abdullah, a *daf*-playing dervish in Sulaymaniyah (Simo 2007, p. 125). This song which refers to the legend of Farhad and his tragic love story introduces the theme of lost love and heartbreak which is dominant throughout the play:[3]

---

[3] According to this famous Iranian romance, a sculptor named Farhad falls in love with Shirin, an Armenian princess, who is also coveted by Khosrow, king of Iran. Khosrow sends Farhad to Mount Behistun and sets him the impossible task of carving the cliff rocks.

*Ferhad way lê neqewmawe*
Even Farhad has not been afflicted by this pain
*Wek min rencî nekêşawe*
He has not suffered like me
*Rencero xom yar torawe*
Oh the misery, the beloved is gone
*Ba bimrim canane*
Let me die valiantly
*Sînet baxçe w baxî îrem*
Your chest is the heavenly gardens
*Seyrangay rom û ecem*
Where the Ottomans and Persians trod
*Lêt têr nabim maçit nekem*
I cannot kiss you enough
*Ba bimrim canane...*
Let me die valiantly.... (Salar 1999b, p. 15)

It is in this distinctly Kurdish setting that the story of *Nalî w Xewnêkî Erxewanî* takes place. The play depicts the life of Nali (1797–1870), the poet in the court of Ahmad Pasha Baban, the last independent Kurdish ruler of Sulaymaniyah. The account of Nali's exile in the aftermath of the fall of Babans in the 1840s, his nostalgic homesickness, and his longing for Habiba of Qaradaq, the object of his affection in several of his poems, has enabled Salar to draw parallels which conjoin Kurdistan's past and present in an emotionally powerful and resonant piece of theatre.

Many Kurds mythologize the period from the sixteenth to mid-eighteenth centuries as a 'Golden Age' of freedom and political independence. The existence of semi-autonomous Kurdish principalities during this period of relative stability and the rise of Kurdish high culture has led many to see this period as the pinnacle of Kurdish history. Scholars have suggested that this presentation rests upon a prior assumption that no political divisions existed among Kurds during this time (e.g. O'Shea 2004, p. 133). *Nalî w Xewnêkî Erxewanî* can be interpreted in much the same way in its nostalgic homesickness – here the rule of Baban princes is presented as a 'golden' heritage that has been lost and which needs to be restored by those who are, like Nali, in love with their homeland.

It is significant that Salar chose Nali as the hero of his first attempt at an authentic Kurdish drama. This is a reflection of Nali's contribution to Sorani dialect and its rise as a literary language. With Baban rulers as his patrons, he initiated a literary school named after himself that utilized the Sulaymaniyah region's dialect, thus helping to make it the Iraqi Kurds' intellectual and literary language for generations to come. The poets of Nali School lived through the profound political and social changes that accompanied the fall of the principalities. A nostalgia for the bygone days when the Babans of Sulaymaniyah ruled independently from both the Ottomans and the Persians clearly emanates from their work. This is particularly true of the writings of Nali, whose later poetry was strikingly melancholic and pessimistic. In his work, the bitterness and regret of old age becomes coupled with the pain of exile and foregone love (see Bajalan 2013, p. 7).

From the outset, it is clear that Salar's rendering of the story of Nali's love for the beloved and his exile has a wider significance. Following the *daf* performance mentioned earlier, the characters of *mamosta* (teacher) and his students enter the stage. The teacher announces that 'today's lesson is about the poet Nali and love. Life and dying for the sake of life. The poet who stepped into exile . . . the poet's love for his beloved and his homeland are both part of a great pain' (Salar 1999b, pp. 15–16). The teacher's speech is followed by the sounds of storm and thunder and voices that express dark foreboding about a pregnant woman whose labour pain seems to be never ending in this ominous night (p. 16). The town crier enters the stage to warn the people that the enemies, the Romans, are approaching (p. 16). When this is followed by a chorus singing the famous lines '*Le bîrim dê Suleymanî, ke darulmulkî Baban bû*' (p. 17), it becomes clear that the 'great pain' mentioned earlier by the teacher is the invasion and subjugation of the motherland. This is embodied by the broken body of Habiba and the figure of a pregnant mother in labour pain.

The characters of *gêrerewe* (narrator) and the Kurdish poet, Pîremêrd, interject to describe the story of Nali's departure from Sulaymaniyah by quoting lines Pîremêrd had written on the subject over fifty years prior. After their emotional rendering of the event and Pîremêrd's statement that Nali 'wanted Kurdistan with Kurds in it' (Salar 1999b, p. 19), Nali enters the stage and reads his famous poem in which he bids farewell to his friends and declares his love for them. The first line of the poem reads,

> *Refîqan min ewa royim le latan*
> Friends, I am leaving you now
> *Le mezlûman bila çol bê wilatan...*
> Let the lands be empty of the oppressed. (Salar 1999b, p. 20)

To intensify the emotional impact of Nali's departure, a chorus then proceeds to sing the poem. Now, away from home, Nali writes to Salim (1805–1869), his friend and fellow poet, and, in verse form, asks about the conditions of life in Sulaymaniyah and whether he could return home,

> *Qurbanî tozî rêgetim ey badî xoş mirûr; Ey peykî şareza be hemû şarî şarezûr*
> Oh dear wind, the messenger from Shahrizor[4]
> *Aya meqamî ruxsete lem beyne bêmewe; Ya meslehet tewequfe ta yewmî nefxî sûr?*
> May I return or is it best to wait until the Judgement Day? (Salar 1999b, p. 26)

Salim responds to him in verse and, in rendering the fall of the Babans and the brutality of the Ottomans, seeks to dissuade him from returning home. The narrator of the play also invokes Kurdi (1812–1850), another Sorani poet, when he laments the fall of the Baban emirate in the following terms:

> *Saeqe w berqî nihûset zulmetî da şerq û qerb*
> The ominous thunder has struck east and west with darkness
> *Berde barane be mexsûsî le ser mulkî Beban*
> Stone falls from the sky, especially on the lands of Baban
> *Çawî 'ibret helbire ey dil le wesfî dehrî dûn*
> Look and learn my heart, how the cruel world works
> *Seyr ke sa felek çî kird be zumrey kurd ziman*
> Look what fate did to the Kurdish-speaking people. (Salar 1999b, p. 34)

---

[4] Shahrizor Eyalet was an *eyalet* of the Ottoman Empire that encompassed the area covered by contemporary Iraqi Kurdistan.

In the play, the Baban rule is glorified as the mythical 'Golden Age' when the Kurds lived freely. In one scene, the bygone glory of this principality is celebrated onstage by a traditional Kurdish dance. Both the narrator and the chorus recount a time when Sulaymaniyah was free from the rule of Istanbul and Tehran (Salar 1999b, p. 17). This sense of nostalgia is also evident in the work of Sheikh Reza Talabani (1842–1910), another follower of the Nali School whose idealized image of the Baban emirate, as rendered in Salar's play, has been wistfully sung by contemporary singers. As mentioned earlier, when the approach of the Ottoman army towards Sulaymaniyah is announced, a chorus sings these well-known lines from Sheikh Reza's poem:

> *Le bîrim dê Suleymanî, ke darulmulkî Baban bû*
> I remember Sulaymaniyah when it was the capital of the Babans
> *Ne mehkûmî ecem, ne suxrekêşî alî usman bû*
> It was neither subject to the Persians nor slave-driven by the Ottomans.
> (trans. Edmonds 1957, p. 57)

For their affection for their homeland and idealization of the time when the Babans were the rulers of Sulaymaniyah, the poets of the Nali School have been described as 'proto-nationalists' (see Bajalan 2013, p. 8). For Nali, Salim and Sheikh Reza Talabani, the present was synonymous with disappointment and the pain of subjugation, while the past was a time of splendour and glory. This clearly resonated with the late 1980s Iraqi-Kurdish theatre audiences who had finally achieved autonomy in 1970 only to see it collapse in less than five years and the leader of their long-established national movement defeated and exiled.

The hero's exile in Salar's play leaves the heroine helpless and vulnerable. The narrator recounts how, after Nali's departure, Habiba is attacked by a black-clad group of thugs. The chorus informs the audience that 'the greedy enemies who had coveted Nali's fiancée, cut off her breasts, chopped off her hair, blinded her eyes, and beheaded her' (Salar 1999b, p. 22). She turns into dust and flies up to the sky. Henceforth, she is the goddess of love, worshipped by all who seek light (p. 22). The graphic description of the violence imposed on Habiba's body, while it is not depicted or enacted onstage, clearly recalls Diana Taylor's criticism of the play, *Paso de dos*, which draws attention to the fact that the construction of national identity is predicated on female destruction (Taylor 1997, p. 9). She contends that, in the struggle for national identity, male intellectuals 'need the woman's naked and abused body to express [their] objections and redeem [their] audiences' (p. 10). In Salar's play, the ravaged female body is a politically inscribed entity that reproduces the familiar woman-as-the-nation trope. The image of Habiba presents the familiar metaphor of a nation violated by the invaders.

The woman/mother-as-nation metaphor is reproduced within yet another female figure in the play: a pregnant woman who is absent from the play but her body is used to issue a call to arms. Disembodied voices call for help for 'the mother': 'Pain, pain, pain. Folks, for the sake of God, help that woman; she is dying. Be valiant boys, act manly' (Salar 1999b, p. 32). The sound of thunder and blizzard is heard and voices that bemoan a dark night that is apparently without end, 'Oh that poor woman, when is the baby going to be born? Is that poor mother going to survive? . . . the pain has lasted too long . . . she is short of breath . . . her heartbeat is weakening' (p. 32). This association between pain of childbirth and national liberation recalls Ibrahim Ahmad's novel *Janî Gel* (The People's Pain) which, although written in 1956, had come out in 1972. In justifying revolution and its costs, Ahmad's revolutionary character compares it to the pain of childbirth which is necessary for the birth of a free nation: 'Revolution is a people's labour pain . . . It is no surprise that a people's labour pain should be filled with so much agony, sweat, tears and blood. That's how it is. But there is no doubt that the birth of a brave, proud and happy people should come with even worse pain' (Ahmad 2008, p. 184).

The birth of the new nation, however, is only possible through men's action. The trope of homeland as a sick pregnant mother is, to borrow a term of Najmabadi's, deployed in the language of 'warning and awakening' (Najmabadi 1997, p. 461). The neglected weak motherland is in need of care and cure, and requires her sons' medical and emotional attention. 'The recitation of the suffering of the mother's fevered and tormented body,' Najmabadi says, is 'employed to incite fear and panic over the loss of the mother, thus arousing her children out of their slumber' (p. 461). In *Nali w Xewnêkî Erxewanî*, the threat of the mother's death is understood to provide a basis for political action. Nali's sense of loss and nostalgic longings for the motherland are invoked in order to call for a revolution. Salar alludes to legendary heroic figures in Kurdish tradition to boost his audience's morale. He asserts, towards the end of the play, that if Nali returns to retrieve his beloved/homeland, every mother will have a brave son, a *Kawey Asinger* to protect her (Salar 1999b, p. 36) – like the twelve legendary riders of Mariwan who fought and defeated the Persian army (p. 36).

After the assault on Habiba, the rest of the play depicts Nali's grieving for Habiba/homeland in exile. The narrator, the teacher and Pîremêrd interject at different points to answer the students' questions about Nali's life. They all explain that Nali's love for his beloved and homeland endured despite his exile. Pîremêrd observes, 'Like the mythical lover who survived the cold by staring at a distant fire', Nali survived with the thoughts of love for his love and homeland (Salar 1999b, p. 34). Throughout the play, Nali himself enters the stage to recite lines from his poems. In reflecting on his love for Habiba he recites,

> *Şew hat û emin mestî xeyalatî kesêkim*
>
> Night has come and I am drunk with the thoughts of someone
>
> *Meşqûlî nefes-girtinî muşkîn nefesêkim…*
>
> I breathe in the fragrant air of her presence
>
> *Bawer meke roh sextî qemî firqetî to bûm*
>
> Do not think that I have become accustomed to the pain of your absence
>
> *Bo hatinî to baqîye nîwe nefesêkim*
>
> My last breaths are taken in the hope of your visit. (Salar 1999b, p. 24)

In a spiritual state, Nali sees the image of Habiba flicker in front of him. Overcome with grief, he falls to his knees and recites the following lines in nostalgic longing for her. These lines are also sung by the chorus which further intensifies the impact of Nali's distress:

> *Ey taze ciwan, pîrim û uftadew kewtûm*
>
> Oh young love, I am old and broken-down
>
> *Ta mawe heyatim*
>
> While I am still alive,
>
> *Destê bidere destî şikestem ke be ser çûm*
>
> Put your hand in my broken hand, I do not have long
>
> *Qurbanî wefatim*
>
> My faithful love. (Salar 1999b, p. 31)

Exhausted with emotion, Nali falls asleep and dreams of 'his mother, his village, his town, anything that smells of his beloved' (Salar 1999b, p. 31). His hometown of Sulaymaniyah, however, as the narrator informs us, is burnt down, covered in ash and smoke, and smells of blood and bullets (p. 32).

In the play, the occupied motherland and the Kurds in need of rescue are embodied by the image of Habiba and the woman enduring labour pain. In the final scene of the play, the chorus reminds the students/spectators not to forget the woman in labour and to reassure her that the day will come when her baby is finally born (Salar 1999b, p. 36). This also alludes to the Kurdish nationalist movement that, as the author prophesies, will bear fruit when the men unite to fight and 'die valiantly' for their nation. As the school bell sounds, the teacher announces the end of the lesson, along with the hope that Habiba will not be forgotten. The actors pick up the *dafs* and leave the stage singing the song they had sung at the beginning of the play.

The image of the motherland being abused by strangers has a unique precedent in the history of Kurdish theatre. It dates back to April 1945 when one of the most prominent examples of drama contributing to nation-building took place in the Kurdish town of Mahabad in Iran. This play was *Daykî Nîştiman* (Motherland) which was scripted and staged by a Kurdish political party (namely the Society for the Revival of Kurdistan or *Komeley Jiyanewey Kurdistan*) before the short-lived Republic of Kurdistan in Mahabad was created.[5] The play depicted the white-haired and black-clad Motherland in chains reciting a poem which called upon her sons to liberate her from the yoke of Iranian, Turkish and Iraqi rule. Her call was answered in the next act when her sons picked up arms, defeated the occupiers and freed her from the chains. The play ended with the coming to power of the Motherland and the creation of the Kurdish state. *Daykî Nîştiman*, which was over three hours long, drew heavily on the poetry of Haji Qadiri Koyi, the late-nineteenth-century poet and a forerunner of Kurdish nationalism, and several nationalist songs. Each act ended with a chorus singing patriotic songs to the accompaniment

---

[5] The Republic of Kurdistan was proclaimed on 22 January 1946 in Mahabad (northwestern Iran), with the support of the Soviet Union. The Republic collapsed after negotiations between Iran and the Soviet Union cleared the way for Iranian military action. The Iranian military regained control in December 1946, and the leaders of the Republic were executed in March 1947.

of clarinet, drums and trumpet. These songs included *Xwaye Weten Awa Key* (God, Bless the Homeland), *Erê Hey Kurdistan, Kurdistanî Ciwan* (Oh Kurdistan, Beautiful Kurdistan) and *Dînimî Ayînimî* (You Are My Religion; You Are My Faith) (see Farshi 1995, p. 7). The play concluded with the creation of the Republic, the raising of the Kurdish flag and the introduction of the 'president', who spoke at length about Kurdistan's long history of enslavement and the need to struggle for liberation. The theatrical speech of the president of Kurdistan was followed by a speech by Qazi Muhammad (1893–1947), the future president of Kurdistan, who stepped onto the stage to speak, with great excitement, about Kurdistan's colonial history and future struggle.

The Motherland's cry for help and rescue in the form of a heart-wrenching song brought tears to the eyes of a Kurdish audience who were able, for the first time, to appreciate the power of 'serious' theatre – as opposed to popular forms of entertainment of the time. On the play's impact, Roosevelt writes in a rather sensational tone, 'The audience, unused to dramatic representations, was deeply moved, and bloodfeuds generations old were set aside as life-long enemies fell weeping on each other's shoulders and swore to avenge Kurdistan' (Roosevelt 1993, p. 126). As this and other accounts suggest, *Motherland* was an immediate and resounding success, not only in Mahabad but also in other Kurdish towns. In fact, the play was so successful in attracting people to *Komele*'s doctrine that the party had to open new branches to respond to a fast-growing membership.

In contrast to *Daykî Nîştiman*, Salar's play does not conclude with the actual liberation of motherland but with a dream of it. During this dream episode, the narrator recounts a different ending to Nali's story: that of his return and uprising. He states,

> Nali rebelled; he picked up his sword and polished it. He charged his horse and it went so fast that sparks flew from its hooves scaring away the fiends and ogres. It looked like it had already conquered several Ararats,[6] Helgurds[7] and Qezebs[8] and would soon turn the world upside down. (Salar 1999b, p. 35)

---

[6] A mountain located in the Eastern Anatolia Region of Turkey near the border with Armenia and Iran.
[7] The highest mountain in Iraq (3,607 m), Helgurd is located 81 km northeast of the city of Erbil.
[8] A mountain located in Iranian Kurdistan.

Nali finally reaches Pîremegrûn Mountain in Sulaymaniyah. Uproar ensues and 'two hundred winters of foreign rule' are undone by one spring. The heroism of Kurdish fighters restores the 'Golden Age' of Kurdish self-rule, symbolised by the blossoming of gardens belonging to Abdurrahman Pasha, the mighty Baban ruler (Salar 1999b, p. 36). This victory is of course, not limited to Sulaymaniyah, or Iraqi Kurdistan – references to mountains in the Kurdish regions of Iran and Turkey make it clear that what is ultimately desired and envisaged by the dramatist is the liberation and independence of Greater Kurdistan.

This, however, is only a dream described by the narrator. The mother/land is still in pain and awaiting rescue, and Salar leaves her fate to be decided by the students/spectators. This shows a clear Brechtian influence in that the spectators become observers and are asked to contemplate the actions presented on stage. In Brecht's plays, characters ask the audience to reflect on how the play could end differently. This embodies Brecht's belief that the world is changeable and events are not inevitable. This open-endedness is also a characteristic of Berrechid's works which all end without a conclusion and therefore continue to be written in the minds of the spectators (cited in Ghazoul 1998, pp. 17–18). In Brecht's *Good Person of Sechzuan*, Shen Te addresses the audience and asks,

> How can a better ending be arranged?
>
> Can one change people? Can the world be changed?…
>
> It is for you to find a way, my friends,
>
> To help good men arrive at happy ends. (cited in Innes and Shevtsova 2013, p. 129)

Similarly, in *The Exception and the Rule* the final chorus sings,

> You have seen what is common, what continually occurs.
>
> But we ask you:
>
> Even if it is usual, find it hard to explain.
>
> What here is common should astonish you.
>
> What here's the rule, recognize as an abuse,
>
> And where you have recognized an abuse, provide a remedy. (Innes and Shevtsova 2013, p. 129)

*Nalî w Xewnêkî Erxewanî* encompasses three ethnic myths that are central to all cultural nationalisms: it begins by glorifying a Kurdish 'Golden Age', proceeds to lament its loss and then concludes with the myth of regeneration. The myth of regeneration, according to Smith (1999, pp. 67–8), is a prescriptive account of how to restore the 'Golden Age' and renew the Community as 'in the Days of Old'. It is a rationale of collective mobilization which informs the central concept of nationalism. Smith no that regeneration, with its metaphors of 'rebirth' and 'reawakening', continues the nationalist drama 'by placing the act of liberation in an ideal world of heroic imagery and naturalistic metaphor' (p. 68).

In *Nalî w Xewnêkî Erxewanî*, the myth of regeneration is presented in the form of the rebirth and heroism of a Kurdish literary icon who experienced the rise and fall of the Baban principality. This historical event, as with all cultural nationalisms, is endowed with a deeper symbolic significance. Nali re-enacts the drama of liberation by restoring this symbolic 'Golden Age'. Therefore, Nali represents more than the poet; in the words of the chorus, '*Nalî xewnêki erxewaniye; Nalî goranî Kurdewariye* (Nali is a violet dream; Nali is the Kurdish people's song).' *Erxewan* or Judas-tree is a spring bloomer with pink-purple flowers that grows throughout Kurdistan. By associating the dream of freedom to *erxewan*, Salar both perpetuates the myth of Newroz and Kurdish liberation in springtime and indicates that the dream of freedom is red with the blood of Kurdish fighters.[9]

While Salar's *Nalî w Xewnêkî Erxewanî* does not end with the liberation of the mother/land, Salar evokes the possibility of a free Kurdistan in a dream episode in which victory is achieved in Derbendî Baziyan[10] where the 'Mongols, Tatars, Ottomans and Persians' are defeated (Salar 1999b, p. 36). *Nalî w Xewnêkî Erxewanî* was written at a time when the oppression of the Kurds in Iraq was at its height. This oppression took the form of massive campaign of Arabization, Baathization, cultural suppression, mass deportation, arrests and executions. In spite of all this, *Nalî w Xewnêkî Erxewanî* raised the public's

---

[9] *Erxewanî* translates to purplish-red. I have chosen to translate it as 'violet' because, in addition to being close to the purplish-pink colour of Judas-tree flowers, it also signifies a spring bloomer like the Judas-tree.

[10] This location, which is near to Sulaymaniyah, was the setting for an armed confrontation between the British and Sheikh Mahmud in June 1919.

spirits by envisaging the return of self-rule and the end of oppression (even if in a dream) and thus kindled the patriotic spirit of the audience who were, throughout the performance, reminded of their national cultural identity.

On the impact of the performance on the audience, Kamal Hanjira recalls a scene when Nali stood among the audience and started screaming and crying, and for a few minutes the whole theatre fell into complete silence. 'It was as if Nali still lived among us, as if he lived within us, guiding us like a prophet,' says Hanjira who described the play as 'a ritual on the destruction of villages' and 'a ritual for revolution' (Zangana 2002, p. 99). Rauf also recalls how, in the small auditorium of Sulaymaniyah Fine Arts Institute, the audience was so engrossed in the play it was as if they were students attending Salar's class (Rauf 1995, p. 146). The audience spontaneously participated in the performance as a chorus, singing along with the folkloric songs which were performed on the stage (p. 147). Rauf observes, '*Nalî w Xewnêkî Erxewanî* took us to a tour of Kurdish culture, to a spectacular land, full of colour and magic . . . [The play] in a ritualistic manner, with the sound of *daf* and *santur*, and the scent of incense and wistful longings of the characters, immortalised the story of Nali's exile and his love for Habiba' (pp. 147–8). *Nalî w Xewnêkî Erxewanî* not only upheld the national heritage of an oppressed and denigrated people at a historical moment of national crisis; it also demonstrated the contribution that theatre could make to imagining a better future during one of the darkest times in Kurdistan's national history (Simo 2007, p. 126).

Holdsworth notes that theatre plays a central role within countries seeking political autonomy, stateless nations or countries in the aftermath of colonial or quasi-colonial rule. In each of these instances it helps to reassert a remembered or emergent cultural identity and therefore functions as a form of confidence-building and empowerment (Holdsworth 2014, p. 6). This clearly applied in the case of the Kurds who lacked national institutions to safeguard and promote their vernacular language and the cultural heritage. Salar's indigenous theatre made an important contribution by boosting morale, promoting cultural expression and also mobilizing the public. In incorporating local elements in his plays, Salar sought to create a distinctively Kurdish theatre that would uphold and promote the national identity against the assaults made against it. This reiterates the important contribution theatre made to reaffirm Kurdish

**Figure 24** Actors playing Daf in *Nalî w Xewnêkî Erxewanî*. *Source:* Ahmad Salar's personal archive.

**Figure 25** A musical ensemble in *Nalî w Xewnêkî Erxewanî*. *Source*: Salar's personal archive.

identity in the face of an onslaught that sought to eradicate the very basis of Kurdish existence.

## *Katê Helo Berz Defrê* (When the Eagle Flies High, 1988)

Written and directed by Ahmad Salar, this play was first staged at the Baghdad Festival for Arab Theatre in February 1988. Due to the large number of spectators, it went on stage twice a day for three days. The play was equally well received by the Arab artists. In March 1988, it was staged in the annual festival of the Sulaymaniyah Institute of Fine Arts and in April of the same year, it ran for several days in Sulaymaniyah Workers' Guild Hall (*Niqabey Kirêkaranî Silêmanî*) (Danish 2009b).

*Katê Helo Berz Defrê*, like *Nalî*, has a nationalistic subject. Once again, the love of a woman is associated with the love of the homeland in order to construct a national identity that is grounded within male bonding. The play engages with the Hamawand, from which Ahmad Salar himself descends, a family renowned in Kurdish history for their bravery and military prowess (Simo 2007, p. 190), who Jwaideh describes as the most noted fighting tribe in southern Kurdistan (Jwaideh 2006, p. 161). They supported the Baban princes of Sulaymaniyah until their rule came to an end around 1850. After the fall of the Kurdish principality, the Hamawand refused to submit to the Ottomans. They refused to pay taxes to Turks or to serve in their army and demanded local self-rule. They considered those who submitted to foreign rule to be traitors and their properties to be halal. As such, they began a life of brigandage, raiding caravans and merchants, at times closing the road from Kirkuk to Baghdad and Sulaymaniyah and bringing the trade and transportation to a standstill. For decades, they created trouble for both the Ottomans and the Iranian governments with their systematic brigandage in the whole area between Baghdad, Kermanshah and Mosul. Before the Ottomans lost control over Iraq, they made attempts to put an end to the Hamawand lawlessness by applying extreme measures. Lyon observes,

> [The Hamawand] in the past had ranged from Mosul in the north to the gates of Baghdad and eventually so disrupted trade with Persia that the Turks dispatched an expedition to round them up, men, women and children and herd them into exile at Tripoli in Libya some 2,500 miles off. But even there

they could not be contained for long, and soon they had stolen enough arms and transport animals to enable them to escape . . . they rode back to their homes and renewed their forays until the Turkish authorities were obliged to pardon them. (Lyon and Fieldhouse 2002, p. 101)

European officers have, in general, made unflattering remarks about the Hamawand. Colonel Lyon describes the Hamawand as a lawless tribe of notorious rievers [robbers] (Lyon and Fieldhouse 2002, p. 101) while Armand Pierre Comte de Cholet, the French officer, maintains they were cruel and merciless ruffians (cited in Henning 2012, p. 1). These unsympathetic appraisals are perhaps entirely to be expected given the Hamawand's role in the Kurdish uprisings and the murder of foreign officers across the region.

Kurdish historians instead admire the Hamawand for their valour in the face of Ottoman and Qajar forces, likening the tales of Hamawand bravery and heroism to legends (Amin 2008, p. 30). Amin's book on the history of the Hamawand maintains that they 'loved and protected their homeland' (p. 16). This is premised on the fact that they served the Kurdish administrators of the region and fought with them against their enemies. As referred to in the play (Salar 1999a, p. 60), the Hamawand always supported the Baban rulers and fought their enemies throughout their rule: in 1787, they supported the mir of Qela Çolan against the Ottoman government; in 1819 they supported Abdurrahman Pasha against Najib Pasha of Baghdad; and in 1834 and 1836, they, respectively, supported Ahmad Pasha and Aziz Beg against the Ottomans (Amin 2008, pp. 16–17). In the early twentieth century, they also staunchly supported Sheikh Mahmud Barzanji's rebellion against Iraq and Britain.

Hamawand's and Sheikh Mahmud's popularity among Kurds is attested to by the fact that their deeds are immortalized in traditional Kurdish *lawiks* (mournful songs), which include the following:

*Babî babim Şêx Mehmûd be melik daniraye*

My dear Sheikh Mahmud has become king

*Bexoy le çiya w çolan eskerî le sehraye...*

He is on the mountains while his army is on the plain

*Pêncsed feley teyarê sê hakimî legerdaye*

He has five-hundred soldiers and three commanders

*Kerîmî Fetah Begî eskerî telîm daye...*
Karim Fattah Beg has trained the army...
*Kurdan çek bibestin, pişt meden le qezaye...*
Kurds, arm yourselves, do not back away from this battle. (Rasul 2004, p. 29)

Inspired by historical events but retaining the spirit of Kurdish folk tradition, *Katê Helo Berz Defrê* similarly romanticizes the Hamawand and elevates them to the status of national heroes. The story of the Hamawands' bravery and their support of Kurdish uprisings against the Ottomans and the British is told in the form of a *beyt* by an old *beytbêj* called Lalo. The stage is decorated in the form of a Kurdish nomadic tent and it contains traditional Kurdish items such as *çîq*,[11] *mafûr*,[12] *mêxekbeng*[13] and *milwankey siml*.[14] The actors enter the stage singing *Gulale Surey Ser Kulmî Yarim* (The Red Flower on My Lover's Cheeks), a folkloric love song. The narrator, who hosts the event, welcomes the spectators/guests and informs them that 'tonight we celebrate the reunion of two lovers after the war' (Salar 1999a, p. 39). The *beytbêj*, in the tradition of Kurdish celebration, invites the guests to 'light candles, illuminate the place, burn incense, sprinkle rosewater, give out drinks, eat sweets' and dress up. Also, in the tradition of Kurdish storytelling, he asks the guests to curse the Satan and send blessings to the Prophet Muhammad – at this point the actors start playing *daf* and perform the sufi whirling dance (p. 39). The narrator informs the audience that everything is ready: the musicians, the singer (*goranîbêj*), and the storyteller (*beytbêj*) whose rich reserve of stories includes *Las û Xezal*, *Leylê w Mecnûn*, *Memê Alan*, *Mem û Zîn*, *Nasir û Mal Mal*, *Qelay Dimdim*, *Şîrîn û Ferhad*, *Şîrîn û Xusrew*, *Xecê w Siyamend* and *Zembîlfiroş*, along with many others (p. 40). In addressing himself to the immediate task at hand, the narrator announces his intention to convey the story of Halo in a *beyt* called *Katê Helo Berz Defrê*.

In the scene that is depicted, it is 1924 and Mahmud Khidir of Hamawand, known as *helo* (eagle), is injured in a battle against the British and lies on his deathbed in Qeretamûr, the village of his birth. A British officer, delighted

---

[11] The tent's wall made with reeds, goat hair and wool.
[12] A Kurdish carpet.
[13] Decorations made with carnation.
[14] Long strings of hyacinth.

with the news of his fierce enemy's imminent death, pays him a visit with the intention of witnessing the legendary leader's demise. Mahmud, who is unwilling to be seen in a distressed and weak state, asks his soldiers to sit him up before the arrival of 'that *kafir* (infidel)' (Salar 1999a, p. 44). When the officer enquires about his health, Mahmud answers, 'Don't you see how firm I am before a dog?' (p. 44) At this point, the chorus enters the stage and sings *Berî Beyane Rûnake Aso*, a nationalistic song by Goran,

> *Berî beyane rûnake aso; asoy hîway Kurd mujde bê le to*
>
> The sun is rising; the Kurds' dream is coming true
>
> *Dengî bang helat le mizgewtî dê; baldar hêlaney xoy be cê dêlê*
>
> The call to prayer is coming from the town's mosque; the birds leave their nests
>
> *Helse ey lawî nîştimanî Kurd; demî helsane herkesêk nûst mird*
>
> Get up, you, the youth of the Kurdish homeland; it's time to get up, those who sleep die
>
> *Qespeqespî kew aşkira elê, katî fermane Kurd nabê binwêt*
>
> The birds are singing it's time for action, Kurds should not sleep
>
> *Ho bextî yarî w serbexoyî gel, le gel hawrêta bel bide le bel*
>
> For the freedom of your people, put your hands in your friends' hands. (Salar 1999a, p. 44)

When Mahmud dies, heart-rending cries are heard in the tradition of Kurdish mourning. An actor recites lines from Pîremêrd's play, *Şerîf Hemewend*, which was written to honour Hama Sharif Chalabi, another member of the Hamawand family, who rebelled against the Ottomans in the nineteenth century following the fall of the Babans. This song is in fact inspired by folkloric songs that became integrated into the Kurdish oral tradition after Sharif's heroism and defiance in the face of the Ottoman occupiers of Sulaymaniyah in the nineteenth century,

> *Nemirdûwe, Helo namrê, Helo ser xew deşkênê*
>
> He is not dead, Halo is immortal, Halo is only sleeping a short spell
>
> *Qelqanî zerde, mayinî çon dênê*
>
> Holding a golden shield and riding a mare

*Hewrî le serî ba deyşekênê*

So fast that his silk turban flies in the air

*Şerîf mekujin lawî germênê*

Do not kill Sharif, the lad from Garmiyan

*Çendem pê degutî meço qelatê*

I told you many times not to go to Qelatê

*Şînkekem hukme şeşxan detgatê*

You will be shot by a *şeşxan*.[15] (Salar 1999a, pp. 44–5)

Shukriyah Rasul's study clearly demonstrates that the last three lines of the preceding quote can also be found in the Kurdish folklore. These folksongs, which are also evidenced in the dialects spoken in Erbil, Koya and Raniya (Rasul 2004, p. 21), reflect both the profound grief felt across Kurdistan at the loss of a native hero and also the popular resentment towards the tyrannical Turkish governor of Sulaymaniyah. Two examples of these folksongs follow:

*Qelqanî zerde, mayinî baleban*

He holds a golden shield and rides a mare

*Dengî teplyan dê le girdî sîvan*

The sound of drums is heard from *Girdî Sîvan*[16]

*Şerîf mekujin roley qareman*

Do not kill Sharif, the brave lad (Rasul 2004, p. 20)

And,

*Qelqanî zerde, mayinî dênê*

He holds a golden shield and rides a mare

*Hewrî le ser ba deşekênê*

His *hewrî*[17] dances in the wind

*Şerîf mekujin lawî germênê*

Do not kill Sharif, the lad from Garmiyan (Rasul 2004, p. 20)

---

[15] A type of gun.
[16] The place where the battle took place.
[17] Traditional Kurdish headwear.

The resemblance between Pîremêrd's version and the folksongs means that even if Salar's audience had no knowledge of the former, the lines, which retained Kurdish historical memory of national struggle, would have still resonated with them. In the aftermath of the mourning scene, the story refers back to the two lovers from the Hamawand family: Nuri Muhammadi Sharif (who is referred to as 'Rider' (*sware*) during the course of the play) and Gulê, his beloved.

**Rider:** Dear Gulê, look at the tulips and how black they are inside. Do you know why their hearts have turned to ash? . . . They say the pain of separation from their loved one has burned their insides.

**Gulê:** And who is that loved one?

**Rider:** The short-lived spring that died young.

**Beytbêj:** Since the Romans (Ottomans) turned the spring of the Baban land to the cold winter of death and plunder, the flowers never saw the spring again, they went blind.

**Rider:** And the tulip's redness is the blood that's shed. (Salar 1999a, pp. 45–6)

The *beytbêj* enters the stage and complains about the pain of separation and, in reminding the audience of Mam and Zin and their sad fate, expresses his sincere wish that the story of Rider and his lover does not end similarly. In a musical episode, Mam and Zin enter the stage while Zin recites the following lines from Pîremêrd's *Mem û Zîn*:

> *Min wam dewê le dûrewe xomî nîşan dem*
> I want to show myself to him from a distance
> *Giyanim be dewrya bigerê w hîç nelêm be dem*
> Let my heart beat fast and not say a word
> *Bem eşqe pakewe wekû dû kotirî beheşt*
> With our pure love, like two heavenly birds
> *Lem xelke dûr kewînewe rû bikeyne beheşt*
> We leave this crowd and head to heaven (Salar 1999a, p. 46)

A singer (*goranîbêj*) then appears on the stage and sings Zin's lines from Pîremêrd's play which articulate the pure love between Mam and Zin,

*Xencer bo dile ger rastit dewê*
It is only fair to stab the heart with a dagger
*Ax Memî tiyaye nek berî kewê*
Oh but Mam is in it, I fear I stab him
*Ba destit le mil keyn, yekcariye*
Mam, let us embrace, once and for all
*Ne ray bêgane w ne bedkariye*
It does not matter what people think, for it's not a sin. (Salar 1999a, p. 46)

The *beytbêj* and narrator both, in poetic terms, describe the bravery of Hamawand men who voluntarily fought against the Ottomans. 'The Ottomans had coveted this land for a long time, savagely attacking it for hollow reasons since 1830,' says the narrator (Salar 1999a, p. 47). A voice is heard calling the Kurdish youth of the *eşîret* (family) to pick up guns if they love God, their land and their honour (p. 48). Rider and Gulê enter the stage again and share their final words before Rider leaves for the battle. A silent episode then illustrates war and martyrdom[18] before Goran, the poet, enters the stage while reciting lines from his poetry which link the love of the homeland to the love of the female beloved whose protection is a matter of honour:

*Bilê be bûkî tazey yekem şewim ger hate ser neşim*
Tell my new bride, if she stood over my dead body
*Nelê xoy bo weten kuşt û le rêy eşqî mina nejya*
Not to complain that I got myself killed for the country and did not live for her love
*Wezîfem bû le pênawî wilatêka serim bexşim*
It was my duty to give my head for a country
*Ke toy perwerde kird bo min le dawênî çiyaw kejya*
Which raised you for me within its mountains
*Eger xway gewre bexşî pêt hetîwê pêy bile: role*
If the almighty God gave you an orphan, tell him: child
*Le min firmêskî wîst bawkit, le toş dawa eka tole*
Your father wanted tears from me, and from you revenge (Salar 1999a, p. 48)

---

[18] This is described in the play simply as '*bînrawî ceng û şehîdbûn*' (visualisation of war and martyrdom) with no further explanation.

As is the case throughout the play, the love of the beloved is equated with the love of the homeland. 'Homeland is one's brother, father and family' (Salar 1999a, p. 55) and return to homeland is return to beloved. This sentiment is clearly expressed in the scenes which engage with the Hamawands' exile to North Africa, an event which took place in 1896. The narrator recounts how Halo and his followers including Faqi Qadiri Hamawand, the nationalist poet, were exiled by the Ottomans to Africa and how Faqi Qadir died in Benghazi, away from home and loved ones (p. 52).

In clearly conveying Rider's pain of separation from his beloved and his longing for home, Faqi recites lines from Haji Qadiri Koyi's poetry which were written when he was in Istanbul. The Sorani-speaking Koyi (1817–1897), who experienced the Ottoman government's abolition of the Kurdish emirates, is considered to be a forerunner of Kurdish nationalism. He is Sorani literature's equivalent of Ahmadi Khani, 'a predecessor to whom later generations of nationalists could always turn for inspiration, and whose poems they could quote to give expression to their own nationalist sentiments' (Bruinessen 2003, p. 48). Salar's play typifies Koyi's influence upon contemporary nationalist literature. In the poem that Faqi recites, the land, and in particular its mountains, is projected as a heavenly place that constitutes the essence of Kurdishness:

> *Gorey beharîye êstêke şax û daxî wilat*
> Now that it is the height of spring, the mountains of the homeland
> *Pire le lale w nesrîn û nergisî şehla*
> Are filled with tulips, wild roses and daffodils
> *Le girme girmî sehab û le hajey baran*
> And the roar of the thunderstorm and the sound of rain
> *Çiya pir le heraw newaye pir le seda*
> The mountains are full of sounds
> *Pire le seyl û gulaw û kanî rûy zemîn*
> The lands are full of streams and flowers
> *Pire le birq û brîqey brîskey cûy sema*
> And the sky lights up with flashes of lightning (Salar 1999a, p. 55)

Here, Kurdistan is not only a geographical-topographical entity; it is also 'a sacrosanct, mythic-metaphysical force inspiring love and reverence' (Strohmeier 2003, p. 160). Romantic descriptions of homeland in exile are recited by the narrator and sung by the singer,

> Bonî gijûgiya, hajey şetawan
> 
> The scent of flowers, the flowing of streams
> 
> Xirney bazinî, qulî nazdaran
> 
> The rattling of bracelets on pretty girls
> 
> Şineşinî werd, rûy mêrguzaran
> 
> The dance of the grass in meadows
> 
> Beheşt ebexşê, be diluzaran
> 
> Is a lover's paradise. (Salar 1999a, p. 58)

In historical plays, female figures have been used for nationalist purposes.[19] In Salar's plays, the Kurdish homeland is represented as a female body to construct a national identity based on male bonding among a nation of brothers (Salar 1999a, p. 67). The beauties of the homeland are envisaged as the outlines of a female body for which the male heroes fight and die. Below are some examples of this in *Katê Helo Berz Defrê*:

> 'Be ser kêwî Eraratda be lawik Pîremêrd serkewt
> 
> Elê şwênim kewin kurgel, şewî serkewtine emşew.' (Salar 1999a, p. 66)
> 
> (Pîremêrd climbed the Ararat Mountain to the summit singing a *lawik*
> 
> Saying, follow me boys, tonight is the night of victory.)
> 
> 'Eşret, ho kurgel, cam pir bê lêy erjê, wa dagîrkerî xwanenas, le enazey be der kirdûwa, ca ew kesey şeref û xwa w xakî xoş dewê . . . dest date tifeng.' (Salar 1999a, p. 48)
> 
> (Hey Families, hey boys, enough is enough, the godless occupier has gone too far, if you love your honour, God and land . . . pick up guns.)
> 
> 'Kurîne, demê sale çawyan lem wilate birîwe, bitanbînim rojî êweye.' (Salar 1999a, p. 62)

---

[19] In nationalist literature, female figures such as Joan of Arc have been used as metaphors for struggle against foreign oppressors. While characters such as Britannia, Germania and Marianne in France have been represented as militant figures, others have been depicted in more motherly guise.

(Boys, they have coveted this land for many years, I hope today is your day.)

*'Be tifengî birnew senger çolekem*

*Em şere le ser nerm û nol ekem.'*

(I head to the battle with my gun

I fight this fight for the sake of my sweetheart.) (Salar 1999a, p. 63)

Male bonding takes place in order to liberate the female characters who are mainly used as metaphors for the homeland and the need to struggle against a foreign oppressor. The characters of Nali's beloved (Habiba), the pregnant woman in pain, and Rider's beloved (Gulê) feed into the iconography that depicts women as representations of the nation. Nali's and Rider's agony of separation from their loved ones and their eroticization of homeland as female bodies rearticulate men's duty to their homeland as lovers, protectors and saviours.

In 1896, some of the exiled Hamawand managed to escape and return home from North Africa. The pain of their exile is highlighted in the play by allusions to Kurdish poetry and music. *Xaley Rêbwar* (Travelling Uncle) is perhaps unparalleled in its ability to convey the pain of exile and separation from loved ones: it is sung when the returning refugees search for the remaining members of their family in their hometown:

*Ho xaley rêbwar, gyana xo minîş rêbwarim*

Hey uncle, I am a traveller too my dear

*Rêm pê nîşan be, gyana xizmî xutanim.*

Show me the way, I am your kin my dear (Salar 1999a, p. 56)

Halo, who remains resilient in the face of the many hardships he endures, declares that 'until our last breath, we must persevere... not to become victims of misery and exile' (Salar 1999a, p. 55). With this imperative in mind, he and his followers resume their fight against the Ottoman forces. In a scene that clearly recalls Habiba in Salar's first play, Gulê is arrested and sent to Istanbul in retribution for Halo's rebellion. Again, as in *Nalî w Xewnêkî Erxewanî*, a woman in distress becomes the symbol of motherland in need of protection and liberation – in this respect, it is clearly significant when Gulê calls on her 'heroes' and Rider to come to her rescue (p. 61). As Gulê wails and calls out to 'her brave soldiers', folkloric music and a song by the *beytbêj* compound the emotional intensity of the scene (p. 61).

The next scene depicts the trial of Sheikh Said of Palu who led an uprising against the Turkish government in March 1924. He is portrayed as a nationalist who sacrificed everything for the sake of his nationalistic ideals. In the court, he is accused of treason and being a stooge for foreign powers. Sheikh Said vehemently denies these accusations and asserts that Kurds are not puppets in the hands of others but have their own legitimate national demands for which they sacrifice everything (Salar 1999a, p. 60). A folk music performance then follows before the narrator informs the audience that Sheikh Said and his followers were executed in 1925, before proceeding to draw a historical parallel with the mythical heroes of the Dimdim fortress (p. 60). In the tradition of Kurdish lamentation, Sheikh Said's execution is followed by a *lawik* lamenting the martyred heroes,

*Were lê, lawolê, lawolê, lawolê, lawolê, lawo*

Come on young man

*Sware mezinî bemin mezinî*

You are a great rider

*Serit le pola, çing le asinî*

Your head is of steele, your hands are of iron (Salar 1999a, p. 61)

The Kurdish mourning tradition of *çemer*, which involves singing to the accompaniment of *daf* and *zurna* is also performed for the martyrdom of Jwamer Hamawand, one of the Hamawand's most-feared fighters who was made ruler of Qasre-Shirin and Zuhaw by the Shah of Iran in 1881. He was killed six years later after the Ottomans and the Qajar plotted against him. *Goranîbêj* (the singer) sings lines from the *beyt* of Jwamer Hamawand,

*Dayk be qurban qulî zîneket*

May your mother die for your saddle (mourning expression)

*Çekmey musilî pir le xwêneket*

And your blood-filled boots

*Dayk be qurban rojî bêkesit*

May your mother die for your lonely day

*Tereqey helnesaw demançey destit*

For the bullet that did not leave the gun in your hand

*Dayk be qurban hey law hey lawit*

May your mother die for your battle cries

*Swar frê danî deştî zehawit*

When you threw off riders from their horses in Zehaw plain.[20] (Salar 1999a, p. 62)

The play refers back to the events following the First World War, when the British occupied Kurdish lands. The British officer, who is simply referred to as Captain, maintains that Britain is not the occupier; instead, he presents his country as a liberator whose rule is purely motivated by benevolence and pity – upon this basis, he invites Halo to give up resistance (Salar 1999a, p. 64). Halo defiantly scoffs at this charade and refuses London's offer to pardon him in exchange for his surrender (p. 64). The rebellion continues and the narrator names several British military officers who died as a consequence – they include Captains Lewis, McDonald, Newton, Pearson, Salmon, Scott and Walker, along with Colonel Leachman (pp. 67–8). Karim Beg who kills two British officers (Captains Bond and Makant) is depicted on stage as a hero and a friend of Halo's whose conversation with Halo about the killing of Captain Bond (who was tasked with engaging the Hamawand) is followed by (unspecified) jovial music (p. 67).

This scene is immediately followed by the trial of Sheikh Mahmud Barzanji in a British military court. He questions the legitimacy of any decision made by the court and contends, 'I was fighting against you. Now I am your prisoner; you, the enemy of Kurds. Of course you won't treat your enemy fairly' (Salar 1999a, p. 68). At the conclusion of the trial, when Sheikh Mahmud is sentenced to death, the narrator relates the following: 'Upon hearing the verdict . . . Sheikh, who was empty-handed, threw his headgear onto Greenhouse's chest' (p. 68). Sheikh Mahmud's brave words and gesture are followed by music and Halo's brave anti-colonial speech about the Kurdish right to self-rule.

After bringing out the inextricable unity of landscape and nation in full detail, and depicting the heroism of the men of the nation, who have been

---

[20] A plain west of Kermanshah.

raised by their mothers to fight and die for the country and women they love, the play ends with Halo extending congratulations to Rider for being a true lover and a worthy candidate to protect the land. He observes that 'those who want to climb mountains, before wearing their iron shoes and leather shin-guards, have to really believe in their goal and be determined to achieve it . . . their desire should be so great that even the darkness of grave cannot extinguish it' (Salar 1999a, p. 70). After pausing and looking into Rider's eyes he speaks again: 'Well done, this is true love. I can see Gulê's eyes in your eyes. Now you deserve to be trusted with a holy task' (p. 70).

While the Hamawand continue to live up to their fame as accomplished fighters,[21] their historical resistance to government pressure has long been idolized in Kurdish folktales; a fact which the *beyts* of *Cwamêr Hemewend* and *Şerîf Hemewend* attest to. Salar's play continues the same performance tradition but in a different mode of fiction, which is enacted in a theatre and for the benefit of a late twentieth-century Iraqi Kurdish audience. In reinforcing his idealized depiction of the Hamawand as a patriotic family, Salar incorporates the old *beyts* – this enables him to revive old memories, myths, symbols, traditions and values (Salar 1999a, pp. 44–5, 62). The Hamawand are depicted as true patriots whose rebellions against the Ottomans and the British were for a nationalistic cause. Halo can smell the soil of his homeland when he returns from exile (p. 57), while Rider is a romantic who sees his beloved's image in all beauties of nature (pp. 54, 57).

The idealization of the Hamawand family is not only conveyed through characters' dialogues and the narrator's descriptions. It is also reproduced through choral singing and recitations of Kurdish nationalistic poems such as those by Goran and Fayiq Bekas (Salar 1999a, pp. 44, 48, 51). For example, lines from Sheikh Salami Azabani's poem are recited to bemoan the Hamawand's exile to Libya as an assault on Kurdish people and a further national tragedy upon innumerable antecedents:

---

[21] On 15 January 2003, the *New York Times* published a front-page article on the Hamawand who were simultaneously engaged in wars of resistance against Saddam Hussein (in the North) and Ansar al-Islam, a militant group connected to Al-Qaeda (in the East). The article noted that Karim Agha led the fighting in the North and his son Halat led the war effort in the East. See: http://www.nytimes.com/2003/01/15/world/threats-and-responses-hussein-s-foes-iraqi-kurds-fight-a-war-that-has-two-faces.html.

> *Êşî sexte gil eka herdû gilêney çawî Kurd*
>
> This is a terrible pain which brings tears to the eyes of the Kurds
>
> *Derdî bê dermane derdî qewmî lê qewmawî Kurd*
>
> What has plagued the Kurdish people is an illness with no cure. (Salar 1999a, p. 56)

The idealization of the Hamawand involves glorification of their main place of activity, the Bazyan Pass – this is the commercially and strategically important gateway that connects the mountain regions east of the Qara Daq with the Mesopotamian plain and the outside world. The Hamawand used to loot caravans and entrap Ottoman forces in the Bazyan Valley. In Salar's play, these are acts of resistance that are undertaken in the service of the homeland (Salar 1999a, p. 50). The Bazyan Valley is also of particular importance to Kurdish nationalists because it was where Sheikh Mahmud and his allies, including the Hamawand, fought the British army.

Historical plays in the vernacular language which portray heroic national characters from the past or images from national folklore or rural life have been part of the common patterns of nationalist cultural expression in the artistic work of the nineteenth century, and this feature has further extended into the twentieth and even twenty-first centuries. In depicting male heroes fighting, and perhaps even dying, for the author's native land, historical plays assert the uniqueness of their culture and challenge the dominant discourse of imperial rule. In this manner, Salar's plays draw on the historical legends of local heroes and romanticize the lives of historical Kurdish characters in order to revive and strengthen the sense of national identity among the public, who come to view themselves as a distinct nation, with a distinct culture, history, and homeland. Also in a time when Kurds were in armed conflict with the central government, the plays further fuelled the revolutionary spirit.

As with Saman's plays examined in the previous chapter, Salar's theatre of the late 1980s falls within the Kurdish cultural-nationalist discourse. His theatre employed folklore, myths, historic struggles and depictions of idyllic rural life as a means of demonstrating the distinctiveness of Kurdish culture and calling upon young Kurds to join the uprising. However, while Saman's plays always evidenced leftist leanings and situated the Kurdish question in the universal struggle of the oppressed against their oppressors, Salar's theatre was unequivocally nationalist. His plays deployed Kurdish iconography upon an impressive scale, and made extensive use of Kurdish costumes, handicrafts, instruments and songs. This represented a strong aural and visual refusal of the state's denial of Kurdish presence in the region and its policy of Arabization of their lands.

The shift from Saman's socialist nationalism to Salar's quintessentially Kurdish nationalism should be understood in the wider context of atrocities that were committed against rural Kurdish areas in 1987 and 1988. The Baathist regime's policies of forced assimilation and elimination further fuelled the flames of Kurdish nationalism as virtually no individual or family remained unaffected by the Iraqi army's actions in Kurdistan (Stansfield and Resool 2006, p. 121–2). This commonality of suffering consolidated Kurdish identity in the face of overwhelming oppression (p. 121), as the theatrical output of Ahmad Salar during the late 1980s clearly attests.

Salar's extensive and exclusive use of Kurdish dance, folkloric songs, historical figures, musical instruments, myths and poetry made theatre a public medium for the collective expression and experience of a distinct Kurdish identity that the Baathist regime had sought to dilute since 1975. It fostered a sense of pride in Kurdish cultural traditions which were shown to be appropriate components of a distinctively Kurdish theatre. Salar's musical theatre not only acted as a site for the staging of national history, folklore and culture, and thus strengthening a sense of national identity, it also served as a cultural medium that implicitly commented on contemporary political issues by glorifying those Kurdish characters from the past who, for one reason or another, had fought against foreign rulers of Kurdistan.

*Katê Helo Berz Defrê* is an example of a political Kurdish drama that follows on from Brecht's Epic and Berrechid's Ceremonial Theatre. It presents events from Kurdistan's recent history and casts the characters in a form that brings together dancing, drama, mime, singing and slides. In following on from Berrechid's notion of performance, the play takes the form of a collective game wherein stage and auditorium combine together to constitute a unified platform of collective ceremony. The dramatic script is active and alive and it appears as an unfinished product that is to be fulfilled within a theatrical festivity (Amine and Carlson 2011, p. 166). While the effects of this ceremonial performance, as well as other productions by Ahmad Salar, can only be properly judged and appreciated on stage, the play's political significance can be assessed through a closer examination of its text and the context in which it was created. In staging myths of Kurdish common ancestry, heroic age, its loss and the need for its restoration, Salar's plays conform to Smith's suggestions that myths of origin and descent place 'the act of liberation in an ideal world of heroic imagery and naturalistic metaphor' (Smith 1999, p. 68). In constructing a strong nationalist identity on stage, Salar's plays captured the public imagination, and mobilized the general public toward political activism.

**Figure 26** *Katê Helo Berz Defrê. Source*: Şano, no. 12, 2009.

## Conclusion

Salar's quest for an authentic, indigenous Kurdish theatre led him in the direction of a Ceremonial Theatre that made extensive use of folk culture, including costume, music, songs, stories and traditions. It has already been noted that folklore has functioned as one of the key elements of national identities in modern history. The nationalist use of folklore can be traced back to the eighteenth-century Romantic Movement and the works of innovators such as Herder who glorified folk songs, ballads, fairy tales and legends for their vigour and emotional impact. Ever since, folklore has assumed an important role in mobilizing the masses for nationalistic causes.

In Salar's plays, folk songs, dance and music are combined with modern poetry and history as the basis for a new national theatre. Folk poetry, according to Herder, is the 'nation's archive', 'a mirror of a nation's sentiments, a channel to the history, language, mores and thinking of a community' (Wilson 1973, p. 30). The combination of this oral national history with Kurdish nationalist poetry of the twentieth century not only nurtures a strong sense of unique identity and national grandeur but also perpetuates the national myths which locate the 'Golden Age' of the nation in its past – that is, the Baban era and the heroes of Hamawand. The crushing of the Hamawands' resistance to central government, much like the fall of the Dimdim fortress, is endowed with deeper symbolic significance, thus re-enacting the early drama of the loss of freedom and the decline of the 'Golden Age'.

The playwright draws on all these symbols and memories to inspire revolt. The loss and the necessity to restore the mythical 'Golden Age' are reflections of the present day and 'a route of vernacular mobilization whereby an indigenous intelligentsia uses folk culture to mobilize middle and lower strata and create ethnic nations' (Smith 1999, p. 18). At a time when this ethnic nation has been conquered and humiliated by foreigners, public performance of its folk culture, literature and nationalist myths to packed eager crowds becomes a call for revolution. Therefore, the production of Salar's plays in the late 1980s, when the Iraqi Kurds suffered one of the most brutal campaigns against them, is of great significance to any study of Kurdish national struggle that is interested in uncovering marginalized narratives and forgotten stories of cultural and theatrical resistance.

# Conclusion

Theatre is a significant source and viable genre for witnessing and studying the construction of identities. However, in the Kurdish context, it has not been considered to be capable of providing evidence germane to the understanding of history. This book refutes this assumption by offering insight into the role of theatre and its potential to contribute to an enhanced understanding of Kurdish history. In exploring the history and voices of those involved in making theatre, it hopefully brings to light hidden, marginalized or suppressed narratives and moments that indicate the critical importance of the theatre as a charged political space for the development of Kurdish nationalism.

This book affirms the cultural nationalist approach to the study of nationalism by stressing the essential role that intellectuals and intelligentsia played in introducing and promoting Kurdish theatre during its early years and also in utilizing it as a modernizing tool which helped promote education and retrieve national cultural heritage. However, as it has been repeatedly asserted, there was no divide between cultural and political nationalism in Iraqi Kurdistan – this was a reflection of the fact that the ultimate aim of theatre artists was an independent and free Kurdistan. Ever since its nascence, Kurdish theatre frequently acted as a site for staging national history, folklore and myths and for formulating nationalist ideology. It played, to this extent, an essential role in constructing and disseminating Kurdish nationalist identity.

Although efforts to create an independent Kurdistan had transparently failed, Kurdish intellectuals spoke of the need for a national theatre to serve the Kurdish 'homeland' and 'nation'. In deploying theatrical representation as a site of cultural formation, artists and scholars used the theatrical imaginary as a legitimizing force for this imagined homeland. Therefore, despite the manifest failure of political efforts to preserve a sovereign Kurdish state, the Kurdistan of cultural imagination was maintained in dramatic texts and theatrical performances. In clearly depicting Kurdish national culture, the nationalistic works of the twentieth century served to sustain a belief that the political state would one day be resurrected. The stage insisted upon the existence of a Kurdistan that had been partitioned but had not yet perished.

Theatre not only upheld Kurdish nationalism but also helped to create the very idea of the nation itself. In its early years, theatre was recognized as a useful means for promoting education and women's rights; to the same extent, it also fought against superstitions and outmoded beliefs. Theatre was therefore used to promote modernization and social progress, along with the end goal of nation-building. It was also utilized to represent the national character and to formulate and solidify notions of national identity. Pîremêrd had, in returning to Sulaymaniyah in the early twentieth century, begun the process of maintaining Kurdish national identity by honouring Kurdish national heroes and the nation's past in his plays. His collection of folktales, controversial celebration of Newroz and translation of literary classics into the Sulaymaniyah dialect were all part of his wider effort to construct a shared national identity and to promote national solidarity.

Strohmeier notes that the main arguments that early Kurdish nationalists advanced for distinction and pride derived from the glorious days of the Kurdish principalities, *Mem û Zîn*, the great epic poem, along with important historical figures who could be considered great Kurds, such as Saladin (Strohmeier 2003, p. 200). The contribution that dramatists made to this discourse in Iraqi Kurdistan is clear in their choice of plays. *Saladin*, a play based on the life of the Kurdish hero of the Third Crusade, was repeatedly staged during the 1930s. *Mem û Zîn* received a similar treatment in the period which extended from the 1930s to the 1960s. Theatre itself, as a Western genre, was understood to denote progress and sophistication. As part of their modernization project, the educated class, especially those based in Sulaymaniyah, promoted theatre and utilized it to educate the masses and enlighten them about wider political developments. They sought to remind the masses of their national heritage and thus solidify their national identification, fight outmoded beliefs and encourage women to defy social taboos by appearing on stage.

Despite attempts by the educated elite, the sociopolitical context did not allow for a strong theatre tradition to be established in Kurdistan until the early 1970s. With the creation of the autonomous Kurdistan region in 1970 and the emergence of a small group of drama graduates, Kurdistan saw the first instances of serious theatre which thrived in the free political environment. There was an upsurge of national themes in theatre performances during this era. Dramatists found in national history, legend and myth, a fertile source of subject matter to celebrate the Kurdish national identity and the ultimate defeat of their oppressors. Mythical and historical heroes, such as Kawa in *Kawey Asinger* and Muhammad Pasha Kor in *Kotayî Zordar*, were revived in order to express revolt against tyranny. Meanwhile, themes of freedom fighting and resistance in foreign countries were rendered in plays such as *Nirxî Azadî* and *Çawî Vietnam*, both of which clearly resonated with the Kurdish audiences. Foreign struggles for national freedom and identification provided Kurdish artists with important sources of dramatic power.

The loss of autonomy and the defeat of the Kurdish armed struggle in 1975, in addition to the Iraqi government's massive campaign of Arabization, Baathization, cultural suppression, mass deportation, arrests and arbitrary executions, did not put an end to the appearance of nationalist themes within Kurdish theatre performances. On the contrary, the influence of the increasingly politicized Arab theatre of the post-1967 era, which heavily utilized folk elements, inspired Kurdish artists to draw on their national heritage and to conceive of it as legitimate material for theatre.

Kurdish folklore, myths, legends and local history fed into notions of national identity and provided the raw materials for the creation of dramatic works. The interaction between the romantic idealization of Kurdish history and culture, political liberalism and a strong national consciousness resulted in the creation of several nationalist plays between 1975 and 1991. Drama was utilized as a powerful tool for awakening people to a common heritage and encouraging them to seek out national identity and liberty. By drawing heavily upon Kurdish nationalist myths, national folklore and national heroes, theatre directly contributed to the Kurdish national struggle in Iraqi Kurdistan.

Talat Saman's plays, which were staged in the late 1970s and the early 1980s, not only asserted the uniqueness of Kurdish culture by using images from national folklore but also, by portraying heroic national characters, helped disseminate resistance within a disillusioned Kurdish community that had just lost its freedom. Whether calling for unity among the Kurds in the face of foreign invasions, highlighting the absurdity of borders that divide Kurdistan, or satirizing the presidential election process in Iraq, Saman's body of works attests to Kurdish theatre's engagement with nationalist themes even in the immediate aftermath of the collapse of Kurdish rebellion. His theatre was the continuation of the Kurdish national struggle in Iraq by acting as a social space for upholding and promoting national Kurdish consciousness, identity and solidarity and also encouraging resistance.

It is significant that the first play of Saman that was staged after the fall of the autonomous Kurdistan region was an adaptation of Khani's *Mem û Zîn*, which is perhaps the most frequently quoted Kurdish literary text in nationalist discourse. Saman's play, however, was not just a retelling of an old folktale but a window into Kurdistan's social and political environment which, in the aftermath of Barzani's defeat, leaned towards socialism, anti-feudalism, anti-tribalism, anti-bourgeois-rightism and anti-imperialism. These were the core commitments of the PUK and also the defining characteristics of Kurdish intellectual circles at the time who blamed the tribal mindset for the failure of their national uprisings.

The theatre of Ahmad Salar ushered in a new kind of theatre whose sole purpose was to celebrate Kurdish identity and heritage and promote their protection. The shift from Saman's socialist approach to the plight of Kurds to Salar's purely nationalist approach is comprehensible when the backdrop of the Baath government's increased violence against the Kurds and the genocidal Anfal campaign is taken into account. In fact, the violence inflicted upon Kurdish villages and the displacement and mass murder of their inhabitants triggered Salar's *Nalî w Xewnêkî Erxewanî*, which was his first attempt at an exclusively Kurdish theatre.

In promoting an ideology of common heritage, tradition and belief, Salar's theatre sought to establish a sense of commonality among the audience members that overrode their ideological and cultural differences. Salar's retelling of Kurdish folktales, history and myths contributed to a cultural discourse which sought to create a common cultural history that united audiences from different backgrounds. The promotion of Kurdish culture through performance, therefore, came to function as an important vehicle for asserting a sense of Kurdish identity during one of the most brutal phases of Iraq's campaign against the Kurds.

Smith suggests that ethnic nationalism may promote a new national identity that draws many members of the community into a new type of politicized vernacular culture which creates 'the nucleus of the future ethnic nation and its political identity, even when secession is prevented and the community fails to obtain its own state' (Smith 1991, p. 137). This politicized vernacular culture includes arts, crafts, dress, poetry and songs, each of which features prominently in Salar's plays. Both Saman's and Salar's plays demonstrate the politicization of cultural heritage through the cultivation of its poetic spaces. This is described by Smith as identifying a sacred territory that belonged historically to a particular community. This also signified 'a process of turning the natural features of this sacred homeland into historical ones, and naturalizing historical monuments' (p. 127). This meant romanticizing the homeland's landscapes, legends and monuments, through which Saman's and Salar's nationalist plays evoked powerful sentiments of nostalgia and identification among large and receptive audiences.

These dramatists were also drawn to portrayals of virtue from the past with the prospect of inspiring emulation by contemporary generations. Their accounts of idealized heroes and sages (such as Halo, Goldenhand and Mam) and the 'Golden Age' of Kurdish self-rule and bravery, reiterated the nation's antiquity, noble heritage and ancient glory, thus strengthening the audience's sense of national pride and patriotism. The decline and loss of the 'Golden Age' through oppression and neglect provided the audiences with a vivid panorama of their current history, in which clear parallels were established between past and present tragedies. It was the desire to recover the liberties and rights enjoyed in the 'Golden Age' that fuelled the nationalist sentiments and reinforced the spirit of resistance among live audiences.

The fact that even during the various trials and tribulations of the Iran–Iraq, which had caused extreme financial duress, the public, and the working classes in particular, were willing to pay to see theatre performances reveals the appeal that nationalist theatre had for all social classes. It is important to note that during the latter stages of the Iran–Iraq war, economic and social circumstances were extremely difficult, and it was therefore extremely significant that a worker was willing to spend their daily earnings on a theatre performance.

In her *Utopia in Performance*, Jill Dolan (2005) asks, 'Why do people come to watch other people labor on stage?' (p. 36). She contends that, in addition to the obvious draw of theatre as a provider of cultural capital, 'people are drawn to attend live theatre and performance for other, less tangible, more emotional, spiritual, or communitarian reasons' (p. 36). She explains,

> Audiences are compelled to gather with others, to see people perform live, hoping, perhaps, for moments of transformation that might let them reconsider the world outside the theatre, from its micro to its macro arrangements. Perhaps part of the desire to attend theatre and performance is to reach for something better, for new ideas about how to be and how to be with each other to articulate a common, different future. (Dolan 2005, p. 36)

Theatre's possibilities as a place of inspiration and vision, 'a space of desire, of longing, of loss,' (Dolan 2005, p. 37) can be witnessed in the 'Golden Age' of Kurdish theatre, when theatre provided one of the few public spaces in which Kurdish nationalism could be expressed. While Dolan tries to find meaning in Western theatre by appealing to the small, but powerful, moments that performance can provide to make the audience affectively imagine or experience a better world, those who witnessed plays such as *Katê Helo Berz Defrê* and *Qelay Dimdim* were so galvanized by them that decades later they still recall the ambience in the theatre. For the Kurds who lived under the brutal Baath regime, entering a space where their heroes and their golden history were brought back to life was itself magical and utopian.

Ethnic nationalism is one of the most powerful forces of collective identification and action. Identification with a specific nation implies a strong emotional investment able to foster solidarity bonds among its members. When the nation is denied, humiliated, oppressed or threatened, what can be more uplifting to its members than a public performance of its uniqueness and grandeur? What better way to assure the Kurdish nation of its antiquity and self-worth than a dramatic performance of *Mem û Zîn*, one of its oldest literary texts? At a time when economic and political conditions forced many to leave Kurdistan, what could possibly be more emotionally powerful than witnessing an exiled classic Kurdish poet weep over the loss of his beloved/homeland?

The theatre of the 1970s and 1980s is widely acknowledged to be the 'Golden Age' of Kurdish theatre because, in contrast to contemporary Kurdistan, there was an eager theatre-going public who was connected to the performers through a mutual pain. Theatre for them was a space in which they experienced 'communitas' – this is a term that Victor Turner uses to describe moments when audiences 'feel themselves become part of the whole in an organic, nearly spiritual way'; at this point, their individuality becomes attuned to those around, and they bathe in a cohesive, albeit fleeting, sensation of belonging to a wider group (cited in Dolan 2005, p. 11). In the case of Kurdish theatre, this sense of belonging was unambiguously defined in national terms.

While discussing the affective and political possibilities of theatre, Dolan argues that emotions might move us to social action. Likewise, examples such as *Mem û Zîn*, *Qelay Dimdim*, *Nalî w Xewnêkî Erxewanî* and *Katê Helo Berz Defrê* clearly demonstrate that theatre, especially during the period 1975–91, definitely participated in the process of collective mobilization and action by promoting myths central to the concept of nationalism. In defying the strict censorship of the Baathist regime, Kurdish theatre continued to, through the creative application of Kurdish folk culture and literature, promote Kurdish nationalism and resistance, thus reassuring a denigrated, disenfranchised and persecuted people of their self-worth. More importantly, it brought the public together and aroused a spirit of resistance by portraying heroic and legendary national characters from the past. This inspired the audiences to emulate the heroism they witnessed on stage and bring forth the act of liberation out from the realm of dramatic imagery and into reality.

# Timeline: Iraqi Kurds

## A Chronology of Key Events

| | |
|---|---|
| 1918 | After the defeat of the Ottoman Empire in the First World War, British forces occupy the oil-rich Ottoman vilayet (province) of Mosul, bringing extensive Kurdish-populated areas under British rule. |
| 1919 | Mosul area is added to the new Iraqi state, which comes under a British mandate. |
| 1920 | Treaty of Sèvres, signed by the defeated Ottoman government, provides for a Kurdish state, subject to the agreement of the League of Nations. Article 64 of the treaty gives Kurds living in the Mosul vilayet the option of joining a future independent Kurdistan. |
| 1921 | Emir Faysal crowned king of Iraq, including Mosul. |

## Uprising

| | |
|---|---|
| 1923 | Sheikh Mahmud Barzanji rebels against British rule and declares a Kurdish kingdom in northern Iraq. |
| 1923 | Kemal Ataturk's newly founded Turkish Republic gains international recognition with the Treaty of Lausanne. The Treaty of Sèvres is not ratified by the Turkish parliament. |
| 1924 | Sulaymaniyah falls to British forces. |
| 1932 | Uprising in the Barzan region to protest at Iraq's admittance to the League of Nations, while Kurdish demands for autonomy are ignored. |

| | |
|---|---|
| **1943** | Mulla Mustafa Barzani leads another uprising, and wins control of large areas of Erbil and Badinan. |
| **1946** August | British RAF bombing forces Kurdish rebels over border into Iran where they join Iranian Kurds led by Qazi Muhammad, who founds an independent Kurdish state in Mahabad. |
| **1946** | Kurdistan Democratic Party (KDP) holds its first congress in Mahabad. Within a few months, the 'Mahabad Republic' collapses under attack from Iranian forces, and Barzani flees to the Soviet Union. |
| **1951** | A new generation of Kurdish nationalists revives the KDP. Barzani is nominated president while in exile in the Soviet Union, but the real leader of the KDP is Ibrahim Ahmad, who favours close ties with the Iraqi Communist Party. |
| **1958** | Overthrow of the Iraqi monarchy allows Kurdish nationalists to organize openly after many years in hiding. A new Iraqi constitution recognizes Kurdish 'national rights' and Barzani returns from exile. |
| **1960** | Relations between the Iraqi government and Kurdish groups become strained. The KDP complains of increasing repression. |
| **1961** | KDP is dissolved by the Iraqi government after Kurdish rebellion in northern Iraq. |

## Autonomy Granted

| | |
|---|---|
| **1970** March | Iraqi government and the Kurdish parties agree a peace accord, which grants the Kurds autonomy. The accord recognizes Kurdish as an official language and amends the constitution to state that 'the Iraqi people is made up of two nationalities, the Arab nationality and the Kurdish nationality'. |

| | |
|---|---|
| **1971** August | Relations between the Kurds and the Iraqi government deteriorate. Barzani appeals to the United States for aid. |
| **1974** March | Iraqi government imposes a draft of the autonomy agreement and gives the KDP two weeks to respond. Barzani rejects the agreement, which would have left the oilfields of Kirkuk under Iraqi government control, and calls for a new rebellion. |
| **1975** March | Algiers Accord between Iran and Iraq ends Iranian support for the Kurdish uprising, which collapses. Barzani withdraws from political life. |
| **1975** June | Jalal Talabani, a former leading member of the KDP, announces the establishment of the Patriotic Union of Kurdistan (PUK) from Damascus. |
| **1978** | Clashes between KDP and PUK forces leave many dead. |
| **1979** | Barzani dies, his son Masoud Barzani takes over the leadership of the KDP. |

## Iran–Iraq War

| | |
|---|---|
| **1980** | Outbreak of war between Iran and Iraq. |
| **1983** | PUK agrees to a ceasefire with Iraq and begins negotiations on Kurdish autonomy. |
| **1985** | Under increasing Iraqi government repression, the ceasefire begins to break down. |
| **1986** | Iranian government sponsors a meeting reconciling the KDP and PUK. Now both major Kurdish parties are receiving support from Tehran. |
| **1987** | Talabani and Barzani join forces with a number of smaller Kurdish factions to create the Kurdistan Front. |
| **1988** | As the Iran–Iraq War draws to a close, Iraqi forces launch the 'Anfal Campaign' against the Kurds. Tens of thousands of Kurdish civilians and fighters are killed, and hundreds of thousands forced into exile, in a systematic attempt to break the Kurdish resistance movement. |

| | |
|---|---|
| **1988** 16 March | Thousands of Kurdish civilians die in a poison gas attack on the town of Halabjah near the Iranian border. Human rights watchdogs and Kurdish groups hold the Iraqi regime responsible. |
| **1991** March | After the expulsion of Iraqi troops from Kuwait in March 1991, the uprising grinds to a halt and US-led forces refuse to intervene to support the rebels. Around 1.5 million Kurds flee before the Iraqi onslaught, but Turkey closes the border forcing hundreds of thousands to seek refuge in the mountains. |

## Safe Haven

| | |
|---|---|
| **1991** April | Coalition forces announce the creation of a 'safe haven' on the Iraqi side of the border. International aid agencies launch a massive aid operation to help the refugees. Meanwhile, Talabani and Barzani open negotiations with Saddam Hussein on autonomy for Kurdistan. |
| **1991** July | Talks continue in Baghdad, but Kurdish peshmerga forces take control of Erbil and Sulaymaniyah, in defiance of Iraqi government orders. |
| **1991** October | Fighting between Kurdish and Iraqi government forces breaks out. Saddam Hussein fortifies the border of Kurdish-held northern Iraq and imposes a blockade. |
| **1992** May | Elections held in areas under Kurdish control give KDP candidates 50.8 per cent of the vote, while the PUK takes 49.2 per cent. The two parties are equally balanced in the new Kurdish government. |

# Bibliography

Abdulhamid, S. (2010) *Aḍwā' 'alá al-ḥayāh al-masraḥīyah fī al-'irāq, ārā' naqdīyah wa-taḥlīlīyah lil-ẓawāhir wa-al-mu'assasāt wa-al-nitājāt al-masraḥīyah khilāla al-qarn al-'ishrīn*. Dimashq: Dār al-Madá lil-Thaqāfah wa-al-Nashr.

Abdurrahman, S. (1984) Raportî Hewlêr Dîdarî Şanoy Kurdî w Hengaw (A Report on the Erbil Theatre Meeting). *Beyan*. 82–7.

Afazeli, A. (1998) *Tūsheī az Tārīkhe Golpāygān va Mardome ān (A Selection of the History of Golpāygān and Its People)*. Tehran: Abjad.

Ahmad, I. (2008) *Janî Gel (The People's Pain)*. Hewlêr: Aras.

Ahmadmirza, K. (1983) 'Komelî Hunere Cwanekanî Pêşû' ('The Old Fine Arts Society'). *Karwan* 6, 49–54.

Ahmadmirza, K. (2011) *Şanoy Kurdî-Silemanî: Le Damezrandiniyawa ta Raperînî 1991 (Kurdish Theatre in Sulaymaniyah from Its Inception to the 1991 Uprising)*. Silêmanî: Karo.

Akyol, H. (2008) *Zargotina Kurdî: Ji Devê Nêrgiza Hemê, Hawîşana Palê û Zîna Elîxan*. Istanbul: Weşanên Do.

Al-Khalil, S. [Kanan Makiya] (2003) *Republic of Fear: The Politics of Modern Iraq*. Berkely: University of California Press.

Allison, C. (2001) *The Yezidi Oral Tradition in Iraqi Kurdistan*. Richmond, VA: Curzon.

Allison, C. (2010) 'Kurdish Oral Literature', in Philip G Kreyenbroek and Ulrich Marzolph (eds) *Oral Literature of Iranian Languages: Kurdish, Pashto, Balochi, Ossetic, Persian and Tajik*. London: I.B. Tauris. pp. 33–69.

Allison, C. (2013) 'From Benedict Anderson to Mustafa Kemal: Reading, Writing and Imagining the Kurdish Nation', in H. Bozarsalan and C. Scalbert-Yücel (eds) *Joyce Blau: l'éternelle chez les kurdes*. Paris: L'Institut Kurde de Paris.

Al-Mufraji, A. F., Abd al-Hameed, S., Kamaal ud-Deen, A., Abbaas, A., al-Nusair, Y., and al-Ani, Y. (1999) 'Iraq', in D. Rubin (ed.) *The World Encyclopaedia of Contemporary Theatre Volume 4: The Arab World*. London: Routledge. pp. 103–119.

Amin, O. A., and Danish, A. O. (2009) 'Xwalêxoşbû Umerî Elî Amin le Dwayîn Dîdarda' ('The Late Omar Ali Amin in His Last Interview'). *Şano* 12, 47–54.

Amin, S. M. (2008) *Hemewend le Serdemî 'Usmanida (Hamawand during the Ottoman Rule)*. Sulaymaniyah: Kurdistan Printing House.

Amine, K., and Carlson, M. (2011) *The Theatres of Morocco, Algeria, and Tunisia: Performance Traditions of the Maghreb*. Houndmills: Palgrave Macmillan.

And, M. (1963–4) *A History of Theatre and Popular Entertainment in Turkey*. Ankara: Forum.

Anderson, B. (1991) *Imagined Communities. Reflections on the Origins and Spread of Nationalism*. London: Verso.

Aras, R. (2013) *The Formation of Kurdishness in Turkey: Political Violence, Fear and Pain*. London: Routledge.

Ashna, O. (2009) *Pîremêrd û Pêdaçûneweyêkî Nwêy Jiyan û Berhemekanî* (*Pîremêrd and a New Exploration of His Life and Works*). Vol. 1. Hewlêr: Aras.

Ashurpur, S. (2010) *Namāyesh-hāye Irānī* (*Iranian Performances*). Tehran: Sūreye Mehr.

Aydin, D. (2014) 'Mobilising the Kurds in Turkey: Newroz as a Myth', in Cengiz Gunes and Welat Zeydanlioğlu (eds) *The Kurdish Question in Turkey: New Perspectives on Violence, Representation, and Reconciliation*. London: Routledge. pp. 68–88.

Azimpur, P. (2006) *Būka Bārāna va Hola Bārāna: Arūsakhāye Bārānkhāhī – Kurdistan* (*Buka Barana and Hola Barana: Rain Ritual Dolls – Kurdistan*). Tehran: Moaseseye Anjomane Namāyesh.

Aziz, H. S. (2013) *Komelêk Bînînî Şanoyî* (*Some Observations of Theatre Performance*). Hewlêr: Berêweberayetî Hunerî şano.

Aziz, M. (2011) *The Kurds of Iraq: Ethnonationalism and National Identity in Iraqi Kurdistan*. London: Tauris Academic Studies.

Badawi, M. M. (1987) *Modern Arabic Drama in Egypt*. Cambridge: Cambridge University Press.

Badawi, M. M. (1988) *Early Arabic Drama*. Cambridge: Cambridge University Press.

Badawi, M. M. (1992) 'Arabic Drama Early Developments', in Muhammad Mustafa Badawi (ed.) *Modern Arabic Literature*. Cambridge: Cambridge University Press. pp. 329–57.

Bajalan, D. R. (2013) 'Early Kurdish "Nationalists" and the Emergence of Modern Kurdish Identity Politics: 1851 to 1908', in Fevzi Bilgin and Ali Sarıhan (eds) *Understanding Turkey's Kurdish Question*. Plymouth: Lexington Books.

Balaghi, S. (2002) 'The Iranian as Spectator and Spectacle: Theatre and Nationalism in the Nineteenth Century', in Fatma Muge Gocek (ed.) *Social Constructions of Nationalism in the Middle East*. Albany: SUNY series in Middle Eastern Studies. pp. 193–216.

Baldyga, N. (2005) 'Reconstructing the Nation: Conflicting Cultural Imaginaries in Eighteenth Century Poland', in Kiki Gounaridou (ed.) *Staging Nationalism: Essays on Theatre and National Identity*. Jefferson: McFarland.

Bamarni, Q. (2011) 'Şanovanê Kurd Qazî Bamernî Ewê Pitir Ji 30 Salan Dûrî Welat' ('Kurdish Theatre Artist, Qazi Bamarni, after over 30 Years in Exile'). *Şano* 21, 85–90.

Barzanji, Y. Q. (2007) *Şanoy Kurdî (Kurdish Theatre)*. Silêmanî: Govarî Şano.

Beeman, W. O. (1981) 'A Full Arena: The Development and Meaning of Popular Performance Traditions in Iran', in Michael Bonine and Nikki Keddie (eds) *Modern Iran: The Dialectics of Continuity and Change*. Albany, NY: State University of New York Press. pp. 361–82.

Beeman, W. O. (1988) '(Theatre in the) Middle East', in Martin Banham (ed.) *Cambridge Guide to World Theatre*. Cambridge: Cambridge University Press. pp. 664–76.

Beeman, W. O. (2010) 'Music at the Margins: Performance and Ideology in the Persianate World', in John Morgan O'Connell and Salwa El-Shawan Castelo-Branco (eds) *Music and Conflict*. Urbana: University of Illinois Press. pp. 141–54.

Bekas, S. (2008) Şano w Awênekanî Yadewerî (Theatre and Memories of the Past). *Şano* 11, 8–12.

Bengio, O. (2002) *Saddam's Word: Political Discourse in Iraq*. New York: Oxford University Press.

Berrechid, A. (2008) 'Le Théâtre Ceremoniel (al Ihtifaliyya)', in Mohammed Habib Samarkandi (ed.) *Le Théâtre Arabe au miroir de lui-même et son contact avec les créations des deux rives de la Méditerranée*. Toulouse: Presses Universitaires du Mirail.

Beyzai, B. (2004) *Namāyesh dar Irān (Theatre in Iran)*. Tehran: Roshangarān va Motāleāt-e-Zanān.

Bhatia, N. (2004) *Acts of Authority, Acts of Resistance: Theater and Politics in Colonial and Postcolonial India*. Ann Arbor: University of Michigan Press.

Blandford, S. (ed.) (2013) *Theatre and Performance in Small Nations*. Bristol: Intellect.

Blau, J. (2010) 'Kurdish Written Literature', in Philip G Kreyenbroek and Ulrich Marzolph (eds) *Literature in Iranian Languages Other Than Persian: Companion Volume II*. London: I.B. Tauris. pp. 33–69.

Bogad, L. M. (2005) *Electoral Guerrilla Theatre: Radical Ridicule and Social Movements*. London: Routledge.

Bois, T. (1966) *The Kurds*. Beirut: Khayats.

Boon, R., and Plastow J. (eds) (1998) *Theatre Matters: Performance and Culture on the World Stage*. Cambridge: Cambridge University Press.

Boynukara, C. (2008) *Arîn & Mem û Zîn (Arin & Mam and Zin)*. Istanbul: Evrensel Basım Yayın.

Bozarsalan, H. (2003) 'Some Remarks on Kurdish Historiographical Discourse in Turkey (1919-1980)', in Abbas Vali (ed.) *Essays on the Origins of Kurdish Nationalism*. Costa Mesa, CA: Mazda.

*British Foreign Office Documents on the Kurds* (1944). University of Exeter Special Collection: Omer Sheikhmous Archive.

Brockett, O. G. (1967) 'Research in Theatre History'. *Educational Theatre Journal* 19 (2), 267-75.

Bruinessen, M. van (1986) The Kurds between Iran and Iraq. *MERIP Middle East Report* [Online] 141, 14-27.

Bruinessen M. van, and Boeschoten, H. (eds) (1988) *Evliya Çelebi in DiyarBakr: The Relevant Section of the Seyahatname*. Leiden: E.J. Brill.

Bruinessen, M. van (1992) *Agha, Shaikh, and State: The Social and Political Structures of Kurdistan*. London: Zed Books.

Bruinessen, M. van (1994) 'Kurdish Nationalism and Competing Ethnic Loyalties'. English version of 'Nationalisme kurde et ethnicités intra-kurdes'. *Peuples Méditerranéens* 68-9, 11-37. Available from: https://dspace.library.uu.nl/bitstream/handle/1874/20671/bruinessen_94_kurdishnationalismandcompeting.pdf?sequence=1&isAllowed=y (accessed 12 January 2019).

Bruinessen, M. van (2000) *Kurdish Ethno-Nationalism versus Nation-Building States: Collected Articles*. Istanbul: Isis Press.

Bruinessen, M. van (2003) 'Ehmedi Xani's Mem u Zin and its Role in the Emergence of Kurdish National Awareness', in Abbas Vali (ed.) *Essays on the Origins of Kurdish Nationalism*. Costa Mesa, CA: Mazda.

Carlson, M. (1994) 'Nationalism and the Romantic Drama in Europe', in Gerald Gillespie (ed.) *Romantic Drama*. Amsterdam: J. Benjamins.

Carlson, M. (2008) 'National Theatres: Then and Now', in S. E. Wilmer (ed.) *National Theatres in a Changing Europe*. Basingstoke: Palgrave Macmillan. pp. 21-33.

Çelik, D. (2017) *Dengbêjî Tradition and Its Effects on Kurdish Theatre in Turkey*. PhD Thesis. Istanbul: Istanbul University.

Çeliker, A. G. (2009) 'Construction of the Kurdish Self in Turkey through Humorous Popular Culture'. *Journal of Intercultural Studies* 30 (1), 89-105.

Celîl, C. (ed.) (2011) *Kela Dimdimê û Xane Lepzêrîn*. Çapa 1. Vezneciler, İstanbul: Nûbihar.

Chewar, O. (1980) Faylî 67 (File no. 67). *Rojî Kurdistan*, Special Issue. 83-95.

Chivers, C. J. (2013) Threats and Responses: Hussein's Foes; Iraqi Kurds Fight a War That Has Two Faces. *The New York Times*. 15 January.

Chyet, M. L. (1991) *'And a Thornbush Sprang Up between Them': Studies on Mem u Zin, a Kurdish Romance*. Berkeley: University of California.

Cusack, G. (2009) *The Politics of Identity in Irish Drama W.B. Yeats, Augusta Gregory and J.M. Synge*. New York: Routledge.

Danish, A. O. (2009a) Hunermend Mamosta Telet Saman (The Artist and Master Talat Saman). *Kurdistannet* [Online]. Available from: http://kurdistannet.org (accessed 12 January 2019).

Danish, A. O. (2009b) 'Şanogerî Katê Helo Berz Efrê' ('The Performance of When the Eagle Flies High'). *Govarî Tîpî Şanoy Salar* 12.

Danish, A. O. (2009c) 'Tîpî Şanoy Zanko' ('The University Theatre Group'). *Şano* 13.

Darvishian, A. (2000) *Sāl-hā-ye Abrī (Cloudy Years)*. 4 vols. Tehran: Cheshmeh.

Daryaee, T., and Malekzadeh S. (2014) 'The Performance of Pain and Remembrance in Late Ancient Iran'. *The Silk Road* 12, 57–64.

Davidson, S. N. (1933) 'The Termination of the Iraq Mandate'. International Affairs 12, 60–78.

Dieckhoff, A. (2006) 'Beyond Conventional Wisdom: Cultural and Political Nationalism Revisited', in Christophe Jaffrelot and Alain Dieckhoff (eds) *Revisiting Nationalism: Theories and Processes*. New York: Palgrave Macmillan. pp. 62–77.

Dolan, J. (2005) *Utopia in Performance: Finding Hope at the Theatre*. Ann Arbor: University of Michigan Press.

Dönmez, R. O. (2012) 'Constructing Kurdish Nationalist Identity through Lyrical Narratives in Popular Music'. *Alternative Politics* 4 (3), 318–41.

Doyle, M. W. (2002) 'Staging the Revolution: Guerrilla Theater as a Countercultural Practice, 1965–1968', in P. Braunstein and M. D. Doyle (eds) *Imagine Nation: The American Counterculture of the 1960s and '70s*. New York: Routledge. pp. 71–97.

Dzhalilov, O. D. (1967). *Kurdski geroicheski epos "Zlatoruki Khan": Dimdim (The Kurdish Heroic Epic "Gold-Hand Khan": Dimdim)*. Moscow: Nauka. pp. 5–26, 37–9, 206.

Eagleton, T. (1981) *Walter Benjamin: or, Towards a Revolutionary Criticism*. London: Verso/NLB.

Eagleton, W. (1963) *The Kurdish Republic of 1946*. Middle Eastern Monographs 5. London: Oxford University Press.

Edensor, T. (2002) *National Identity, Popular Culture and Everyday Life*. Oxford: Berg.

Edmonds, C. J. (1957) *Kurds, Turks, and Arabs: Politics, Travel, and Research in North-Eastern Iraq, 1919–1935*. London: Oxford University Press.

Edmonds, C. J. (1968) 'The Kurdish War in Iraq: The Constitutional Background'. *The World Today* 24 (12), 512–20.

Edwards, P. (1979) *Threshold of a Nation: A Study in English and Irish Drama*. Cambridge: Cambridge University Press.

Erol, A. (2010) 'Re-Imagining Identity: The Transformation of the Alevi Semah'. *Middle Eastern Studies* 46 (3), 375–87.

Farokhi, B., and Kiyayi, M. (2001) 'Marāseme Chamar dar Īlām' ('The Chamar Ritual in Ilam'). *Ketābe Māhe Honar* 39–40, 22–5.

Faroqhi, S. (2005) *Subjects of the Sultan: Culture and Daily Life in the Ottoman Empire*. London: I.B. Tauris.

Farouk-Sluglett, M., and Sluglett, P. (2001) *Iraq since 1958: From Revolution to Dictatorship*. Revised edition. London: I.B. Tauris.

Farshi, B. (1995) 'Kurteyek le ser şanoy "Daykî Nîştiman"' ('A Brief Note on the Play, "The Motherland"'). *Gzing* 7, 23–8.

Fayzi, G. S. (2006) *Barî Edebî Kurdî le Şarî Hewlêr: Le Nêwan Salanî 1935–1958* (Kurdish Literature in Erbil between 1935 and 1958). Hewlêr: Aras.

Fîdan, M. (2014) *Çîrokên Gelêrî* (*Folktales*). Istanbul: Berbang.

Floor, W. (2005) *The History of Theater in Iran*. 1st edn. Washington, DC: Mage.

Fraser, J. B. (1840) *Travels in Koordistan, Mesopotamia, &c., Including an Account of Parts of Those Countries Hitherto Unvisited by Europeans*. London: R. Bentley.

Frazer, J. G., and Fraser, R. (1998) *The Golden Bough: A Study in Magic and Religion*. Oxford: Oxford University Press.

Galip, O. (2015) *Imagining Kurdistan: Identity, Culture and Society*. London: I.B. Tauris.

Galawej (2009) *Bîrewerîye Hergîz le Bîr Nekrawekanî Min* (*My Never-Forgotten Memories*). Hewlêr: Aras.

Gellner, E. (1983) *Nations and Nationalism*. Ithaca, NY: Cornell University Press.

Ghazoul, F. J. (1998) 'The Arabization of Othello'. *Comparative Literature* 40 (1), 1–31.

Goran, A. (2005) *Dîwanî Goran* (Goran's Book of Poetry). 2nd edn. Tehran: Paniz.

Gounaridou, K. (ed.) (2005) *Staging Nationalism: Essays on Theatre and National Identity*. Jefferson, NC: McFarland.

Gunter, M. M. (1996) 'The KDP-PUK Conflict in Northern Iraq'. *The Middle East Journal* 50 (2), 225.

Haji, M. (1989) 'Afretî Kurd û Peywendî le Gel Hunere Cwanekan' ('Kurdish Woman and Her Association with the Fine Arts'). *Karwan* (81), 91–7.

Hamadbeg, J. (2007) *Mêjûy Serheldan û Geşesendinî Şano w Drama Le Koye 1931–2007* (The Rise and Development of Theatre and Drama in Koya 1931–2007). Hewlêr: Dezgay Mûzîk û Kelepûrî Kurd.

Hamelink, W. (2014) *The Sung Home: Narrative, Morality, and the Kurdish Nation*. PhD Thesis. Leiden: Leiden University Press.

Hammond, A. (2007) *Popular Culture in the Arab World: Arts, Politics, and the Media*. Cairo: American University Cairo Pres.

Hassanpour, A. (1992) *Nationalism and language in Kurdistan, 1918–1985*. San Francisco, CA: Mellen Research University Press.

Hassanpour, A. (1996) 'Dimdim'. *Encyclopaedia Iranica VII*. pp. 404–5.

Hassanpour, A. (1997) 'Med-TV, Großbritannien und der türkische staat: Die suche einer staatenlosen nation nach souveränität am äther (MED-TV, Britain and the Turkish State: A Stateless Nation's Quest for Sovereignty in the Sky)', in C. Brock, E. Savelsberg and S. Hajo (eds) *Ethnizität, Nationalismus, Religion und Politik in Kurdistan*. Münster: Lit Verlag. pp. 239–78.

Hassanpour, A. (2003) 'The Making of Kurdish Identity: Pre-20th Century Historical and Literary Discourses', in A. Vali (ed.) *Essays on the Origins of Kurdish Nationalism*. Costa Mesa, CA: Mazda.

Hassanpour, A. (2012). 'The Indivisibility of the Nation and Its Linguistic Divisions'. *International Journal of the Sociology of Language* 217, 49–73.

Hawrêyanî Gezîze (Gaziza's Friends) (2009). *Şanokar* 5, 46–69.

Hawri, A. B. (2002) *Berhemî Xebat: Beşêk Le Berhemekanî A. B. Hewrî* (*The Fruit of Labour: A Collection of A. B. Hawri's Works*). Hewlêr: Aras.

Heidari, M. (29 December 2013) Kūse Nāghāldī dar Ostane Markazī: A'īnī Bāstānī va dar Hāle Farāmūshī (Kūse Nāghāldī in Markazi Province: An Ancient Forgotten Tradition). *Islamic Republic News Agency*. Available from: http://www.irna.ir/fa/NewsPrint.aspx?ID=80971468 (accessed 12 January 2019).

Henning, B. (2012) *Dealing with the Kurdish Hamawand Tribe in Northern Iraq: Opportunities of the Ottoman-Iranian Borderland in the late 19th century*. MA thesis. Bamberg: Universität Bamberg.

Hawrami, H. K. (2001) *Dramay Kurdî Le Naw Dramay Cîhanda* (Kurdish Drama and Its Place in the World Drama). Hewlêr: Çapxaney Wezaretî Perwerde.

Hirschler, K. (2001) 'Defining the Nation: Kurdish Historiography in Turkey in the 1990s'. *Middle Eastern Studies* 37 (3), 145–66.

Holdsworth, N. (ed.) (2014) *Theatre and National Identity: Re-Imagining Conceptions of Nation*. New York: Routledge.

Holdsworth, N. (ed.) (2010) *Theatre and Nation*. Basingstoke: Palgrave Macmillan.

Hooshmandrad, P. (2004) *Performing the Belief: Sacred Musical Practice of the Kurdish Ahl-i Haqq of Guran*. PhD Thesis. Berkely: University of California.

Hourani, A. H. (1947) *Minorities in the Arab World*. New York: AMS Press.

Hutchinson, J. (1987) *The Dynamics of Cultural Nationalism: The Gaelic Revival and the Creation of the Irish Nation State*. London: Allen & Unwin.

Hutchinson, J. (1994a) 'Cultural Nationalism and Moral Regeneration', in John Hutchinson and Anthony D. Smith (eds) *Nationalism*. Oxford: Oxford University Press.

Hutchinson, J. (1994b) *Modern Nationalism*. London: Fontana Press.

Innes, C., and Shevtsova, M. (2013) *The Cambridge Introduction to Theatre Directing. Cambridge Introductions to Literature*. Cambridge: Cambridge University Press.

Isakhan, B. (2012) *Democracy in Iraq*. Burlington, VT: Ashgate.

Jaffar, S. (1992) 'Le Théâtre Kurde', in D. Baram and Halkawt Hakim (eds) *Les Kurdes par delà de l'exode*. Paris: L'Harmattan. pp. 207–32.

Jaffar, S. (2012) 'La Question d'Identité dans le Théâtre Kurde', in M. Gonzalez and H. Laplace-Claverie (eds) *Minority Theatre on the Global Stage: Challenging Paradigms from the Margins*. Newcastle upon Tyne: Cambridge Scholars Publishing. pp. 119–34.

Jaffar, S. (2015) 'Badea Dartash: Comédienne et Dramaturge Irakienne', in A. Fouque, M. Calle-Gruber and B. Didier (eds) *Dictionnaire Universel des Créatrices*. Paris: des Femmes Antoinette Fouque.

Jamal, R. R. (2007) *Bizava Şanoyê li Dihokê 1930–2006* (Theatre Movement in Duhok 1930–2006). Duhok: Hawar.

Jwaideh, W. (2006) *The Kurdish National Movement: Its Origins and Development*. Syracuse, NY: Syracuse University Press.

Karakeçili, F. (2008) *Kurdish Dance Identity in Contemporary Turkey: The Examples of Delilo and Galuç*. MA Thesis. Toronto: York University. Available from: http://www.academia.edu/6546183/Kurdish_Dance_Identity_In_Contemporary_Turkey (accessed 12 January 2019).

Karim, S. F. (2009) *Geşesendinî Dramay Kurdî 1975–1995* (*The Flourishing of Kurdish Drama 1975–1995*). Silêmanî: Melbendî Kurdolocî.

Karim, K. Y. (2011) 'Şano Le Nêwan Dwêne w Emro Da' ('Theatre between Yesterday and Today'). *Raman* 173, 143–9.

Karim, K. Y. (2013) 'Şanoy Kurdî Le Nêw Heftakan û Êstaa' ('Kurdish Theatre between the 70s and Today'). *Tiyater: Jimarey Ezmûnî Taybet be Sêyem Fîstîvalî Nêwdewletî Hewlêr bo Şano*, 75–7.

Khaksar, A. (2018) 'Vākāvi-e Jāygāh-e Namād va Namādpardāzi dar Marāseme Āini-Namāyeshi-e Chamar' ('Analysis of Symbols and Symbolism in Ritual of Chamar'). *Nāme-ye Honar-hā-ye Namāyeshi va Mūsiqi* (Journal of Dramatic Arts and Music) 15, 5–21.

Khaznadar, M. (2005) *Mêjûy Edebî Kurdî* (History of Kurdish Literature). Vol 5. 1st edn. Hewlêr: Dezgay Çap û Biławkirdnewey Aras.

KNN TV's Special Programme on Refiq Chalak. [Online]. Available from: https://www.youtube.com/watch?v=TATy6TQ0qV8 (accessed 12 January 2019).

Kotte, A. Maanen, H.,and Saro, A. (eds) (2009) *Global Changes Local Stages: How Theatre Functions in Smaller European Countries*. Amsterdam: Rodopi.

Kreyenbroek, P. G. (1992) 'On the Kurdish Language', in P. G. Kreyenbroek and S. Sperl (eds) *The Kurds: A Contemporary Overview*. London: Routledge. pp. 68–83.

Kreyenbroek, P. G., and Allison, C. (1996) *Kurdish Culture and Identity*. London: Zed Books.

Kreyenbroek. P. G. (1998) 'On the Study of Some Heterodox Sects in Kurdistan'. *Les Annales de l'autre Islam* 5, 163–84.

Kruger, L. (2008) 'The National Stage and the Naturalized House: (Trans)National Legitimation in Modern Europe', in S. E Wilmer (ed.) *National Theatres in a Changing Europe*. Basingstoke: Palgrave Macmillan. pp. 34–48.

Kurdish Students Society in Europe – UK Branch (1975) *Kurdistan Week: Cover-up for New Conspiracy*. University of Exeter Special Collection: Omer Sheikhmous Archive.

Levitas, B. (2002) *The Theatre of Nation: Irish Drama and Cultural Nationalism, 1890–1916*. Oxford: Oxford University Press.

Lyon, W. A., and Fieldhouse, D. K. (2002) *Kurds, Arabs and Britons: The Memoir of Wallace Lyon in Iraq, 1918–44*. London: I.B. Tauris.

Mahfuz, N. (1975) *Miqdad Alley*. African Writers; series 151. London: Heinemann.

Malakarim, M. (1980) *Dîwanî Goran: Sercemî Berhemî Goran* (*The Diwan of Goran: The Complete Works of Goran*). Baghdad: Korî Zaniyarî Iraq.

Malakarim, M. (2009) *Bîrî Komelayetî w Siyasî Pîremêrd* (*Pîremêrd's Social and Political Thought*). 2nd edn. Hewlêr: Aras.

Marranca, B. (1996) *The Theatre of Images*. Baltimore, MD: Johns Hopkins University Press.

Martin, C., and Bial, H. (1999) *Brecht Sourcebook*. London: Routledge.

Maziri, S. (2006) *Al-Takwīn al-Siyāsī wa al-Thaqāfī lil-Aḥzāb wa al-Jam'iyāt al-Kūrdīyah min Sina 1880 li-ghāyat 1958*. Baghdad: Jiya.

McDowall, D. (2004) *A Modern History of the Kurds*. London: I.B. Tauris.

Mda, Z. (1998) 'Current Trends in Theatre for Development in South Africa', in Derek Attridge and Rosemary Jolly (eds) *Writing South Africa: Literature, Apartheid, and Democracy, 1970–1995*. Cambridge: Cambridge University Press.

Meskub, S. (1971) *Sūg-e Siyāvash (Mourning Siyavash)*. Tehran: Khārazmī.

Metîn, M. (2014) *Jêrzemîn (Underground)*. Istanbul: Diyarbakir Metropolitan Municipality.

Mirawdeli, K. (2012) *Love and Existence: Analytical Study of Ahmadi Khani's Tragedy of Mem u Zin*. Bloomington: AuthorHouse.

Muhammad, M. (2010) 'Şanoy Ezmûngerî Le Kurdistan Paşî Çareke Sedeyek (Experimental Theatre in Kurdistan after a Quarter of a Century)'. *Şano* 20, 70–3.

Muhammad, M. (2011) 'Pêşekî' ('Introduction'), in *Mem û Zîn* (Mam and Zin). Silêmanî: Berêwberêtî Çap û Bilawkirdinewey Silêmanî. pp. 7–9.

Murray, C. (1997) *Twentieth-Century Irish Drama: Mirror up to Nation*. Manchester: Manchester University Press.

Najmabadi, A. (1997) 'The Erotic Vatan [Homeland] as Beloved and Mother: To Love, to Possess, and To Protect'. *Comparative Studies in Society and History* 39 (3), 442–67.

Narshakhi, A. M. J. (1938). *The History of Bukhara*. M. Razavi (ed.). Tehran: Sanāī.

Nezan, K. (1996) 'The Kurds: Current Position and Historical Background', in Philip G Kreyenbroek and Christine Allison (eds) *Kurdish Culture and Identity*. London: Zed Books.

Nyberg, M. M. (2012) *Connecting through Dance: The Multiplicity of Meanings of Kurdish Folk Dances in Turkey*. MA Thesis. Bergen: University of Bergen.

O'Shea, M. T. (2004) *Trapped between the Map and Reality: Geography and Perceptions of Kurdistan*. New York: Routledge.

Özoğlu, H. (2004) *Kurdish Notables and the Ottoman State Evolving Identities, Competing Loyalties, and Shifting Boundaries*. Albany: State University of New York Press.

Patriotic Union of Kurdistan (PUK) (1977) *Revolution in Kurdistan: The Essential Documents of the Patriotic Union of Kurdistan (PUK)*. New York: PUK Publications.

Peymangay Hunere Cwanekanî Silêmanî (Sulaymaniyah Institute of Fine Arts) (2009). *Govarî Tîpî Şanoy Salar* (12).

Pirbal, F. (2001) *Mêjûy Şano Le Edebiyatî Kurdîda: Le Konewe ta 1957* (The History of Theatre in Kurdish Literature from its Emergence to 1957). Hewlêr: Aras.

Pirbal, F. (2006) *Mêjûy Hunerî Şêwekarî Le Kurdistanda: Le Konewe ta Pencakan (The History of Painting in Kurdistan: From Its Beginnings to the 50s)*. Hewlêr: Aras.

Pîremêrd (1968) *Mem û Zîn (Mam and Zin)*. Sulaymaniyah: Jîn.

Plastow, J. (1996) *African Theatre and Politics: The Evolution of Theatre in Ethiopia, Tanzania and Zimbabwe: A Comparative Study*. Amsterdam: Rodopi.

Postlewait, T. (1991) 'Historiography and the Theatrical Event: A Primer with Twelve Cruxes'. *Theatre Journal* 43 (2), 157–78.

Postlewait, T. (2009) *The Cambridge Introduction to Theatre Historiography*. Cambridge: Cambridge University Press.

Qarib, H. (2009) 'Ezmûngerî Kurdî: Deq û Ekter le Jêr Sêberî Derhênerda' ('Kurdish Experimentalism: Text and Actor Overshadowed by Director'). *Şano* 20, 77–80.

Qazi, Q. F. (2009) *Sê Beytî Folklorîk: Mem û Zîn, Xec û Siyamend, Ehmed Şeng (Three Folkloric Beyts: Mam and Zin, Khaj and Siyamand, Ahmad Shang)*. Hewlêr: Aras.

*Question of the Frontier between Turkey and Iraq: Report submitted to the Council of the League of Nations by the Commission instituted by the Council Resolution of Sept. 30th, 1924* (1925). Lausanne: League of Nations. Available from: https://biblio-archive.unog.ch (accessed 12 January 2019).

Rasul, I. M. (1979) *Aḥmadī Khānī 1650–1707: shāʿiran wa-mufakkiran faylasūfan wa-mutaṣawwif* (Ahmadi Khani 1650–1707: A Poet, Thinker, Philosopher and Mystic). Baghdad: Maṭbaʿat al-Ḥawādith.

Rasul, I. M. (2010) *Lêkolînewey Edebî Folklorî Kurdî (Studies of Kurdish Folkloric Literature)*. Hewlêr: Aras.

Rasul, S. (2004) *Silêmani Le Edebî Folklorda (Sulaymaniyah in Folkloric Literature)*. Çapî yekem. Silêmanî: Instîtutî Kelepurî Kurd.

Rauf, D. (1995) *Gutarî Ezmûngerî Le Rewtî Şanoy Kurdîda* (Essays on Experimentalism in Kurdish Theatre Movement). Stockholm: n.p.

Rauf, D. (2010) Dana Reûf: Ezmûnkarêkî Raber û Hemîşe Dil le Nîştiman (Dana Rauf: A Veteran Experimentalist Whose Heart Is always with the Homeland). *Şano* 20, 97–105.

Reinelt, J. (2008) 'The Role of National Theatres in an Age of Globalization', in S. E. Wilmer (ed.) *National Theatres in a Changing Europe*. Basingstoke: Palgrave Macmillan.

Rich, C. J. (1836) *Narrative of a Residence in Koordistan and on the Site of Ancient Niniveh: with Journal of a Voyage Down the Tigris to Bagdad and an Account of a Visit to Shirauz and Persepolis Volume.1*. Westmead: Gregg.

RonîWar (2011) *Mem û Zîn: Roman* (Mam and Zin: A Novel). Istanbul: Ava.

Roosevelt, A. (1993) 'The Kurdish Republic of Mahabad', in Gerard Chaliand (ed.) *A People without a Country: The Kurds and Kurdistan*. London: Zed Books. pp. 122–38.

Sadeqi, Q. (2013) 'Amalkard va Janbehāye Namādīne "Halparke" ya Raqshaye Āīnī-Bāstānīe Kordī' ('The Functions and Symbolic Meanings of "Halparke" or Ancient Ritualistic Kurdish Dances'). *Namāyesh* 161, 79–82.

Sadgrove, P. (1996) *The Egyptian Theatre in the Nineteenth Century: 1799–1882*. Reading: Ithaca Press.

Sagvand, A. (1999). 'Āīnhāye Sūgvāri dar Lorestān va Rīshehāye Ān' ('Mourning Rituals in Lorestan and Their Roots'). *Keyhāne Farhangī* 149, 10–13.

Salar, A. (1999a) 'Katê Helo Berz Defrê' ('When the Eagle Flies High'), in *Şanoy Salar* (Salar's Theatre). Hewlêr: n.p. pp. 38–70.

Salar, A. (1999b) 'Nalî w Xewnêkî Erxewanî' ('Nali and a Violet Dream'), in *Şanoy Salar* (Salar's Theatre). Hewlêr: n.p. pp. 14–36.

Salar, A. (2012) 'Pêşekî (Introduction)', in *Xec û Siyamend*. Hewlêr: Aras.

Salar, A. (2013) 'Ezmûnî Şanom (My Theatre Experience)'. *Raman*. 194, 110–13.

Salih, N. (2006) 'Çwar Roj ber le Raperînî Silêmanî Rijêm Beniyaz Bûe Jimareyek Hunermend û Nûser Bikate Barmete' ('Four Days before Sulaymaniyah Uprising Regime Decided to Arrest Several Artists and Writers'). *Silêmanî Nwê*. 190, 8.

Salimi, H. (2003) *Zemestān dar Farhang-e Mardom-e Kord* (*Winter in the Culture of the Kurdish People*). Tehran: Surūsh.

Saman, T. (2010) *Qel û Rûte* (*The Raven and the Pauper*). 21. Silêmanî: Govarî Şano.

Saman, T. (2011a) *Mem û Zîn* (*Mam and Zin*). Silêmanî: Berêwberêtî Çap û Bilawkirdinewey Silêmanî.

Saman, T. (2011b) *Şarî Evîn* (*The City of Love*). Hewlêr: Aras.

*Şano: Govarî Tîpî Şanoy Salar* (*Theatre: Salar Theatre Group's Journal*) (Dec 2008) no. 11.

*Şano: Govarî Tîpî Şanoy Salar* (*Theatre: Salar Theatre Group's Journal*) (March 2009) no. 12.

*Şano: Govarî Tîpî Şanoy Salar* (*Theatre: Salar Theatre Group's Journal*) (2009) no. 14.

Saritaş, S. E. (2010) *Articulation of Kurdish Identity through Politicized Music of Koms*. MS thesis. Ankara, Turkey: Middle East Technical University. [Online]. Available from: http://etd.lib.metu.edu.tr/upload/12611651/index.pdf (accessed 12 January 2019).

Sattari, J. (2008) *Zamīneye Ejtemāīye Ta'ziyeh va Teātr dar Īrān* (The Social Context of Taziyeh in Iran). Tehran: Nashre Markaz.

Scalbert-Yücel, C. (2009) 'The Invention of a Tradition: Diyarbakır's Dengbêj Project'. *European Journal of Turkish Studies. Social Sciences on Contemporary Turkey*. (10), [Online]. Available from: http://ejts.revues.org/4055 (accessed 12 January 2019).

Schechner, R. (2002) *Performance Studies: An Introduction*. London: Routledge.

Şemo, E. (2007) *Dimdim: Roman*. Yenişehir/Diyarbakır: Lîs.

Sheikh Mahmud, C., and Sheikh Mahmud, M. E. (2011) *Jiyanî Pêşmerge (The Life of the Peshmerga)*. Silêmanî: Patriotic Union of Kurdistan.

Sheikhmous, O. (n.d.) 'The Self-made Tragedy in Kurdistan: Kurdish intellectuals Should Have the Civil Courage to Say Enough to Their So-called "Leaderships"'. University of Exeter Omer Sheikhmous Archive.

Sheyholislami, J. (2011) *Kurdish Identity, Discourse, and New Media*. New York: Palgrave Macmillan.

Simo, I. A. (2007) *Şanoy Kurdî Le Nêwan Deqî Xomalî w Biyanîda (Kurdish Drama between Kurdish and non-Kurdish Plays)*. Silêmanî: Govarî Şano.

Smith, A. D. (1986) *The Ethnic Origins of Nations*. Oxford: Basil Blackwell.

Smith, A. D. (1991) *National Identity*. Reno: University of Nevada Press.

Smith, A. D. (1999) *Myths and Memories of the Nation*. New York: Oxford University Press.

Smith, A. D. (2009) *Ethno-Symbolism and Nationalism: A Cultural Approach*. London: Routledge.

Smith, J. (2004) 'Karagoz and Hacivat: Projections of Subversion and Conformance'. *Asian Theatre Journal* 21 (2), 187–93.

Southgate, H. (1840) *Narrative of a Tour through Armenia, Kurdistan, Persia and Mesopotamia with an Introduction, and Occasional Observations upon the Condition of Mohammedanism and Christianity in Those Countries*. New York: D. Appleton.

*Spark (Organ of the Patriotic Union of Kurdistan (PUK))*. University of Exeter Special Collection: Omer Sheikhmous Archive.

Stansfield, G., and Resool, S. H. (2006) 'The Tortured Resurgence of Kurdish Nationalism in Iraq, 1975–1991', in Mohammed Ahmed and Michael Gunter (eds) *The Evolution of Kurdish Nationalism*. Costa Mesa, CA: Mazda. pp. 98–122.

Stone, C. (2007) *Popular Culture and Nationalism in Lebanon: The Fairouz and Rahbani Nation*. London: Routledge.

Strohmeier, M. (2003) *Crucial Images in the Presentation of a Kurdish National Identity: Heroes and Patriots, Traitors and Foes*. Leiden: Brill.

Subhan, K. (2012) *Ferhengî Şanoyî* (Dictionary of the Theatre). Hewlêr: Berêweberayetî Hunerî Şano.

Suleiman, Y., and Muhawi, I. (eds) (2006) *Literature and Nation in the Middle East*. Edinburgh: Edinburgh University Press.

Tanya, H. (1985) *Şano û Şanoy Kurdewarî* (Theatre and Kurdish Theatre). Baghdad: Afaq.

Taylor, D. (1997) *Disappearing Acts: Spectacles of Gender and Nationalism in Argentina's 'Dirty War'*. Durham, NC: Duke University Press.

Taymur, M. (1988) '*Derwazeyêkî Rixney Dramay Nwêy Kurdî, Beşî Yekem* (A Critical Window to Modern Kurdish Drama, Part One)'. *Karwan* 64, 60–9.

Tejel, J. (2009) *Syria's Kurds: History, Politics and Society*. London: Routledge.

Tezcür, G. M. (2009) 'Kurdish Nationalism and Identity in Turkey: A Conceptual Reinterpretation'. *European Journal of Turkish Studies. Social Sciences on Contemporary Turkey* 10 [Online]. Available from: http://ejts.revues.org/4008 (accessed 12 January 2019).

Thoman, R. E. (1972) 'Iraq under Ba'thist Rule'. *Current History* 62 (365), 31–7.

Thompson, J., Hughes, J., and Balfour, M. (2009) *Performance in Place of War*. Calcutta: Seagull Books.

Toynbee A. J., and Boulter V. M. (1935) *Survey of International Affairs 1934*. London: Oxford University Press.

Vali, A. (2003) *Essays on the Origins of Kurdish Nationalism*. Costa Mesa, CA: Mazda.

Wannous, S. (1988) Bayanat Li Masrah 'Arabi Jadid (Manifestos for a New Arabic Theatre). Beirut: Dar al-Fikr al-Jadid..

Weill, K. (2000) 'Gestus in Music', in C. Martin and H. Bial (eds) *Brecht Sourcebook*. London: Routledge.

Wilmer, S. E. (2002) *Theatre, Society, and the Nation: Staging American Identities*. Cambridge; New York: Cambridge University Press.

Wilmer, S. E. (ed.) (2004) *Writing and Rewriting National Theatre Histories*. Iowa City: University of Iowa Press.

Wilmer, S. E. (2005) 'Herder and European Theatre', in Kiki Gounaridou (ed.) *Staging Nationalism: Essays on Theatre and National Identity*. Jefferson, NC: McFarland. pp. 63–85.

Wilmer, S. E. (ed.) (2008) *National Theatres in a Changing Europe*. Basingstoke: Palgrave Macmillan.

Wilmer, S. E. (2009) 'Theatrical Nationalism: Exposing the Obscene Superego of the System'. *Journal of Dramatic Theory and Criticism* 23 (2), 77–88.

Wilson, W. A. (1973) *Folklore and Nationalism in Modern Finland*. Bloomington: Indiana University Press.

Yavuz, M. H. (2001) 'Five Stages of the Construction of Kurdish Nationalism in Turkey'. *Nationalism and Ethnic Politics* 7 (3), 1–24.

Yüksel, M. (2010) *Dengbej, Mullah, Intelligentsia: The Survival and Revival of the Kurdish-Kurmanji Language in the Middle East, 1925–1960*. Doctoral Thesis. Villanova, PA: Villanova University.

Zakaryaei, H. (11 June 2013) ASOSAT Album Nigar Hasib Qaradaxi. Available from: https://www.youtube.com/watch?v=AQ3pE_0KDxU (accessed 12 January 2019).

Zangana, H. (2002) *Theater als Form des Widerstands in Kurdistan*. Hildesheim: Internationales Kulturwerk.

Zarifian, M. (2009) 'The Symbolic and Mythical Ritual of Garwanaki', in *Kermashan*. Erbil: Aras Publication. pp. 200–20.

Zarrilli, P. B., and Williams, G. J. (2010) *Theatre Histories: An Introduction*. New York: Routledge.

Zimmern, H. (1883) *The Epic of Kings: Stories Retold from Firdusi, by Helen Zimmern. With Two Etchings by L. Alma Tadema, R.A., and a Prefatory Poem by Edmund W. Gosse*. London: T.F. Unwin.

# Index

Abdulhamid, Sami 127, 128, 156, 182
Ahmad, Ibrahim 87, 163–4
   *Janî Gel* 191
   *Menûçer* 89
Ahmadmirza, Kawa 9, 10, 71n. 13, 93, 101, 102, 105, 107, 133
Allison, Christine 6n. 7, 19, 25n. 2, 45, 46, 111, 171–2, 173, 178
Amin, Omar Ali 96, 103
Amine, Khalid 5n. 6, 32, 43–5, 182, 213
*Anfal* 3, 10, 15, 130, 132, 151, 183, 220, 227
al-Ani, Yusuf 126–8
Arab Theatre
   influence on Kurdish theatre 125–9, 182–3, 185
Arif, Hussein 134
Ashna, Omid 63–5, 81–3
Azabani, Sheikh Salam 211
Azawi, Fazil 145
Aziz, Simko 112, 119, 141

Baath party/regime
   Arabization 113–14
   cultural suppression 114–19, 132–4
Baban, Ismail Haqi 64
Babans 9, 30, 45, 50–3, 187–90, 195–6
Bahiya Khan 68
Bamarni, Qazi 103–5, 107, 118–19, 155
*Bangî Heq* 56
*Bangî Kurdistan* 74
Barzani, Mulla Mustafa 84, 113, 164
Barzanji, Sheikh Mahmud 30, 43, 52, 54–6, 60, 61, 68, 74, 79, 200, 210, 212
Barzanji, Yasin Qadir 9, 10, 69–70, 72, 75–7, 79–82, 86–7, 89–90, 93–5, 99, 108, 120–1
Bekas, Fayiq 211
Bekas, Sherko 92–3
Berrechid, Abdelkarim 135, 182–3, 195, 213
*Beyan* 12, 99, 112, 129, 134
*beytbêj* 46–7, 52, 172, 201, 204–5, 209
Bois, Thomas 30, 32–4, 37, 83

Brecht, Bertolt
   influence on Arab and Kurdish theatre 126–9, 144–6, 174, 177, 182, 185, 195, 213
Bruinessen, Martin van 1–2, 24–5, 54, 76, 122–3, 131–2, 162, 206

Carlson, Marvin 5n. 6, 32, 43–5, 182, 213
Celîl, Casim 173, 178
Celîl, Ordîxan (Ordikhan Dzhalilov) 171–2
*çemer* 40–2, 149n. 15, 209
Cevdet, Abdullah 62
Chalak, Rafiq 71n. 13, 72, 91–4
Chewar, Osman 123, 129
Chyet, Michael L. 44–5, 75n. 14, 161, 168
*çîrokbêj* 46
Committee for Union and Progress (CUP) 58
cultural nationalism 2–3, 11, 74, 78–9, 108, 111, 166, 179, 196

dance-drama 22–5
Danish, Asayish Osman 89, 119, 174, 198
*Darkar* 57, 85
Dartash, Badea 105, 115, 118, 124, 134, 136
   *Ey Gelî Felestînî Rapere* 115, 118
   *Nexşey Xwênawî* 124
Darvishian, Ali-Ashraf 37
*Daykî Nîştiman* 193–4
*dengbêj* 6, 44–7
*Diyarî Kurdistan* 60
Dolan, Jill 222–3
Dragun, Osvaldo 125, 145

Edmonds, Cecil J. 29–30, 50, 52–6, 60, 190
*elem and kotel* 41–2
Erbil
   Arab troupes in 71
   first theatrical performances 67
   non-Muslim artists of 67, 67n. 9, 73
Erbil theatre groups
   *Komeley Huner û Wêjey Kurdî* 129, 156

*Komeley Lawanî Kurd* 67
*Tîpî Hunerî Hewlêr* 102, 133
*Tîpî Nwêy Hunerî Kurdî* 156

Fanon, Frantz
   *The Wretched of the Earth* 140
Faraj, Alfred 126
Fattah, Shakir 52, 90
Fayzi, Goran Soran 71

*garwanekî* 35–6
Gaziza 103–4
George Abyad Troupe 68
Goran, Abdullah 7, 83, 87–8, 90, 92, 99–100, 109, 174, 202, 205, 211
   *Encamî Ejdehak* 99
   *Gulî Xwênawî* 83, 90
guerrilla theatre 13, 17, 140–7

*hakawati* 44, 126–8, 183, 185
Hakkari, Abdurrahim Rahmi 7–8
Halabja 8, 21, 132, 148–9
Hamadbeg, Jawad 88–90, 101–2
Hamawand, Faqi Qadir 206
Hamawands
   in folk culture 200–3, 211
   in Kurdish plays 78, 198–215
Hanjira, Kamal 148, 197
Hassanpour, Amir 2, 6, 9, 77, 112, 162, 168, 172
Hawrami, Hama Karim 8n. 9, 9–10, 31, 49
*Hawrêyanî Gezîze* 103–4
Hawri, A. B. 69
   *Dildarî w Peyman Perwerî* 69
Hilmi, Rafiq 60–1, 64, 85
   *Hîwa* party 57, 61, 85–6
Holdsworth, Nadine 12, 140, 197
Hourani, Albert H. 59–60
Hutchinson, John 2, 74, 78, 108, 180

Ismail, Ismail Fahd
   *Milaff al-Ḥādithah* 67 123

Jaff, Osman Pasha 21
Jaffar, Shwan 27, 133, 135n. 6
Jalal, Ibrahim 119, 127–8, 156, 182
*Jiyan* 8n. 9, 10, 63, 64n. 5, 65, 68–71, 76–7
Jwaideh, Wadie 44, 54–6, 61, 83–4, 86, 199

Kadhim, Adil 125–6
Karakeçili, Fethi 22–5, 162n. 4
Karim, Khalil Yaba 66n. 6, 110–12, 118, 153
Karim, Salam Faraj 9–10, 21, 111, 125, 129–30, 140, 151–2, 181, 183, 185
*Kawey Asinger*
   folk performances 26–7
   stage adaptations 99, 103, 157
   staged by political parties 88–9
KDP (Kurdistan Democratic Party) 87–8, 100–1, 122, 129, 131, 151, 163–5, 170, 226–8
Kemal, Yaşar
   *Teneke* 125
Khaja, Ahmad 52, 67
Khalil, Taha 93, 99, 186
Khani, Ahmad (Ehmedî Xanî) 5, 75–7, 84–5, 160–3, 167–9, 172, 174, 206, 220
Khattab, Fattah 13, 115, 143–6
Kirkuk
   Arabization 113, 118
   leftist movement 85–6
   oil reserves 57
   TV 97, 118
   women's rain ritual 37–8
Kirkuk theatre groups
   *Komeley Huner û Wêjey Kurdî* 105, 107
   *Tîpî Hunerî Xebat* 97
   *Tîpî Lawanî Kerkûk* 97
*Komeley Birayetî* 57, 85
*Komeley Jiyanewey Kurdistan* 28, 193
*Komeley Zanistî Kurdan* 64–6, 68–70, 74–7
*Kose-geldî/Kose-Kose* 33–5
Koya theatre groups
   *Tîpî Şanoy Kekon* 102
   *Tîpî Şanoy Lawan û Qutabiyanî Koye* 89
   *Tîpî Şanoy Mîllî Koye* 88n. 19, 90
Koyi, Haji Qadir 5, 193, 206
Kreyenbroek, Philip G. 5n. 4, 25n. 2, 178
KRG (Kurdistan Regional Government) 150, 152
*Kurd Teavun ve Terakki Cemiyeti* 62
Kurdi (poet) 189
Kurdish movement in Iraq
   14 July Revolution 97
   1970 Agreement 101
   1991 uprising 150

Algiers Agreement 113, 121, 169
Barzani's revolt 84–5
creation of the KDP 87
events after Treaty of Lausanne 57–60
KDP-PUK conflict 122–3, 151, 163–5
PUK's new uprising 122
rise of leftist parties 85–6
September Revolution 100
Sheikh Mahmud's rebellion 55–6
Kurdish Society for Fine Arts 93–4, 99
Kurdish theatre
    banned 115, 118
    between 1970–4, 102–7
    cross-gender acting 80, 96
    decline in the 60s 101
    decline in the 90s 151–2
    early identity-building 66–83
    emergence 66–74
    first female actors 94–6
    first festival 107
    first official groups 102
    histories 7–10
    inspiration from folk culture 129, 135
    leftist influence 86–91, 105–6
    translated plays from Arabic 125
    under the Baath 111–50
    women's participation and rights 79–82, 96–7
Kurmanji 9–10, 46, 122, 161, 171

Lausanne, the Treaty of 57–8
Living Newspaper, the 144–6

Mahabad Republic 28, 92, 120, 174, 177, 179, 193–4
Mam, Muhamad Mawlud 156
    *Pîlan* 116–17, 130, 156
Mandalawi, Sabah 145
Mann, Oskar
    *Die Mundart der Mukri* 47
Mariwani, Dilshad 106–7
    *Çawî Vietnam* 107, 219
*masrah al-ihtifali* (Festive or Ceremonial Theatre) 129, 135, 182–3, 213, 215
McDowall, David 55–6, 58, 74, 85–8, 97, 101, 104, 113, 131–2, 163–4, 166
*Memê Alan*
    folkloric narrative 75, 161, 201
    Hakkari's 7–8

*Mem û Zîn*
    in the 1940s 84–5, 90
    in 1958 73, 94
    folk performances 45
    Khani's 161–3, 167–9, 172, 220
    Pîremêrd's 8n. 9, 75–7, 80–2, 109, 204–5
    Saman's 15, 130, 160–71, 180
Mirawdeli, Kamal 168
*mîrmîran/mîrmîrên* 27–32
Misri, Fuad Majid 119, 137, 182, 186
    *Xec û Siyamend* 119–20
*mor* 41
mosque performances 42–3
Muhammad, Muhsin 12–13, 125, 138, 157, 170
Muhammad, Qasim 125–7
Mukriyani, Hemin 120
Müller, Heiner 145

Naji, Jawad Rasul 73
Najmabadi, Afsaneh 191
Nakam, Narmin 94–6
Nakam, Simko 120, 171
    *Receb û Piyawxoran* 120–1, 171
Nali (poet) 187–8
Naqib, Sheikh Mustafa 21
nationalist myths 15–6
Nawab, Muzaffar 145
*Newroz*
    carnival performances 26–32
    celebrations in Koya 88–9, 101

Omar, Shamal 10n. 10, 136
    *Le Çawerwani Siyamend* 137
Omid, Mahdi 118

Palestine
    in Kurdish theatre 115, 122–5, 177, 179
Partisan Theatre 143–6
Patriotic Union of Kurdistan (PUK) 122, 131, 143–5, 149, 151, 163–5, 180, 220
*Pêşkewtin* 55
Pirbal, Farhad 7–10, 27–8, 42, 62, 64, 67–8, 71, 73, 80, 88
Pîremêrd 5, 8n. 9, 60–4, 69–70, 75–83, 109, 160, 188, 192, 202–7, 218
    *Mehmûd Aqay Şêwekel* 8n. 9, 78–9, 82
    *Şerîf Hemewend* 78, 202
    (see also *Mem û Zîn*)

Piscator, Erwin 144–6, 177
Plastow, Jane 31, 140n. 9

Qaradaqi, Nigar Hasib 115, 136–7, 139
Qasab, Danial 67, 73
al-Qasab, Salah 137, 183
Qasim, Abdulkarim 97, 100
*qissa* 43

Rashid, Fuad 68–9
   *Îlm û Cehl* 68, 80
   *Nîron* 68, 68n. 11, 70
Rasul, Izzeddin Mustafa 21, 44n. 14, 46, 78, 168n. 6, 169, 172, 201
Rasul, Shukriya 45–6, 203
Rauf, Dana 197
Rauf, Midiya 136–9
Resool, Shorsh Haji 102, 111, 114, 131, 141, 170, 173, 181, 213
Rich, Claudius James 50
*Rojî Kurdistan* 56
Roosevelt, Archie 194
*Roşinbîrî Nwê* 134
Rushdi, Fatma 71

Sadeqi, Qotbeddin 23
Saʻdi, Jaʻfar 156
Saʻedi, Gholam-Hossein 145
Saeid, Khalid 73, 88, 93
Salar, Ahmad 13–15, 17–19, 47, 105, 112, 119–20, 125, 128–9, 134–6, 141, 148, 153, 181–215, 220–1
   *Katê Helo Berz Defrê* 15, 128, 135, 181, 184, 198–215, 222–3
   *Nalî w Xewnêkî Erxewanî* 15, 128, 135, 181, 183–198, 220, 223
Salim (poet) 60n. 2, 189–90
Saman, Talat 15, 17, 19, 105, 125, 128–30, 134n. 5, 153, 155–180, 212–3, 219–23
   *Heme Dok* 128–9
   *Nefretlêkiraw* 128
   *Qelay Dimdim* 171–9
   *Qel û Rûte* 128, 157–9
   *Şarî Evîn* 129, 157
   (see also *Mem û Zîn*)
Scott, Sir Walter
   *The Talisman* 67
*Selahedînî Eyûbî* 67, 71
Şemo, Erebê 33, 173

*Serbazî Aza* 69–70, 80
Sèvres, the Treaty of 57
*Shāhnāmeh* 26, 38–40, 46
Shakespeare 182
   *Hamlet* 133
   *Julius Caesar* 134
   *Othello* 73, 91, 119
   *The Merchant of Venice* 91, 133
Shawqi, Azad 73, 93
Sheikh Nuri, Sheikh Salih 74, 79–80
al-Shibli, Haqqi 71
Simo, Ibrahim Ahmad 183, 186
Smith, Anthony D. 2, 15–6, 108, 166, 179, 196, 214–5, 221
Sorani 9–10, 46, 90, 108, 122, 162, 171, 188–9, 206
*Spark* 114, 122, 131, 164
Stansfield, Gareth 102, 111, 114, 131, 141, 170, 173, 181, 213
storytelling 43–7, 73, 128, 185, 201
Strohmeier, Martin 2n. 2, 6, 53–4, 63, 65, 77, 162n. 3, 169, 207, 218
Sulaymaniyah
   Arab troupes visiting 71
   chemical bombings of villages 132
   first theatre performances 49, 67–79
   leftist movement 84–7
   mass demonstrations 58, 66, 114, 131
   mock king festival in 28–32
   nineteenth-century entertainers 21
   notables' petitions to the League of Nations 57
   return of the elite to 60–1
   support for the PUK 123, 151
   theatre in the 1980s 132–140
   under Major E. B. Soane 55–6
   under Sheikh Mahmud 55–6
   under the Baban rule 9, 50–3, 187–8, 190
Sulaymaniyah Institute of Fine Arts 134–6, 140, 197–8
Sulaymaniyah theatre groups
   *Şanoy Salar* 135, 182
   *Tîpî Nwandinî Silêmanî* 102, 107, 119, 141
   *Tîpî Nwandin û Mosîqay Silêmanî* 96, 102
   *Tîpî Pêşrewî Şanoy Kurdî* 102, 107, 119–20, 135, 141, 148, 182

*Tîpî Şanoy Zanko* 119
Suleiman, Yasir 4

Talabani, Jalal 88, 122–3, 163–4
Talabani, Sheikh Reza 52, 190
Tanya, Hasan 8–10, 21, 29–31, 43, 68, 89–90, 94, 127n. 3
Taylor, Diana 12n. 11, 190–1
Taymur, Muhammad 30, 32, 43, 53
*ta'ziyeh* 20–1, 38
theatre of the displaced 148–50
*Tîpî Mosîqay Mewlewî* 93
Tovi, Anwar 73

Wahbi, Tawfiq 21, 30
Wakim, Bishara 71, 92
Wannous, Sadallah 126–7, 145

*al-Wathba* 88
Weiss, Peter 136, 145–6
women
  education 80–2
  first appearance on stage 94–7

Yamulki, Gozida Khanim 80
Yamulki, Mustafa Pasha 31
Yusuf, Sa'di 145

Zaki Beg, Salih 60
Zaki Beg, Muhammad-Amin 64, 79
Zangana, Hawre 9, 10n. 10, 102, 106–7, 119, 137–8, 141–50
Zangana, Jalil 118
Zangana, Muhyuddin 125, 128, 182
Zarifian, Mahmud 35–6

www.ingramcontent.com/pod-product-compliance
Lightning Source LLC
Chambersburg PA
CBHW070028010526
44117CB00011B/1749